T0400293

Architecture's Appeal

This collection of previously unpublished essays from a diverse range of well-known scholars and architects builds on the architectural tradition of phenomenological hermeneutics, as developed by Dalibor Veseley and Joseph Rykwert and carried on by David Leatherbarrow, Peter Carl, and Alberto Pérez-Gómez.

Taking an interdisciplinary approach and drawing on ideas from beyond the architectural canon, contributors including Kenneth Frampton, David Leatherbarrow, Juhani Pallasmaa, Karsten Harries, Steven Holl, Indra Kagis McEwen, Paul Emmons, and Louise Pelletier offer new insights and perspectives on questions such as the following:

- Given the recent fascination with all things digital and novel, what is the role of history and theory in contemporary architectural praxis?
- Is authentic meaning possible in a technological environment that is so global and interconnected?
- What is the nature and role of the architect in our shared modern world?
- How can these questions inform a new model of architectural praxis?

Architecture's Appeal is a thought-provoking book which will inspire further scholarly inquiry and act as a basis for discussion in the wider field as well as graduate seminars in architectural theory and history.

Marc J. Neveu is Chair of the Department of Architecture at Woodbury University, Los Angeles, USA, and the Executive Editor of the *Journal of Architectural Education.*

Negin Djavaherian is an independent scholar currently residing in Montréal, Canada.

"At a time when architectural theory might go unquestioned and the monologue of the technological paradigm and digital age seems to offer the possibility for an endless agenda and sense of progress, a group of well-known scholars addresses the role of poetics and ethics within architecture, providing insight from many and diverse angles. A must-read for all those intending to gaze deeper into their own age from a contemporary perspective in architectural theory."

— Federica Goffi, Associate Professor and Associate Director of Graduate Programs, Azrieli School of Architecture and Urbanism, Carleton University, Canada

"*Architecture's Appeal* is a timely reminder of the role of history and theory in a world so infatuated with technology and gratuitous formal explorations. At the very core of these reflections within the book is the belief that our past is relevant and provides critical insight into new possible realities and roles yet to be invented for the architects of the future."

— Gregory Henriquez, Managing Partner, Henriquez Partners Architects, Canada

ARCHITECTURE'S APPEAL

How theory informs architectural praxis

Edited by
*Marc J. Neveu and
Negin Djavaherian*

LONDON AND NEW YORK

First published 2015
by Routledge
2 Park Square, Milton Park, Abingdon, Oxon OX14 4RN

and by Routledge
711 Third Avenue, New York, NY 10017

Routledge is an imprint of the Taylor & Francis Group, an informa business

© 2015 Marc J. Neveu and Negin Djavaherian

The right of the editors to be identified as the authors of the
editorial material, and of the authors for their individual chapters,
has been asserted in accordance with sections 77 and 78 of the
Copyright, Designs and Patents Act 1988.

All rights reserved. No part of this book may be reprinted or
reproduced or utilised in any form or by any electronic, mechanical,
or other means, now known or hereafter invented, including
photocopying and recording, or in any information storage or
retrieval system, without permission in writing from the publishers.

Trademark notice: Product or corporate names may be trademarks
or registered trademarks, and are used only for identification and
explanation without intent to infringe.

British Library Cataloguing-in-Publication Data
A catalogue record for this book is available from the British Library

Library of Congress Cataloging-in-Publication Data
Architecture's appeal : how theory informs architectural praxis/
[edited by] Marc J. Neveu, Negin Djavaherian.
pages cm
Includes bibliographical references and index.
1. Architecture—Philosophy. 2. Architectural practice. I. Neveu,
Marc J., editor. II. Djavaherian, Negin, editor. III. Kirkbride,
Robert. Reading chamber.
NA2500.A7348 2015
720.1—dc23
2014029403

ISBN: (hbk) 978-1-138-02421-2
ISBN: (pbk) 978-1-138-02422-9
ISBN: (ebk) 978-1-315-77592-0

Typeset in Bembo
by Swales & Willis Ltd, Exeter, Devon, UK

CONTENTS

FIGURES

CONTRIBUTORS

Lawrence Bird
Urban Designer, Gem Equities, Canada

Anne Bordeleau
Assistant Professor, School of Architecture, Waterloo, Canada

Ricardo L. Castro
Associate Professor, School of Architecture, McGill University, Canada

Lian Chikako Chang
Director of Research and Information, Association of Collegiate Schools of
   Architecture, USA

Lily Chi
Assistant Professor, Department of Architecture, Cornell University, USA

Caroline Dionne
Scientist and Lecturer, École Polytechnique Fédérale de Lausanne,
   Switzerland

Negin Djavaherian
Independent scholar, Canada

Paul Emmons
Associate Professor, Washington-Alexandria Architecture Center, Virginia
   Tech, USA

Kenneth Frampton
Ware Professor of Architecture, Graduate School of Architecture, Planning, and Preservation, Columbia University, USA

Marco Frascari
Former Director, David Azrieli School of Architecture and Urbanism, Carleton University, Canada

Karsten Harries
Howard H. Newman Professor of Philosophy, Yale University, USA

Juan Manuel Heredia
Assistant Professor, School of Architecture, Portland State University, USA

Steven Holl
Architect, Steven Holl Architects, USA

Robert Kirkbride
Director of studio 'patafisico and Associate Dean of Constructed Environments, Parsons The New School for Design, USA

Lisa Landrum
Assistant Professor, Department of Architecture, University of Manitoba, Canada

David Leatherbarrow
Professor of Architecture and Chair of the Graduate Group in Architecture, University of Pennsylvania, USA

Graham Livesey
Associate Professor and Associate Dean, Faculty of Environmental Design, the University of Calgary, Canada

Indra Kagis McEwen
Adjunct Professor, Art History, Concordia, Canada

Peter Olshavsky
Assistant Professor, Architecture, University of Nebraska-Lincoln, USA

Marc J. Neveu
Chair, School of Architecture, Woodbury University, USA

Santiago de Orduña
Visiting Faculty, Universidad Veracruzana. México, México

Juhani Pallasmaa
Architect and Professor of Architecture, University of Technology, Helsinki, Finland

Stephen Parcell
Professor, School of Architecture, Dalhousie University, Canada

Louise Pelletier
Professor, l'École de design de l'Université du Québec à Montréal, Canada

Natalija Subotincic
Professor, Department of Architecture, University of Manitoba, Canada

David Theodore
Assistant Professor, School of Architecture, McGill University, Canada

Tracey Eve Winton
Associate Professor and Director of Studies for the Rome Program, School of Architecture, Waterloo, Canada

ACKNOWLEDGEMENTS

It is with great pleasure that the editors of this book express their gratitude to all who helped make this project become more than a conversation.

Warm thanks go to all authors who have contributed to this collection as well as those who read and edited drafts. A special thanks to Louise Pelletier who, in very early discussions of the project, helped to shape the scope and bring focus to the work.

Thank you to all of the institutions and individuals who either contributed or gave permission for the reproduction of the images. Specific sources are listed in the captions.

Finally, thank you to Alberto, a scholar, a mentor, a professor, and a friend to all in this book and many more. Most importantly, thank you for clearing a shared space of becoming.

OPENING

Marc J. Neveu and Negin Djavaherian

> *How can architects reconcile their wish to design a beautiful world and the imperative to create a better place for society?*

This question served as the foundation for the 2007 Reconciling Poetics and Ethics Conference in Montréal at the Canadian Centre for Architecture. The conference brought together an international cast of scholars to deliberate, discuss, and debate many issues surrounding the poetics and ethics of architecture. A secondary objective of the conference was in celebration of the twentieth anniversary of the History and Theory of Architecture Program at McGill University. Indeed many of the questions raised at the conference were those discussed around the seminar table at McGill over the previous twenty-five years. This volume, *Architecture's Appeal*, is a collection of essays from a similar and diverse group of well-known scholars that continues the conversation. Similar to the conference there is an additional purpose, that is, to honor the teaching and scholarship of Alberto Pérez-Gómez.

Situated within the architectural tradition of phenomenological hermeneutics, this book asks innovative and related questions. For example, given the recent fascination with all things digital and novel, what is the role of history and theory in contemporary architectural production? From Greek temples to Buddhist stupas to Gothic cathedrals, architecture has traditionally reconciled the order of the world through built form. Lacking a common worldview, is such reconciliation still possible? We are continually made aware of imminent global crises, environmental, financial and otherwise. Often these are the result of human interaction and underscored by our technological enframing of the world. While avoiding a nostalgic return to nature, is authentic meaning possible in a technological environment that is so global and interconnected? Given the complexity of these questions, what is the nature and role of the architect in this modern world? Further, how might the questions asked inform alternative models of architectural praxis? Rather than attempting to dictate a model to follow, the questions asked in this volume – often developed with ideas from outside of the architectural canon – offer an opening to more deeply consider to the role of architecture and allow us to re-think our role as architect.

Graduates of the History and Theory of Architecture Program at McGill very often arrived to the seminar room with a background in professional practice. Many returned to practice while others have gone on to academic careers. Regardless of their path, many students from the program experienced something indefinable that has profoundly influenced their work, research and life. Rather than finding a prescriptive methodology to approach the history and theory of architecture, discussions around the table offered openness to discovery and interpretation. This shared experience, this shared ground, reminds one of *chora* – a space of becoming – an idea explored by Alberto Pérez-Gómez and demonstrated around the seminar table. With contributions from alumni, friends and colleagues of the program, this book is organized into five parts. Each part is related to the following by a short interlude intended to offer a pause and add character to the texture of the book. It begins with an invocation to the gods, Greek, Roman and other. A fictional account of the architect's fall leads to the second section on the making of worlds. Though separated by centuries the topic of these essays relate to our crafting of a shared world. Through the late Marco Frascari's door of theory we enter into the third part, on eros, which acts as a hinge for the entire collection. After a short (re)visit to Dr. Freud's office, the fourth part includes essays that seek to explore the fusion of horizons, between architecture and other topics. The final set of essays looks more closely at the ground and refiguration of Pérez-Gómez's scholarship. The book ends with two poems, an interlude not meant to close the book but to open up to other horizons.

This collection is not meant to be definitive; rather, it is intended as an open book, inviting questions and awaiting interpretation. In this way, the appeal of architecture may be understood in at least two ways: as something asked of, and as something longed for.

PART I
Invoking the gods

1

THE READING CHAMBER

Robert Kirkbride

Preamble

The Reading Chamber *centers on a chimeric room whose paginated construction has stimulated generations of transcriptions and mistranslations. Originally exhibited in the bend of a copper pipe and later acquired by a permanent collection,[1] the text has been freshly transcribed and illustrated.[2]*

Long ago I overheard, or was told – it is no longer exactly clear to me – of a cylindrical room containing the sum of human knowledge. This document reconstructs a profile of this remarkable chamber from the tangle of hearsay and credible research.

At the center of the room is a column – more precisely, a hinge – said to extend beyond the confines of the azure ceiling and into the heavens, although I am skeptical of such hyperbole. It is conceivable, however, that numerous pages are appended to the central hinge like curtains, or *velæ*, extending from floor to ceiling and completing the radius to within a hair's breadth of an outlying concentric ring of columns.[3] Although details are scarce, it appears that one is to read while walking, by pushing the page in front of oneself.

Curiously, the central hinge rotates in either direction, leading to heated confrontations whenever multiple readers occupy the room, simultaneously pushing the pages in opposing directions. These uprisings have precipitated vastly learned and acutely obtuse debates about the protocols of pagewalking.[4] Rarely has the more disconcerting question about the chamber's original purpose been raised.

These debates carried on for centuries, until it was no longer clear which argument was being defended, or to what end. In the manner that temporary

FIGURE 1.1 *The Reading Chamber,* drawn by Scintilla Paramanu

solutions become unquestioned truths, a provisional rule of thumb was adopted: upon entering the chamber, readers proceed to their right, establishing *recto* and *verso*. To read beyond the text of a given page, one must exit and reenter the chamber at its circumference.

For ages, this unabashedly random solution elicited criticism and conspiracies, although many readers find solace in upholding an established code of etiquette, no matter how dubious. Acceptance, in this view, is more pragmatic and productive than confronting the underlying, abysmal questions concerning the chamber itself. Strangely, no one seems to have considered

FIGURE 1.2 *The Reading Chamber*, drawn by Scott Hsu

altering the physical characteristics of the chamber, and to this day, reputedly, the hinge remains free to pivot in either direction, ambivalent.

Some argue that each page has been inscribed with one single narrative, refracted through an array of languages and colloquialisms – a pinwheel *rosetta stone*. Others speculate that by deciphering all of the texts amassed in the chamber, the key to divining humankind's role in the universe lies close at hand.

I am apprehensive about such grandiloquence. If we have merely repeated the same canon since the kindling consciousness of our ancestors, disputes over the shape of time would favor the eternal return. The chamber would thus embody a truism, a self-fulfilling prophecy, and notions of evolution or enlightenment would be dismissed since one could never emerge from the hermetic cycle of divine recapitulation.

On the other hand, if it is as some have implied (or I have inferred), and each page has been translated in chronological succession, then the notion of evolution and chance is resuscitated. In brief: a translator is a frontiersman who negotiates boundaries, stimulating the commerce of ideas. Exchanges are imperfect: techniques of transcription are notoriously unstable and flawed. As liberty – some might say libertinage, or *vagabondry* – is the hallmark of a pioneer, so it must be acknowledged that each page bears the indelible stamp of a translator's interpretation of another's world. If this assertion is valid, then the exact number of pages within this supposedly small chamber is infinite: even as the ink dries on one page, somewhere else the transcription of another has already begun.

Another plausible interpretation centers on the arts of speaking and listening, as distinguished from the arts of writing and reading, and offers an explanation of the chamber's puzzling peripatetic nature.

Some believe there are closely related linguistic groups, while others share features but fall beyond the family tree. Close inspection of etymologies and oral traditions suggests deeper connections: languages presumed long dead are alive and well, embedded in (if somewhat obscured by) contemporary vocabulary and syntax, following millennia of subtle transmutation.[5]

Across the Roman Empire, for example, Latin became as enmeshed with its expanding territories as its network of laws and highways, enjoying and suffering regional manipulations of the tongue ages before the advent of moveable type. And yet even Latin is a relatively recent skein: traces of the Phoenicians and Celts endure, stretching back beyond written memory along the chthonic sinews of *protolanguages*.

The world is a loom from which words are spun. Language is a textile, woven across the land, and each person introduces a thread by speaking.

FIGURE 1.3 *The Reading Chamber*, drawn by Michael McDowell

Villages separated by the slightest walking distance evolved subtle inflections perceptible only to the ear of a traveler who knots the threads together with every step taken, conversation engaged, village and city visited.[6]

In a pedestrian world, *barbarian* describes a person who travels too quickly to assimilate dialectical variations between two given locations, a phenomenon that explains the horrifying force of the horse-borne war machines of the Goths and Tartars, as well as the sweeping transformations during that effervescent yet nebulous age of aerial transport and hyper communication.[7]

Historically speaking, a pilgrim did not require a dictionary of foreign languages but absorbed subtleties of cadence and idiom at the pace of walking, encouraging the thought that there once may have existed as many tongues in the world as pages contained in the *Chamber*. If nothing else, the hinged

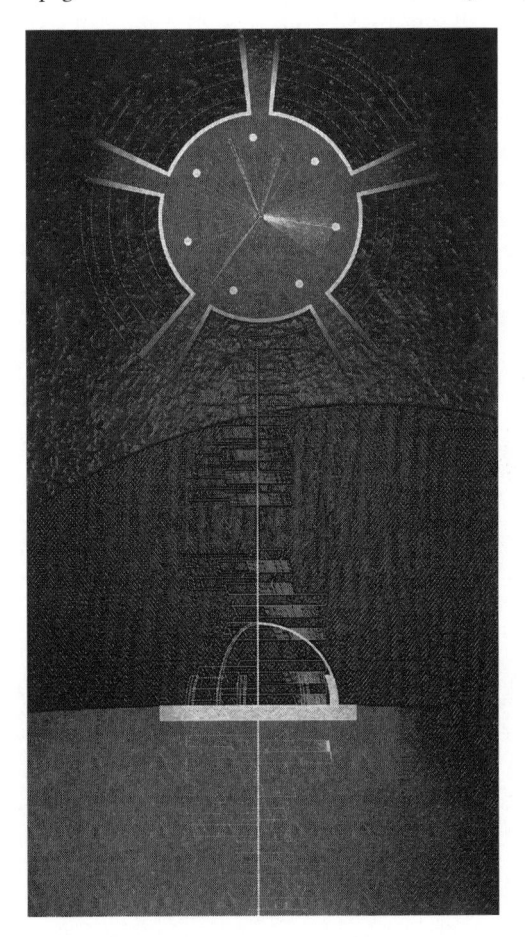

FIGURE 1.4 *The Reading Chamber*, drawn by Andrew Broddle

pages recall the traces of a language borne by the feet and tongue as much as by the hand and pen. *The Reading Chamber* embodies the difference between a barbarian–soldier and a peregrine–vagabond.

Yet the chamber is also an imperfectly constructed metaphor. Although readers must travel through other languages in order to circumnavigate the text, they are free to leave and reenter the chamber at any point, potentially bypassing entire landmasses and peoples. The room's configuration contradicts the traditional seamless weave of land and language.[8]

It has been suggested, uberoptimistically, that this fundamental rift between form and substance is the fertile source of all scholarship.[9] Skeptics countered that the construction of the room was itself the first scholarly wedge driven between our experience of the world and its representation.[10] Detractors have gone as far as denouncing the chamber as humankind's first great vanity, calling it a *revolving door to nowhere*.[11] Others have painted the *Chamber* as an apparatus of calibrated gears that have rusted to a halt, more akin to a scrap yard than clockwork. Cynics simply refuse to entertain its existence altogether.

Supposedly, there are sizable gaps among the pages, prompting the rumor that many have been furtively torn out or surgically removed.[12] In any case,

FIGURE 1.5 *The Reading Chamber*, drawn by Charlotte Ensign

they are irretrievably lost. There is a sect of scholars – bitingly referred to as the *Optimists* – who argue that these lacunae are simply benign gaps, awaiting the insertion of new transcriptions. They also believe that gaps in human expression, including differences in language, are not to be lamented as evidence of the loss of an original state of understanding. Rather, they are the wellsprings of human imagination, plumbed by such devices as metonymy and metaphor.[13]

Attempts to maintain order and discourage theft of or mischievous wrongdoing (some speak of lewd drawings in the margins) have led to the invention of complex and abstruse systems for codifying, cross-referencing, indexing, and inserting glosses. These techniques are under constant debate and revision, and transcriptions that fail to comply with the most recent, authorized annotational habits are subjected to zealous scrutiny. Many have acknowledged that these systems often overlap and contradict one another, leading to impossible entanglements for readers and transcribers alike.

Although earnest and well intentioned, this passion for clarity has spawned an industry of hollow tasks.[14] If each page is self-contained and indivisible, an a-tomic encapsulation of the universe, it would not need the slightest reference to any other page, *each page being itself the authorized edition*.[15]

Whether fact or fiction this elusive structure has endured generations of boundless enthusiasm and meticulous derision.[16] Akin to such epic projects as the *Tower of Babel* and the *Ark of Noah*, *The Reading Chamber* ultimately presents a confounding mirror. One translator has scribbled in a margin, whether in a flash of hope or fit of anguish:

> *In this concise yet endless chamber,*
> *there exists neither time nor direction,*
> *merely unceasing toil.*
> *We are ever filling a vessel*
> *– fabricated in our own image –*
> *with a substance as indifferent and yielding as water or sand.*

Transcribed by Roberto Sposadellachiesa

Addendum

Toward the conclusion of The Reading Chamber, *a sidelong reference is made to the* Tower of Babel *and the* Ark of Noah. *The following elaborates on this notorious remark.*

There is an irresolvable tension between oblivion and our tactics of preservation. Without fear of oblivion we would have no need for containment,

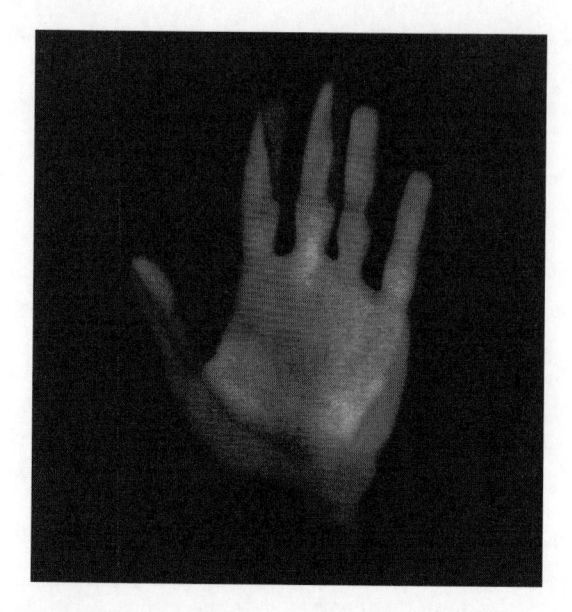

FIGURE 1.6 *The Reading Chamber*, drawn by Rob O'Roboro

neither language nor libraries, and without containment there would be no means of apprehending oblivion. Put another way, without forgetting there would be no memory, and without memory, we would have no fear of forgetting.

The *Tower of Babel* has not yet fallen in the same way that the *Ark of Noah* still has not found land. The *Ark* is the world itself. We are its self-appointed navigators – that is the evidence of our being, embedded in myth and matter. Our task of naming has not yet exhausted the contents of this world, an unfinished project.

Similarly, we are in the midst of the *Tower*. From day to day we contribute to the ebb and flow of its construction and destruction. We build on the foundations laid before us, providing footing for others to follow. And, in the way that the extinction of beings in the world accompanies our discovery of those unanticipated, the foundations crumble as we build anew.

We expend our lives spanning, stitching, and shoring up cracks that open behind even as we cast lines forward. It is difficult to discern the boundary of renewal and progress, for all of the scaffolding. Ancient navigators mended their sailing vessels when and where necessary – a piece at a time – in untiring repair.

The *Tower* manifests a multiplicity of language and fluent expression. It is not carved from a single, monolithic language lost long ago with an illusory

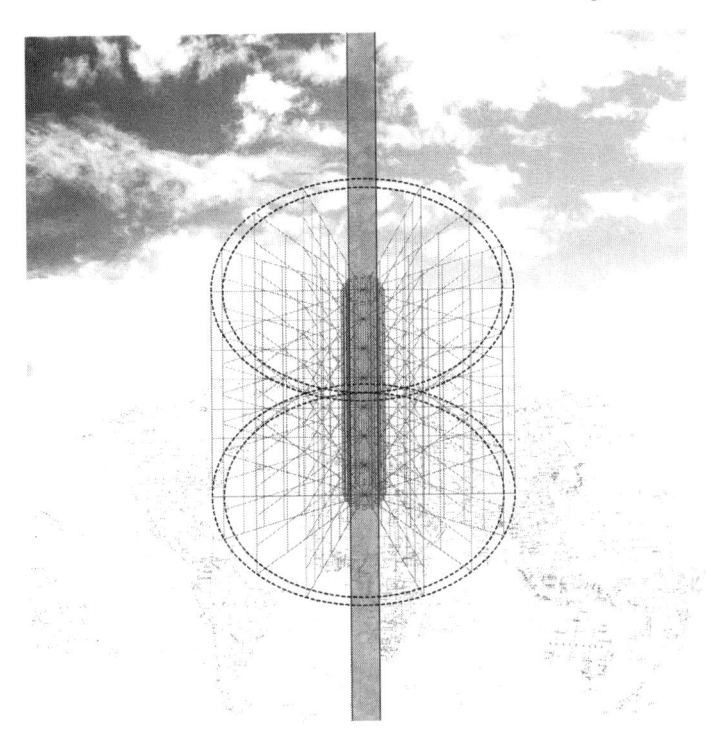

FIGURE 1.7 *The Reading Chamber*, drawn by Angelina Putri

paradise, nor is it an idyllic model where all minds and hearts act as one. We are compelled by our differences to speak and act, expressing our ambits and identities through an *Ark*, a *Tower*, a *Reading Chamber* – by language itself. These vehicles of transformation transport us between certainty and uncertainty, clamor and silence, memory and forgetting.

Notes

1 Portfolio N7433.4.K575 R43 1997b (Rare Book Collection, University of Pennsylvania). Exhibited at Philadelphia Art Alliance in 1997, this iteration of *The Reading Chamber* is described in the rare book collection catalog as follows: "Eight laminated leaves attached by wire to a central, pivoting metal hinge, which is, in turn, attached to copper tubes at top and bottom, which are fixed to ceiling and floor, allowing the book, suspended at approximately eye-level for a standing reader, to be circumnavigated by spinning the text-pages." It is also noted that "one laminated leaf [has] detached from [the] central hinge."

2 The illustrations were produced, in the order of appearance, by Scintilla Paramanu, Scott Hsu, Michael McDowell, Andrew Broddle, Charlotte Ensign, Rob O'Roboro and Angelina Putri.

3 The columns at the room's perimeter are described variously. I have read there are as many as sixteen and as few as six columns, reflecting diverse opinions on the direction of the winds and division of the heavens. There are also conflicting reports on their appearance. Some say the columns have been fashioned in human form, in a manner anticipating caryatids; others fervently argue that only pure geometries would have been used for such a divine fabrication. This issue remains open to speculation.

4 The "directionality" of reading the chamber appears to be subjective. In many cultures pagewalking occurs in the *opposite* direction (to the left). One imagines the turbulence along the borders of neighboring cultures that read and write in contrary directions (cf. *Eugubian Tablets*). Evidence points also to peoples in the dim past for whom writing was performed as an agrarian practice, boustrophedonically plowing the writing instrument back and forth in a continuous, ductile furrow. I have even heard tales of strange peoples for whom the hinge of *The Reading Chamber* extends horizontally, providing readers the possibility to navigate the text from *top to bottom* (and conceivably the reverse). By some accounts, this horizontal hinge is said to encircle the earth as an infinite ring; by others, the hinge merely alights upon the earth as a tangential line, passing through the chamber as it continues along its axis through the heavens.

5 Castiglione observes: " . . . since Italy was not only vexed and ravaged but long inhabited by the barbarians, the Latin language was corrupted and spoiled by contact with those nations, and from that corruption other languages were born: and like rivers that from the crest of the Apennines separate and flow down into the two seas, so also these languages divided, and some of them tinged with Latinity reached by diverse paths, one this country and one that; and one of them remained in Italy tinged with barbarism." Baldassare Castiglione, *The Book of the Courtier* (New York: Horace Liveright, 1929), 43.

6 Ivan Illich and Barry Sanders, *ABC: The Alphabetization of the Popular Mind* (New York: Random House, 1988).

7 Oxford English Dictionary: *Barbary* − L. *barbaria*, land of barbarians, Berber. Applied by Arab geographers from ancient times to natives of North Africa, west and south of Egypt. According to native lexicographers, of native origin, f. Arab *barbar* "to talk noisily and confusedly" (which is not derived from Gr. βαρβαρoζ: according to others, a foreign word, African, Egyptian, or perhaps f. Greek. Actual relations, if any, of the Arabic and Greek words cannot be settled; but in former European langs, *Barbaria, Barbarie, Barbary,* have from the beginning been treated as identical with L. *barbaria*, Byzantine Gr. βαρβαρια, land of barbarians. Committing a *barbarism* was thus *to speak like a foreigner;* historically, anyone speaking a language different from one's own has been considered a *barbarian.*

8 "Ancient Egyptians believed that the seat of the soul was in the tongue: the tongue was a rudder or steering-oar with which a man steered his course through the world." Bruce Chatwin, *The Songlines* (New York: Penguin Group, 1988), 271.

9 There is a slender entry for the *Chamber* in *The Codex of the Flight of the Imagination*, an exceedingly rare volume containing delicate illustrations for an array of fledgling notions and the forces encountered at their birthing, both conducive and inopportune.

10 The anatomist Andreas Vesalius, who fought for the convergence of theory and direct observation, describes the effect of this division: "After the barbarian invasions all the sciences . . . went to rack and ruin. At that time, and first of all in Italy, the fashionable doctors began to despise the work of the hand, in imitation of the ancient Romans . . . When the whole procedure of the manual operation

was handed over to barbers, the doctors not only soon lost the true knowledge of the viscera, but very soon practical anatomy also came to an end. This no doubt was due to the fact that the doctors no longer risked operating; while those to whom this task had been entrusted were too ignorant to read the writings of the teachers of anatomy . . . the dissectionist, ignorant of the art of speech, is not able to explain the dissection to the students and badly arranges the demonstration that should follow the doctor's explanations, while the doctor never lends a hand to the work itself, but disdainfully guides the ship with the help of the manual worker, and he talks . . . " Paolo Rossi, *Philosophy, Technology and the Arts* (New York: Harper and Row, 1970), 7.

11 A few (unfortunately anonymous) rebuttals have quipped that language – and thought itself – is rightfully humankind's first true vanity. There are conflations of *The Reading Chamber* with the *Tower of Babel*, perhaps since the two structures are twin aspects of thought and its articulation – written and spoken language.

12 The loose association known as the *League of Bucologists*, which attends to holes, hovels, and imbroglios, has spawned a microspecialist denomination, the *Culobucologists*, who investigate the ends and means of hollows, hallows, and haloes.

13 George Steiner, *After Babel: Aspects of Language and Translation* (Oxford: Oxford University Press, 1975).

14 Many have observed that the administration of these techniques is as random as the *recto/verso* directionality of pagewalking.

15 And yet, the unstemmed flow of critique and counter-critique reveals a leak in the authority of the monad-pages. Consequently, each of us may introduce a new page in the chamber, provoking the inevitable interpretation and counter-interpretation of endless others. Of particular note are the speculations of Leticia Alvarez de Toledo.

16 Keeping in mind that *fiction is etymologically the figment of fact.*

2

THE TOWER OF BABEL AND JACOB'S PILLAR

Hegel, Heidegger, and the death of architecture

Karsten Harries

Introduction

When we look at Brueghel's representation of the Tower of Babel, hanging in the Kunsthistorisches Museum in Vienna, we are struck by the contrast between the still unfinished tower, already piercing the clouds, literally a skyscraper, and countless much more modest structures in the picture, first of all the houses that make up the surrounding city, but also farmhouses, city walls, and bridges; and the fragile shelters that, somewhat like swallow nests, cling to the tower itself, presumably put up by the workers to satisfy their need for shelter while work on the tower is proceeding. The contrast established in this picture between the monumental architecture of the never to be finished tower and these much more modest buildings must have been quite familiar to Brueghel's contemporaries: in one medieval city after another we meet with the same contrast, where often, as in this picture, the magnitude of the work undertaken, almost always a church, prevented its completion. The painting thus invites a distinction between two kinds of building: between mere buildings and works of architecture.

It is a familiar distinction: the history of building has long turned around two poles, one marked first of all by the house, the other by temple or church, one comparatively private, the other comparatively public, one comparatively profane, the other comparatively sacred. And it is the latter pole that we think of first of all when we think of architecture.[1] Consider, for example, the understanding of architecture presupposed by Nikolaus Pevsner, who begins his *An Outline of European Architecture* with this seemingly self-evident observation: "A bicycle shed is a building; Lincoln Cathedral is a piece of architecture."[2] The distinction seems obvious. To be sure, a cathedral, too, is also a building. But the architect does not only build; he does more. But how are we to understand this "more?" Pevsner's answer is quite expected: what distinguishes works of architecture from mere buildings is that they are "designed with a view to aesthetic appeal." A work of architecture is a functional building that is also a work of art. In support of this distinction between building and architecture one could cite Vitruvius, who demanded that the architect build "with due reference to durability, convenience, and beauty."[3] But despite the authority of Pevsner and Vitruvius, do we really capture the essence of architecture when we follow an approach that understands works of architecture as buildings intended to succeed also as aesthetic objects?

Look once more at Brueghel's painting: a concern for beauty is not what led to the building of the Tower of Babel. Here the Biblical account:

> . . . they said, "Come, let us build ourselves a city and a tower with its top in the heavens, and let us make a name for ourselves, lest we be scattered abroad upon the face of the earth." And the Lord came down to see the city and the tower, which the sons of man had built. And the Lord said, "Behold, they are one people, and they have one language; and this is only the beginning of what they will do; and nothing they propose to do will be impossible for them. Come let us go down and confuse their language, that they may not understand one another's speech." So the Lord scattered them abroad from there over the face of all the earth, and they left off from building the city. Therefore its name was called Babel, because there the Lord confused the language of all the earth; and from there the Lord scattered them abroad over the face of all the earth.
>
> *Gen. 1, 4–9, RSV*

The work of architecture here is understood as the product of a communal act of self-assertion. The tower's builders want "to make a name" for themselves, so that they would "not be scattered about the face of the earth." So understood architecture has not so much an aesthetic, as a political and an ethical function. In this particular case, to be sure, and this invites further reflection, the building of this enormous tower leads not to the desired preservation, but to the destruction of community: "the Lord scattered them abroad from there over the face of all the earth, and they left off from building the city." The story of the fall repeats itself: pride once again robs human beings of their home. There is the suggestion that we humans cannot fashion ourselves into a genuine, lasting community by raising such a work, no matter how gigantic, a suggestion that community and home are, in a sense, a gift.

It is not difficult to come up with modern analogues to Babel's Tower. Consider our cities, where splendid skyscrapers, large-scale aesthetic objects, often by our most distinguished architects, create a disturbing sense of place or rather non-place! Or consider Frank Gehry's Guggenheim Museum in Bilbao! Crucial in all such cases is the way architecture relates or rather fails to relate, responds or rather fails to respond, to the ground provided by the existing buildings and the land. Indeed, to the extent that the intention of the architect is to create aesthetic monuments, a certain disregard of the pre-given context is to be expected. To the extent that the architect understands himself as someone whose task it is to transform buildings into ideally self-sufficient, self-assertive aesthetic objects, he must tear the ever-evolving fabric of the landscape or the city. Alexander Tzonis and Liane Lefaivre thus insist, invoking the authority of Aristotle, that the work of architecture, like every work of art, "is a world within the world, 'complete,' 'integral,' 'whole,' a world where there is no contradiction."[4] Greek temples are cited as an illustration. According to the authors — and I do not want here to challenge the adequacy of their characterization — they "turned a cold shoulder to every structure that happened to be next to them, even if this other structure was another temple."[5] Here I am concerned with a more basic claim that must be affirmed and can be illustrated with countless modern examples: to the extent that architects take their task to be the creation of self-sufficient aesthetic objects, architecture must aim at the creation of works that turn a cold shoulder, not just to their neighbors, but to a world that inevitably constrains them with its demands and necessities. To be sure, the world refuses to be forgotten. As in Brueghel's painting, it provides the inevitable, pre-given point of departure, the ground needed to support whatever figures the architect chooses to put there. But if the work of architecture is to be a self-sufficient aesthetic object, the world should be no more than that.

Brueghel's painting of Babel's tower warns us that such architecture, far from gathering a multitude into a genuine community, scatters and isolates them. How can architecture establish a communal ethos?

Jacob's ladder

Let me turn to another passage from Genesis, one that once was read as part of the consecration rite of every church and served to establish the traditional symbolism of the church as house of God and gate of Heaven.

And he [Jacob] came to a certain place and stayed there that night, because the sun had set. Taking one of the stones of the place, he set it under his head and lay down in that place to sleep. And he dreamed that there was a ladder set up on the earth and the top of it reached the heaven: and behold, the angels of the Lord were ascending and descending on it! And behold, the Lord stood above it and said, "I am the Lord, the God of Abraham your father and the God of Isaac: the land on which you lie I will give to you and to your descendants; and your descendants shall be like the dust of the earth and you shall spread to the west and to the east and to the north and to the south; and by your descendants shall all the families of the earth bless themselves. Behold, I am with you, and will keep you wherever you go, and will bring you back to this land; for I will not leave you until I have done that of which I have spoken to you. Then Jacob awoke and said: "Surely the Lord is in this place. This is none other than the house of God, and this is the gate of heaven."

Gen. 28, 11–17, RSV

We should note these main points: a particular landscape is experienced as filled with the presence of the divine: it is the house of the Lord; God dwells in that landscape. In this place heaven and earth are experienced as somehow linked: it is not only the dwelling place of God but opens up to a higher reality, it is the gate of heaven. The ladder of the dream symbolizes that linkage. That linkage, and this is what matters most in this context, is tied to a trust that extends beyond the individual to his offspring, extends into an indefinite future. The world is experienced as in tune not just with Jacob, but with coming generations.

Jacob responds to this experience by marking the place: he takes the stone on which he slept, turns it into a pillar, transforming the horizontal slab into a vertical post. Later churches reenact that archetypal act: every church once was thought to represent Bethel. The Tower of Babel and Jacob's pillar represent rival approaches to architecture, one self-assertive, the other responsive to what is experienced as sacred.

But what can the latter paradigm still mean to us today? Does it not lie so thoroughly behind us that all attempts to return to it must seem anachronistic? Is there anything that can be put in its place? Could it be that architecture, by its very essence, demands such a return?

Heidegger's promise

An affirmative answer seems implied by Heidegger's much cited but deeply ambiguous description of a Greek temple in "The Origin of the Work of Art."

A building, a Greek temple, portrays nothing. It simply stands there in the rock-cleft valley. The building encloses the figure of the god and lets it stand out in the holy precinct through the open portico. By means of the temple, the god is present in the temple. This presence of the god is itself an extension and delimitation of the precinct as a holy precinct. The temple and its precinct, however, do not fade into the indefinite. It is the templework that first fits together and at the same time gathers around itself the unity of those paths and relations in which birth and death, disaster and blessing, victory and disgrace, endurance and decline, acquire the shape of destiny for human being. The all-governing expanse of this open relational context is the world of this historical people. Only from and in this expanse does the nation first return to itself for the fulfillment of its vocation.[6]

It is difficult to offer a literal reading of this passage. Already the very beginning causes the reader to stumble: "A building, a Greek temple portrays nothing." How are we to understand the "indefinite article": "Ein Bauwerk, ein griechischer Tempel." Into what region does Heidegger's "ein" direct us? Many have wondered which temple Heidegger is talking about. But can it really matter whether he was thinking of a particular temple, say the so-called Poseidon Temple in Paestum? As soon as you substitute some particular temple for what the text leaves indefinite, what Heidegger has to say threatens to become incoherent. If such a temple were indeed to establish "the world of this historical people," each temple for the first time, such establishment would have a revolutionary significance and would cause the Greek world to fall apart, only to found it anew. So understood, a Greek temple would indeed turn a cold shoulder to its pre-given environment as Tzonis and Lefaivre claim, would be apolis, as Heidegger, at about the same time, claimed disturbingly for all genuine creators, including not only poets, but also political leaders, who he wrote must be: "without city and place, lonely, uncanny, without expedients in the midst of all that is, without law and limit, without structure and order, because as creators, they themselves must lay the foundation for all this."[7] Should we understand the temple's architect, too, as such a lonely creator? If so, Heidegger's temple threatens to turn into a version of the Tower of Babel, Heidegger's Greece into a precursor of Hitler's Germany.[8] But the text rules out such a literalization. Heidegger's temple cannot be found on some map. Like the Tower of Babel or Jacob's pillar, it has its place in an ideal space. As an ideal type it challenges the way we build.

The temple is said by Heidegger to establish a particular region as a holy precinct, presided over by a god. But upon entering this precinct and in this sense leaving the world of the everyday, that dimension is not simply left outside and behind. The temple illuminates the everyday. It is this that lets Heidegger say that the temple reveals to the community their world. "World" here does not name the totality of facts, but a meaningful order that assigns to things and persons their proper places. Think of the modern world, or the world of the Middle Ages. "World" is understood here, as already in *Being and Time*, as a space of meanings. But this world is now thought historically as established by human work. Such work Heidegger thinks as "a making space for" (einräumen), although the English here fails to capture the way the German also suggests "furnishing." All such einräumen already presupposes some Raum or room, which without such einräumen would remain an indefinite and uninhabitable open expanse. Heidegger would have us understand the world-establishing of the temple-work as such a "furnishing." Such furnishing presupposes that open expanse for which Heidegger gives us the metaphor of the clearing. His world is that clearing made habitable by human work, thought by Heidegger as an einräumen.

But how are we to think such world-establishing work? Where does it find measure and direction? "The Origin of the Work of Art" offers no clear answer to that question, but only an oracular pointer when it says of the temple that as it stands there, "it first gives to things their look and to men their outlook on themselves. This view remains open as long as the work is a work, as long as the god has not fled from it."[9] But is it not the world that according to Heidegger first gives to things their look and to men their outlook on themselves? Now the world is placed into an essential relationship to the presence of a god. How are we today to understand such a god and his relationship to the world?

Unlike Brueghel's Tower, Heidegger's temple would seem to be more than a product of prideful self-assertion: Heidegger points to how this "more" is to be understood when the temple is said to present the earth:

> The temple's firm towering makes visible the invisible space of the air. The steadfastness of the work contrasts with the surge of the surf, and its own repose brings out the raging of the sea. Trees and grass first enter into their distinctive shapes and thus come to appear as what they are. The Greeks called this emerging in itself and in all things *phusis*. It clears and illuminates also that on which and in which man bases his dwelling. We call this ground the earth. What this word says is not to be associated with a mass of matter deposited somewhere, nor with the merely astronomical idea of a planet. Earth is that whence the arising brings back and shelters everything that arises without violation. In the things that arise, earth is present as the sheltering agent.[10]

Establishing a world, the temple also responds to and interprets the earth, where Heidegger understands "earth" as the ground of our being. We belong to the earth because we have a body. The earth claims and speaks to us through our body. It speaks of life and death, of desire and fulfillment, of pain and of joy.

But again: what does Heidegger's Greek temple mean to us today? Do its gods not lie even more thoroughly behind us than the God who inhabited the cathedrals of the Middle Ages? But already "The Origin of the Work of Art," unafraid of such untimeliness, places the thing, such as a pair of shoes, and the world co-present in it, not just between the open expanse of the sky and the self-secluding earth, but also between mortals and gods. What later will get developed in terms of the Geviert announces itself. But what are Heidegger's, or Hölderlin's, or the Greek gods to us today?

Hegel's challenge

Those who want to draw from Heidegger's temple passage a pointer as to where architecture should be going today will have to contend first with what Heidegger has to say in the epilogue to "The Origin of the Work of Art," where he quotes this famous proposition from Hegel's Lectures on Aesthetics: "Art is and remains for us, on the side of its highest vocation, something past."[11] Today, Hegel suggests, art in its highest sense belongs in a museum. Art has lost the significance it had in ancient Greece or medieval Europe. And architecture is very much included in that judgment. In a figurative sense to be sure, Greek temples and Gothic cathedrals, too, today belong into a museum. Many of the greatest works of architecture have indeed become museums, complete with entrance fees, signs, guides, and guidebooks. There is indeed a sense, if Hegel is right, in which the modern world neither has room nor need for architecture "on the side of its highest vocation."

Consider once more an understanding of works of architecture as public figures on the ground of comparatively private buildings, where temple and church provide the obvious paradigms. These paradigms have lost their authority. The question then becomes how to reoccupy the place once occupied by sacred architecture. A number of building types have presented themselves as possible candidates: towards the end of the Middle Ages city hall and palace emerged as rival building tasks. In the nineteenth-century monument, museum, city and theater engaged the most creative architects. The list of so-called "leading building tasks" can no doubt be increased. But if each of these building types holds some promise, not one of them can offer an altogether convincing answer. The history of architecture thus offers considerable support to the thesis that architecture is and remains for us, from the side of its highest vocation, something past.

Many today have indeed difficulty with the very notion of such a highest vocation, with the attribution of an ethical function to architecture. Is the very idea of a re-occupation of the place once occupied by temple or cathedral not wrong-headed? So we readily embrace some version of the kind of aesthetic approach that would have us understand works of architecture, with Pevsner or Venturi, as decorated sheds in the broadest sense. As Heidegger knows, this aesthetic approach has to mean the death of art, and that includes architecture, in what Hegel took to be its highest sense.

Heidegger glosses Hegel's thesis with the remark:

> The truth of Hegel's judgment has not yet been decided; for behind that verdict stands Western thought since the Greeks, which thought corresponds to a truth of beings that has already happened. Decision upon the judgment will be made, when it is made, from and about this truth of what is. Until then the judgment remains in force.[12]

That is to say, if Heidegger is right, the very shape of modernity, correctly described by Hegel, leaves no place for architecture in its highest sense. This is not to say that what Hegel asserts must be accepted as a last and final word. But for Heidegger it is clear that to challenge Hegel we have to take a step beyond modernity, have to become pre- or post-modern in some sense. On this view architecture in its highest sense and modernity do not go together.

When Hegel speaks of art in its highest sense, he is thinking art in opposition to what I have called the aesthetic approach: according to Hegel, art "only achieves its highest task when it has taken its place in the same sphere with religion and philosophy, and has become simply a mode of revealing to consciousness and bringing to utterance the Divine Nature, the deepest interests of humanity, and the most comprehensive truths of the mind."[13] For Hegel, too, art in its highest sense has what elsewhere I have called an ethical function. Why should this highest task be denied to art today? Hegel could answer: because of the authority of reason. On this point Hegel is close to Nietzsche, who in *The Birth of Tragedy* blames the death of tragedy, and tragedy figures here as the paradigmatically ethical art work, on the Socratic spirit, which is characterized by its confident trust in reason to guide us to the good life. With this art must lose what Hegel considers its highest function. To be sure, art may continue to serve reason, but such service is not essential to the work of reason. To quote Hegel once more:

> The peculiar mode to which artistic production and works of art belong no longer satisfies our supreme need. We are above the level at which works of art can be venerated as divine, and actually worshipped; the impression which they make is of a more considerate kind, and the feelings which they stir within us require a higher test and a further confirmation. Thought and reflection have taken their flight above fine art.[14]

Descartes gave expression to this modern understanding of reality when he made our ability to comprehend the measure of reality. But what we can comprehend we can also master: hence Descartes' promise that his method would render human beings the masters and possessors of nature. The modern understanding of reality culminates in technology; but in this technological world art has no essential contribution to make to our understanding of what matters. It offers a vacation from reality, an escape into beautiful illusion. With this art becomes mere ornament. We can thus say: modernity understands art as a decoration of life. In this sense all the arts could be said to have only a decorative function in the modern world. We moderns could then be said to live in the age of the decorated shed. But if so, architecture in its highest sense is indeed a thing of the past.

What matters here isn't Hegel. Any critique of Hegel would itself be pointless, were it not for the fact that Hegel has given us a profound analysis of certain aspects of our modern world, aspects that do indeed imply the death of architecture in what both Hegel and Heidegger would consider its highest sense.

History

Hegel's understanding of the death of art and architecture in their highest sense is inseparable from his understanding of history. History, if Hegel is right, cannot be understood as a sequence of events without rhyme or reason, but presents itself to us an irreversible process, leading to an ever increasing freedom. Despite countless setbacks, history can be understood as the progress of freedom. As such it is also a process that has to bring with it an increasing spiritual and literal mobility. Is Hegel right? In its general outline the thesis seems difficult to dispute. The other side of this process is that the authority of such natural givens as distinctions of gender or race, or the place one happens to occupy, are granted less and less authority. With this the very meaning of "home" becomes problematic.

Following a tradition going back at least to Plato, Hegel understands the human being as a citizen of two worlds:

> For on the one side, we see man a prisoner in common reality and earthly temporality, oppressed by want and poverty, hard driven by nature, entangled in matter, in sensuous aims and their enjoyment; on the other side, he exalts himself to eternal ideas, to a realm of thought and freedom, imposes on himself as will universal laws and attributions, strips the world of its living and flourishing reality and dissolves it into abstractions, in as much as the mind is put upon vindicating its rights and its dignity simply by denying the rights of nature and maltreating it, thereby retaliating the oppression and violence which in itself has experienced from nature.[15]

This places the human being in opposition to nature. According to Hegel the mind inevitably seeks to assert its mastery over nature. In something as simple as a child throwing stones into the water and enjoying the rings formed Hegel finds evidence of this drive. The human being here seeks to appropriate the natural given by transforming it in his own image and this means first of all in the image of his own spirit.

> This purpose he achieves by the modification of the external things upon which he impresses the seal of his inner being, and then finds repeated in them his own characteristics. Man does this in order as a free subject to strip the outer world of its stubborn foreignness, and to enjoy in the shape and fashion of things a mere external reality of himself.[16]

History is understood as the progress of such appropriation. Art is part of the effort to make the natural and sensible our own, to rob it of its character of being a mute, alien other, and thus to transform it into a dwelling place fit for human beings. Nature is humanized. An expression of such humanization is the city. There is a sense in which, like the Bible, Hegel, too, places humanity between a garden, or in his case rather a wilderness, i.e. nature, and a city.

> The universal need for expression in art lies therefore, in man's impulse to exalt the inner and outer world into a spiritual consciousness for himself, as an object in which he recognizes his own self. He satisfies the need of this spiritual freedom, when he makes all that exists explicit for himself *within*, and in a corresponding way realizes this explicit self *without*, evoking thereby, in this reduplication of himself, what is in him into vision and into knowledge for his own mind and for that of others. This is the free rationality of man, in which, as all action and knowledge, so also art has its soul and necessary origin.[17]

Art brings about an incarnation of the spirit in the sensible. The goal of art is the humanization of the sensible, where humanization means spiritualization. In every work of art we can therefore distinguish a spiritual content and a material embodiment. It should be clear that so understood art prefigures science and technology, which allow for a far more effective mastery of the material.

The place of architecture among the arts

Hegel understands architecture as the original, the first, and that means also as the most primitive of all the arts.

> It is with this that art begins. . . . The idea . . . being itself still in its indistinctness and obscurity, or in vicious, untrue determinateness, is made the import of artistic creations. As indeterminate it does not yet possess in itself that individuality which the Idea demands; its abstractness and one-sidedness leave its shape to be outwardly bizarre and defective. The first form of art is therefore a mere search for plastic portrayal than a capacity for genuine representation.[18]

Unable to find adequate expression, the spirit restlessly compounds images and forms. Hegel is thinking here of Egyptian and Indian art. Characteristic of such art is that it leaves us with a sense of sublimity, mystery and disquiet.

As already mentioned, Hegel associates this symbolic type above all with architecture. Its task, according to Hegel, "lies in so manipulating external inorganic nature that it becomes cognate to the mind, as an artistic outer world."[19] Le Corbusier's similarly tied the origin of architecture to the creation of a geometric spiritual order.

> The material of architecture is matter in itself in its immediate externality and as a heavy mass subject to mechanical laws, and its forms do not depart from those of inorganic nature, but are merely set in order with conformity of the abstract understanding, i.e. with relation of symmetry. In this material and in such forms, the ideal as concrete spirituality does not permit of being realized. Hence the reality which is represented in them remains contrasted with the Idea, as something external which it has not penetrated, or has penetrated only to establish an abstract relation.[20]

Architecture is understood here as the imposition of an abstract spiritual order on inorganic matter. In architecture the abstract mathematical understanding finds expression. Straight lines, rectangles, symmetry, arithmetic and geometric proportions have a decisive importance. But the very abstractness of its vocabulary prevents architecture from doing justice to the concreteness of the Idea.

> It is architecture that pioneers the way for the adequate realization of the god, and in this its service bestows hard toil upon existing nature, in order to disentangle it from the jungle of finitude and the abortiveness of chance. By this means it levels a space for the god, gives form to his external surroundings, and builds him his temple as a fit place for the concentration of spirit and for its direction to the mind's absolute objects.[21]

Architecture creates a space for the deity. But it requires the help of another art, namely sculpture, to make the god truly present. The Greek temple, on this interpretation, thus subordinates architecture to sculpture.

> Architecture, however, as we have seen, has purified the external world, and endowed it with symmetrical order and with affinity to mind, and the temple of the God, the house of his community stands ready. Into this temple, then, . . . the God enters in the lightning flash of his individuality, which strikes and permeates the inert mass, while the infinite and no longer merely symmetrical form belonging to mind itself concentrates and gives shape to the corresponding bodily existence.[22]

In the Greek god Hegel recognizes the perfect reconciliation of spirit and body. That reconciliation is achieved above all by the sculptor. Greek religion is tied to art, on this view, as Christian religion no longer could be. Christianity no longer could seek the sacred in the visible as the Greeks did. Christian spirituality already foreshadows the loss of art's highest vocation. Greek art, according to Hegel, cannot be surpassed as art. Marx later was to concur. Its defect, if we can speak here of a defect at all, is one that attaches to all art, indeed to the entire sensible dimension. Given the inwardness of modern man, his emphasis on reflection, thought alone can do justice to the Idea, by which Hegel thinks the reconciliation of spirit and nature. This is what lets him say that thought and reflection have overtaken the fine arts. Our approach to art is more thoughtful than sensuous. More and more we moderns approach works of art and more especially works of architecture as occasions for reflection. Consider once more our response to a medieval cathedral. And so some modern architects have created buildings that demand to be appreciated as occasions for reflection. Consider Peter Eisenman's all too thoughtful architecture. Or Charles Jencks' characterization of Johnson's Glass House as an architecture with footnotes. Indeed the turn to the text, to words, which is so characteristic of Christian and, to be sure in a very different way, of postmodern architecture can be cited in support of Hegel's thesis.

If we accept any version of the presupposed understanding of history as spiritual progress, we have to accept also that art and more especially architecture have lost their highest function. This is not to question that beautiful buildings will continue to be built and to delight us, as for example, the museum in Bilbao. But given such an understanding of history any attempt to return to architecture its ethical function must seem anachronistic: it fails to take seriously enough the shape of modernity, the way that shape is ruled by reason.

According to Hegel, architecture in its highest sense has to be considered a thing of the past. Some will mourn this, but, if Hegel is right, such mourning is as pointless as wishing to be returned to that wonder which was ours when we were children. Hegel is aware of the loss. He is too close to Winckelmann and to his friend and former roommate, the poet Hölderlin, not to know what has been lost. But he asks those who deplore this death of art in its highest sense to consider the necessity of this death:

> We must, however, not consider this merely an accidental misfortune what befell art from without, due to the insufficiency of the present age, the prosaic sense, the lack of interest, etc. It is rather the effect and development of art itself, which, in bringing the content dwelling in her to objective intuition, by this progress makes a contribution towards her own liberation from the represented content.[23]

Reconsidering Hegel

I would like to conclude with a more searching look at the premises on which this diagnosis rests. Hegel's thesis of the death of architecture is hardly derived from a careful examination of the evidence provided by history. It represents rather an at times willful fitting of the evidence into a schema that is derived from his own determination of art and architecture and their place in the history of the spirit. But regardless of details, that determination is difficult to get around. If we grant Hegel the importance he grants spirit and freedom, we grant him the substance of his case. If human freedom demands that the individual liberate himself from the accidents of what happens to be the case, then our real home should not be sought by looking towards a particular region or genius loci. Rather our real home must be a spiritual home to which the sensible, and that means also art and architecture, cannot do justice. From this point of view, the modern home should have the look of mobility, replaceability. Consider in this connection the recurrent insistence on the inessential nature of what is considered the accident of location, place of birth, gender, and race. Is the attempt to restore to architecture what Hegel considered it highest function or to restore to it what I have called its ethical function, not born of nostalgia that should be resisted? Is it not reason alone that in the end should determine our ethos? Think of Kant's emphasis on pure practical reason and the categorical imperative. Hegel's philosophy, too, is born of the confidence that humanity has finally come of age, that human beings have finally asserted themselves as the masters of nature, including their own nature. On this interpretation the loss of architecture in its highest sense is not really a loss at all, but a sign of humanity's coming of age.

And yet, against Hegel, I would like to insist that the power of the human spirit has here been exaggerated in a way that returns us to the Tower of Babel, where modernity's tower of Babel is not a tower at all, but that spiritual architecture Descartes promised and hoped to build, that Hegel hoped to complete, and on which we are still building. Hegel was unable to effect that reconciliation of spirit and nature that his philosophy promises. He could not effect it, because from the very beginning the spirit was given priority and the assumption was made that reality and the human spirit are finally commensurable.

Against this I would insist that they are finally incommensurable, would insist with Heidegger on the rift between world and earth, spirit and nature, word and reality, insist also that meanings cannot finally be invented, but must be disclosed. It is sufficient to contemplate any natural object, say a rock or a tree, to know about the inadequacy of all our attempts to describe it, to recognize that reality will finally always transcend and thus elude our grasp. Against any understanding of reality that makes our ability to grasp it clearly and distinctly its measure, I want to maintain that we know that something is real precisely because we are aware that we are unable to finally understand it. Reality transcends our understanding. Art recalls us to this transcendence. That is why Heidegger would have the work of art present the earth. Nietzsche might have said that art recalls us to the Dionysian ground of our existence.

In Hegel's philosophy, and to us moderns, what I have here called the transcendence of reality announces itself first of all as the concrete, sensuous, arbitrary, and contingent. The place that as a matter of fact I occupy to reason appears as a place that I just happen to occupy. The sex, which is as a matter of fact my own to reason, appears as a contingent fact that does not touch my essence. This goes for all my physical characteristics, also for my particular background. Reason lets me see the factual as the merely contingent, lets me see the world *sub specie possibilitatis*, from the vantage point of possibility. But if my biological and historical make-up are all understood as merely contingent facts, who or what is the "I"? When I take away all my supposedly accidental, contingent properties, what remains of me? In the end, as Kierkegaard saw, the self itself becomes empty, meaningless and abstract, a mere ghost of a self. And architecture, too, becomes ghostly and insubstantial.

At this point, as Nietzsche put it, reason coils back on itself and begins to recognize its limits. Inseparable from such recognition is an awareness of what I want to call "material transcendence." With that expression I want to point in the same general direction as Kant with his "thing-in-itself," which is present to us only as appearance. What invites talk of a thing-in-itself is the fact that, even if constituted by our language or concepts and as such appearance, what thus appears is not created by our understanding, but given. Inseparable from our experience of things is a sense of this gift, an awareness that our understanding is finite, and that means also that the reach of our concepts and words is limited. Everything real is infinitely complex and thus can never be fully translated into words. The rift between thing and word, between reality and language cannot be closed. Speaking that refuses to recognize this rift must degenerate into idle talk.

Language opens human beings to reality. Yet, as Heidegger emphasized, language conceals even as it reveals. Where this essential concealment is forgotten, language cannot but replace reality with a false, merely linguistic reality. To be sure, human being is essentially a dwelling in language. But the house of language is not a prison. Art may be understood as a way of opening the windows of that house, and that also goes for architecture. Needed is a new realism.

Such talk of a "new realism" is meant to suggest that art has the power to recall us to a sense of the gift of reality, where this means also that art discloses the rift between language and reality, a rift that is a presupposition of all meaning. What puts us in touch with material transcendence, this transcendence within the visible, within the sensible, is first of all the body. Here it is important to keep in mind that the embodied self is also a caring, desiring self. What it discloses is not just an assemblage of mute facts, but an inevitably meaningful configuration of objects of desire or things to be avoided. To be in the world is to be claimed in countless different ways by persons and things. What I call material transcendence may thus not be reduced to the mute presence of things. To be open to it is inevitably to be affected, moved, claimed, and claimed in quite specific ways. Material transcendence thus also refers to the affective base without which all our talk of values, ideals, or divinities is ultimately groundless: idle talk.

Art and architecture are needed to reintegrate the human being, whose essence is threatened by the shape of the modern world, determined as that shape is by an overemphasis on spirit, on logos. And it should be clear that what I called in the beginning of this essay the aesthetic approach cannot effect such a reconciliation. That approach is indeed itself an expression of the inability to place art at the service of life. As Heidegger suggested with his mention of the god, we have to rediscover once more the sacred in the sensible. But this means that there is a sense in which once again we are cast back to the origin of art. If art is to regain its ethical function architecture will have to take the lead. And the works to which such attempts will lead, will of necessity have the same character of indefiniteness, of gesturing towards something which they cannot adequately articulate, that according to Hegel characterizes all symbolic art.

Notes

1 For an extended treatment of this distinction, see Karsten Harries, *The Ethical Function of Architecture* (Cambridge, MA: MIT Press, 1979), 270–282.
2 Nikolaus Pevsner, *An Outline of European Architecture* (Harmondsworth: Penguin, 1958), 23.
3 Vitruvius, *The Ten Books of Architecture*, trans. Morris Hickey Morgan (New York: Dover, 1960), book 1, ch. 3, 17.
4 Alexander Tzonis and Liane Lefaivre, *Classical Architecture: The Poetics of Order* (Cambridge, MA and London: MIT Press, 1986), 9.
5 Ibid., 243.
6 Martin Heidegger, *Holzwege, Gesamtausgabe*, vol. 5 (Frankfurt am Main: Klostermann, 1977), 27–28; and "The Origin of the Work of Art," in Martin Heidegger *Poetry, Language, Thought*, trans. Albert Hofstadter (New York: Harper and Row, 1971), 41–42.
7 Martin Heidegger, *Einführung in die Metaphysik. Gesamtausgabe* (Frankfurt am Main: Klostermann, 1983), vol. 40, 162.
8 See Robert Jan van Pelt, "Apocalyptic Abjection," in Robert Jan van Pelt and Carroll Williams, *Architectural Principles in the Age of Historicism* (New Haven: Yale University Press, 1991), 317–381.
9 Heidegger, "The Origin of the Work of Art," 43.
10 Ibid., 49.
11 Ibid., 79–80.
12 Ibid., 68.
13 Georg Wilhelm Friedrich Hegel, *Introductory Lectures on Aesthetics*, trans. Bernard Bosanquet, ed. and intro. Michael Inwood (Harmondsworth: Penguin, 1993), 5–6.
14 Ibid., 12
15 Ibid., 59–60
16 Ibid., 36.
17 Ibid.

18 Ibid., 82
19 Ibid., 90.
20 Ibid.
21 Ibid., 90–91
22 Ibid., 91
23 Georg Wilhelm Friedrich Hegel, *Vorlesungen über die Aesthetik*, vol. 13 of *Jubiläumsausgabe*, ed. Hermann Glockner (Stuttgart: Fromann, 1937), 231.

3

READING WHAT IS WRITTEN BETWEEN THE LINES

The esoteric dimension of Ebenezer Howard's *Garden Cities of To-Morrow*

Paul Emmons

When an author "writes between the lines," like the purloined letter of Edgar Allan Poe, it is hidden in plain view. These sorts of texts have two faces: one exoteric and straightforward that fulfills widely held expectations, the other esoteric and hidden between the lines. In these situations, readers are active agents engaged in a quest for understanding. How do readers determine when to "read between the lines" as proper textual exegesis and not merely an arbitrary, willful interpretation imposed on a text?

Today's valuation of transparency in all facets of life occludes the possibility of intentionally hidden meanings in writings.[1] This is especially true for topics such as architecture, which tend to be viewed as technical and professional. Yet, whenever censorship and persecution occur, an author's true thoughts often are presented esoterically, a *"ductus obliquus."*[2] Political philosopher Leo Strauss (1899–1973), a German–Jewish refugee writing in the United States during the Second World War and later under McCarthyism, notes that persecution of writers can take many forms – not only in totalitarian states, but also indirectly in places where freedom of expression is presumed.[3] Strauss shows that social ostracism and academic exclusion can themselves be powerful forces toward esoteric authorship.[4]

The case of Ebenezer Howard's famous treatise, *Garden Cities of To-Morrow* (1898/1902) illustrates these issues. As we will see, Howard was enormously influenced by spiritualism, but his references are invisible to the average reader. In Howard's attempt to be taken seriously and expand his audience beyond a small like-minded group, he made his writing on city planning exoterically separate from its latent spiritualism to protect himself from rejection and ridicule, but not so subtly as to defeat his purpose of enlightening those people sensitive to his vision. As a parable proclaims truth like a herald and at the same time conceals truth like an oracle, Howard advanced his views on urbanism while concealing his views on spiritualism. Only an attuned ear listening for clues will hear the hidden story in the text.

Ebenezer Howard

Over the past one hundred years, Ebenezer Howard (1850–1928) has been cast as the father of the garden city movement and more broadly as a founder of the discipline of urban planning.[5] Numerous plaques and monuments honor him, while a substantial and growing body of literature is dedicated to his work and influence.[6] These writings do the (dis)service of locating Howard within the profession of town planning and focus attention on those more professionally oriented sources to study their influence on his development of the garden city. As a result, his image is cleansed and is made worthy as a founding father of the profession, yet this unduly narrows a truer understanding of the origins of his innovative thinking.

Biographies usually describe Howard as a "pragmatic inventor."[7] They occasionally reference his spiritualism, though often minimizing it with innocuous language. Yet, it is often expressed as perplexing how he came to the idea of the garden city. Identification of clear precedents for his urban diagrams is missing. George Bernard Shaw wrote his friend Howard was a "heroic simpleton" and Lewis Mumford described him as "a practical idealist."[8] These oxymorons suggest that there is a side of Howard missing from the construction of him as a practical professional – his spiritualism.

By the late nineteenth century, millions of people worldwide were entranced by spiritualism.[9] Howard endorsed its fundamental claim: "those who have departed from us through the portals of Death, [are understood] no longer as dead, but as living in a new and perhaps more exalted plane of existence."[10] There was a strong affinity between spiritualism and other reform movements, including women's rights, land reform and communitarianism. Sometimes described as a mystical counterbalance to rampant nineteenth-century materialism, it is better understood as an extension of materialist thought into the religious realm where spirits are real entities that could one day be understood scientifically.

Ebenezer Howard's life history reveals an early and continuous involvement in spiritualism.[11] As a young man, Howard taught himself through textbooks the relatively unknown Pitman's Shorthand. Isaac Pitman had accepted the revelations of Christian mystic Emmanuel Swedenborg and included it in his shorthand manuals "to scatter the seeds of truth."[12] Howard then became private secretary to liberal minister Dr. Joseph Parker, a friend and supporter of Pitman. Parker used phrenology to analyze Howard's skull, finding he had the aptitude for preaching.[13] At the age of 21, Howard migrated to the USA to farm and also organized and preached at Ebenezer Church in Howard County, Nebraska.[14] Failing at farming, Howard moved to Chicago where an editor at the *Chicago Times* hired him to create a transcript of a lecture to be given by Cora Scott Richmond. Richmond was a well-known trance medium who channeled the thoughts of long-dead people from the spirit world.[15] Her trance message to Howard was: "I see you in the center of a series of circles working at something which will be of great service to humanity." He later took this as a vision of his garden city and to the end of his life credited her influence for its origins.[16] Howard returned to England but remained in contact with Richmond over the years and also was active with leading Theosophists, such as Annie Besant. He joined the Zetetical Society, a group of freethinkers including Bernard Shaw and Sidney Webb, where he lectured on the scientific basis of spiritualism.[17]

Howard's concern with spiritualism merged with writing his treatise. "The idea of the garden city exists in the spiritual atmosphere . . . [providing] a clear sense of revelation coming into my mind from some mysterious source."[18] George Dickman, a Kodak executive who was "a great admirer of Cora Richmond," provided the funding for publishing *To-morrow: A Peaceful Path to Real Reform*.[19] The famous supporters helping to realize the first garden city in Letchworth were also involved in spiritualism; including H.G. Wells, George Bernard Shaw and Alfred Russel Wallace.[20] Throughout the rest of his life, Howard continued his spiritualist activities, including hosting seances in order to speak with his wife after she died.[21] In 1910, he gave an address to the London Spiritualist Alliance.[22] After its founding, Letchworth was dubbed a place for "cranks" by the popular press and still today is a center of spiritualism.

Over the course of his adult life, almost all of his activities and interests can be understood through his fundamental commitment to spiritualism uniting religion with science. Stenography was associated with spirit writing. Howard also devoted many years to creating an advanced typewriter. The new technologies allowing communication at a distance – including typewriters, telegraphs, telephones, phonographs and photography – were all considered important advances for spiritualist science.[23] While most historians of the garden city movement have overlooked or marginalized this material, it clearly is important to search for its subtle presence in Howard's text and images. Three cases are unfolded below.

The Blake quotation

> I will not cease from mental strife
> Nor shall my sword sleep in my hand,
> Till we have built Jerusalem
> In England's green and pleasant land.[24]

Howard begins at the outset in the first chapter of both editions of *Garden Cities* by quoting William Blake (1757–1827). Commentators, reading it as a rhetorical flourish, have enjoyed its aptness.[25] Yet, is Howard's reason for it appearing at the head of his book quite so obvious? It has not yet been noted that Howard misquotes a word in Blake's poem – *fight* becomes *strife*.[26] It is so well known that is unlikely to be a mistake. Strauss notes that in esoteric writing "errors" which would be obvious to the informed are intentionally used to call attention to a hidden meaning of the text. Another esoteric technique is to cite historical works to present hidden ideas rather than writing in one's own name.[27] Howard's change emphasizes the internal nature of the struggle and signals to careful readers that this has greater import.

The quotation is from the beginning of Blake's *Milton, A Poem* (dated 1804, first engraved 1808), a story of the descent of Milton's spirit from heaven into Blake's body. Blake reported that Milton appeared to him on many occasions.[28] Blake experienced visions since childhood and he often spoke about his spiritual conversations with the deceased. He also drew "visionary heads" or portraits of long-dead people as they appeared before him. Blake was involved in the more exotic aspects of religious enthusiasm: mesmerism, magic, cabbala, eroticism and ritual nudity. He closely studied mystical writings by Swedenborg and Jacob Boehme.

Millennial dreams of creating a heavenly realm on earth were widespread among spiritualists and the poem equates unfallen England with the biblical Garden of Eden.[29] The poem opens Howard's work as a key for a spiritualist reading without unduly alarming the general public who read it as an innocent metaphor. This is what Strauss dubbed a "noble lie," cautioning, "one must not be blinded by those passages that are overtly beautiful or edifying."[30]

The three magnets

Howard describes the different benefits of life in town and in country as two magnets, each attracting people. He proposes a third magnet, the garden city (Figure 3.1), which "partakes in the nature of both."[31] The diagram sets text in approximate concentric circles while the three magnets are related as if on the points of an equilateral triangle with the apex pointing downward.

He describes "the people" as metal filings subject to magnetism. Commentators admire the diagram as clearly conveying a complex problem and identify it as "the most widely reproduced and translated planning document in the world."[32] Read as a useful metaphor, any latent implications are again overlooked. To read esoterically, one must attend to enigmatic elements and, as noted above, resist being blinded by poetic passages in order to discover their hidden significance.

Magnetism along with electricity was important to spiritualism because it demonstrated that invisible forces could impact physical things: "the essence of magnetism is the link connecting mind with matter."[33] The movement of metal filings into orderly patterns by magnets demonstrates the existence of what Howard calls the "etheric substance" that is the pervasive spiritual

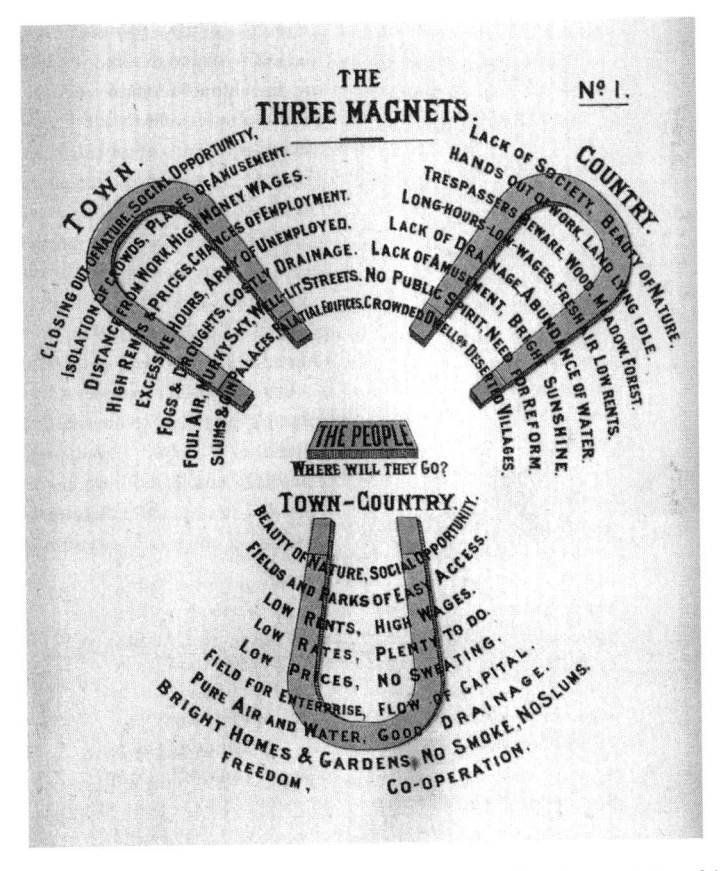

FIGURE 3.1 "The Three Magnets," Ebenezer Howard, *To-Morrow: A Peaceful Path to Real Reform* (1898)

medium forming auras around physical bodies.[34] In 1875, noted scientist and spiritualist William Crookes, whom Howard knew and cited, collaborated with an electrical telegraph engineer to photograph the luminous flames that "sensitive" people could see around magnets.[35] Mesmeric lecturers began showcasing their ability to manipulate the "invisible animal magnetic fluid" to produce fantastic feats of mental and bodily rapport with their subjects, including interaction with the spirit world.[36]

Magnetism also played a central role in creating "spirit circles" at seances. Sitters joined hands in a circle to create a "circuit" or "battery."[37] Sometimes, lightly touching the table would conduct the circle's magnetism. Men and women were alternately seated as positive and negative charges to emanate magnetic spheres.[38] Sitters also held onto a "magnetic cord" to promote spirit contacts.[39]

Howard describes the third magnet in an extraordinary way, as the result of a marriage between the two sexes. "Town and country *must be married*, and out of this joyous union will spring a new hope, a new life, a new civilization."[40] Finding male spiritual aspects in the city and female materic elements in the country, their wedding produces a unity of the sexes in an androgyne, a widespread notion among spiritualists and theosophists.

The garden cities diagram

In the first edition of *To-Morrow*, Howard includes his celebrated diagram of a "Group of Slumless Smokeless Cities" showing circles of six slightly different garden cities surrounding a seventh larger central city (Figure 3.2).[41] He cautions that the diagram should not be taken for a building proposal due to the need to adjust for peculiarities of an actual site. The representation of the garden city corresponds exactly to the textual description and although he cautions it is only a diagram, it is treated thereafter as a literal design. The drawing has a key and a scale like an architectural plan. Omitting the diagram from the second edition may have been regarding concern for it appearing excessively spiritualist. Strauss notes that esoteric writing often uses rarity to achieve secrecy, so that "a statement which occurs least frequently, or even which occurs only once," may be considered by the author to be most true.[42]

Howard includes a footnote below the diagram: "This drawing is, in many respects, very like one to which (after making it) my attention was directed, in a work entitled, *Palingenesia; or, The Earth's New Birth* (Hay, Nisbet & Co., Glasgow, 1894)."[43] He stresses that while similar, *Palingenesia* did not influence the making of his design. Tellingly, there are two errors in Howard's citation and it seems unlikely that they would both be by chance.[44] The ten-year later date error suggests that Howard had seen it prior to his

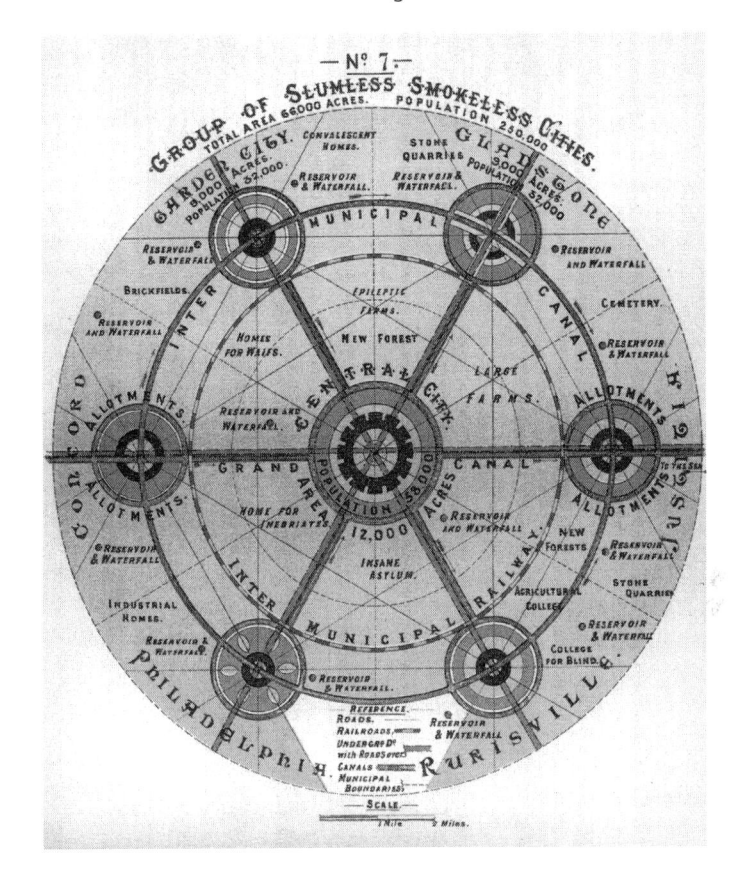

FIGURE 3.2 "Group of Slumless Smokeless Cities," Ebenezer
Howard, *To-Morrow: A Peaceful Path to Real Reform* (1898)

own design. *Palingenesia* had a small publication run of 150 volumes and would certainly only be known to the most ardent spiritualists. Howard could have simply not mentioned it, but in referencing *Palingenesia* and noting a close similarity he is clearly calling attention to it, although quietly as a footnote. Many commentators have searched for sources to Howard's scheme, but almost never mention this one that he chooses to note. Howard may have intentionally included errors in the citation to emphasize that in truth, he meant that *Palingenesia* was an important influence, but wouldn't do so directly to avoid being thought too radically spiritualist.

The book *Palingenesia* reveals the depth of Howard's commitment to spiritualist literature. Its author, Gideon Ouseley (1835–1906), was a member of the clergy suspended for anti-Christian views who founded The Order of At-one-ment.[45] Ouseley credits the writing of his book to two spirits who dictated it to him: "Theosopho, A Minister of the Holies, and Ellora, A Seeress of the Sanctuary." Emphasizing the equality of the sexes, the two spirit authors are male and female.

The book describes future changes brought about by the evolved influence of spirits, beginning with the earth. "The earth's Axis being now restored to its vertical position by the aid of the guardian spirits of the solar system, and the tutelary Angel of the earth in particular, each Zone has its own . . . unvarying climate, throughout the year being of the nature of an eternal Spring, and sudden changes of weather are unknown" (14). Twelve great railways circle the globe, on bridges across the oceans. Subterranean cities of "metallic splendor" are constructed symmetrically with surface cities, which will be covered by glass (157), and "climates of unchanging loveliness" (8) will be controlled by means of electricity and magnetism (161). The "Plan of a Heptapolis, or system of Seven Cities" has "an astonishing similarity" with Howard's plan.[46] They both consist of seven circular cities, each chief city generating six around it (Figure 3.3). Like Howard's plan, the intervening triangular spaces between circles are to be "kept free and open,

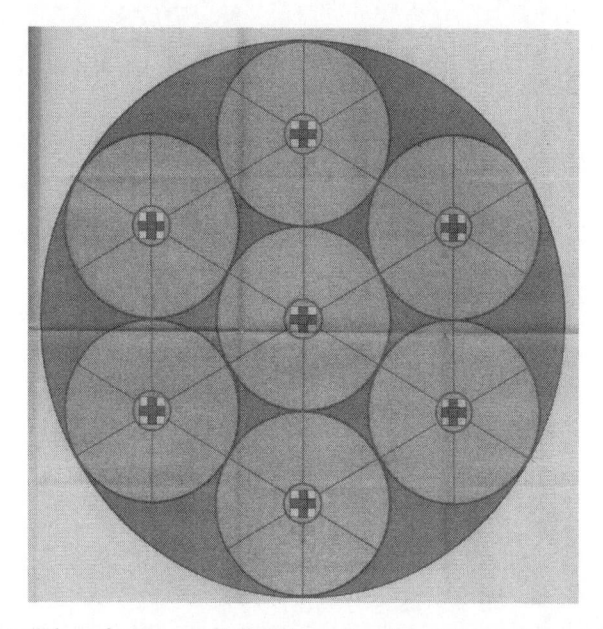

FIGURE 3.3 "Plan of a Heptapolis," Gideon Ouseley, *Palingenesia: or, The Earth's new Birth* (1884). Reproduced with the permission of Rare Books and Manuscripts, Special Collections Library, the Pennsylvania State University Libraries

being laid out as hill, wood, forest, and pasture for milk-giving animals." Both diagrams also include colors, scales and keys.

For Ouseley, the number of seven cities derives from God as a duality, each composed of a triplicity. On the cover and throughout the book, he shows the Seal of Solomon as two overlapping triangles – one red and one blue. The red is male and the blue female, both with a tripartite divinity. When united, they become the one at the center (74). The Deity as One and Bisexual was represented with the figure of an Androgyne, or the Double Equilateral Triangle as its symbol (247). In this way, "seven is a sacred number, symbol of spiritual and divine perfection, made up of the perfect number of nature, six, with divine unity added to it" (265).

A great many spiritual and mystic cosmogonies share this diagrammatic structure.[47] It stretches back into the ancient world, is Christianized in the Middle Ages and appears in the Renaissance with, among others, Giordano Bruno (Figure 3.4).[48] Blake's *Milton*, on the page following the quoted poem, has a cosmogonic diagram with a similar schema. It is reasserted by theosophical writers in the nineteenth century, especially Helene Blavatsky (1831–1891) who had and still has many followers in the first garden city of Letchworth.[49]

FIGURE 3.4 "Area Democriti," Giordano Bruno, *De triplici minimo et mensura* (1591)

Howard's vision of a spiritual city also corresponds quite closely with another proposal that was partly realized in the utopian community *Harmonia* in Kiantone, New York beginning in 1856.[50] This was to be the "beginning of a great circular city, with circular houses radiating out in concentric rings." [51] Simon Crosby Hewitt (b.1816), an ex-Universalist minister turned spiritualist author and editor, was directed by spirit teachers to design the curving "Homes of Harmony" (Figure 3.5). Proposing to magnetize the walls to attract spirits, at least one of the buildings sat on heavy glass cylindrical rollers to allow it to be rotated to enhance receptivity of "atmospheric influences."[52] Hewitt explained that rooms must be either circular or oval to be inviting to spirits.[53] Angularities are to be avoided because spirits are "more perfectly rounded" and "are pained by sharp angles as if pierced by pins."[54] Howard's design showing six cities around one in the center, while never seen previously in urban planning, was a very widely accepted diagram among spiritualists.

While Howard discounted the circular cities image as a mere diagram, he also wrote that as human evolution "to a higher order of society" becomes

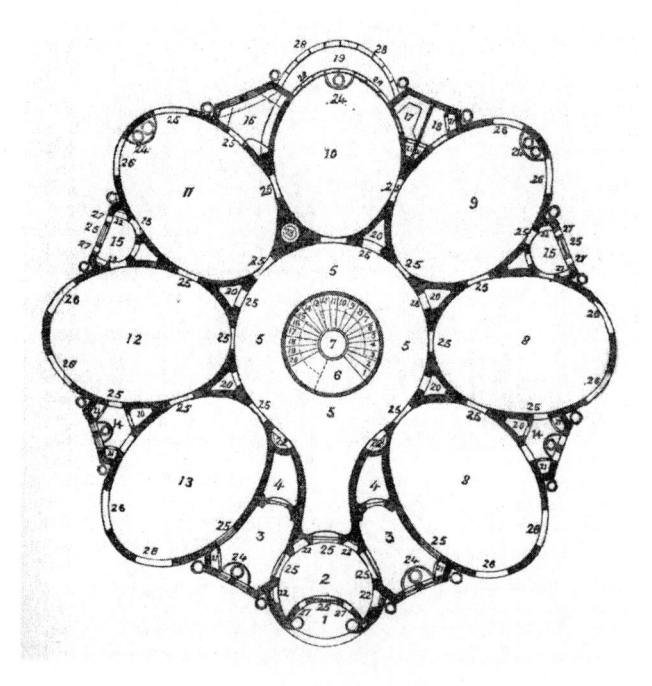

FIGURE 3.5 "Home of Harmony, Ground Plan of First Story," Simon Crosby Hewitt (1856)

"more and more complete does mind become master of matter."[55] Howard is suggesting that the circular diagram could be directly realized on earth as the New Jerusalem when spiritual evolution has unfolded and humanity is raised to another level, able to commune directly with spirits. Howard wrote: "Social progress is the outcome of spiritual forces pushing outward through the hearts and minds of men: . . . those forms taking on higher and higher qualities, as the spiritual powers assume greater and more complete control."[56] The circular Garden City allows humanity to align itself with the divine order.

Conclusion

These three examples of further instances already document Howard's use of esoteric writing.[57] When he emphasizes Garden Cities is not the work of a "fevered brain of an enthusiast," this is because that is exactly what he most feared might be thought.[58] To the extent that authors write esoterically and deliberately hide their deepest and truest thoughts behind a veil of conventionality, by failing to read between the lines we will be blind to their full and true meaning. Furthermore, in treating texts like Howard's exoterically as within the confines of normative concepts of professional knowledge, future thinkers fail to understand the sorts of sources used for past innovative ideas. Exclusively exoteric reading risks future mediocrity.

While the modern world has all but eliminated expectations for esoteric writing, we must appreciate that there are many different currents of thought present at any one time.[59] Esoteric writing provides authors more freedom for heterodox thought and finding inspiration in unexpected places. Even though they may be unpopular at the time or lacking the moment's currency, these views can prove most valuable. Rather than being entrapped by normative professional orthodoxy, truly open scholarship paradoxically requires reading and writing between the lines.

Notes

1　Donald Levine, *The Flight from Ambiguity* (Chicago: University of Chicago Press, 1985); and Arthur Melzer, "On the Pedagogical Motive for Esoteric Writing," *The Journal of Politics* 69 no. 4 (November, 2007): 1015–1031.

2　Sir Thomas More, *Utopia* (1516) 98/30.

3　Leo Strauss, *Persecution and the Art of Writing* (Westport, CT: Greenwood, 1973).

4　Michael Frazer, "Esotericism Ancient and Modern: Strauss Contra Straussianism, on the Art of Political-Philosophical Writing," *Political Theory* 34, no. 1 (February 2006): 33–61.

5　Robert Wojtowicz, "Review," *Journal of Society of Architectural Historians* 51, no. 3 (September 1992): 332–335. The review was of *Patrick Geddes: Social Evolutionist* and City Planner by Helen Meller; The Garden City Utopia: A Critical Biography of Ebenezer Howard by Robert Beevers; and Visionaries and Planners: The Garden City Movement and the Modern Community by Stanley Buder,

6 Peter Hall and Colin Ward, Sociable Cities: the Legacy of Ebenezer Howard (Chichester and London: John Wiley, 1998), 6; John Moss-Eccardt, Ebenezer Howard: An Illustrated Life of Sir Ebenezer Howard 1850-1928 (Aylesbury: Shire Publications, 1973), 44; and Standish Meacham, Regaining Paradise, Englishness and the Early Garden City Movement (New Haven and London: Yale University Press, 1999).

7 Frederic Osborn, "Preface" in Ebenezer Howard, Garden Cities of To-Morrow, ed. Frederic Osborn (London: Faber and Faber, 1946), 21.

8 Evan Richert and Mark Lapping, "Ebenezer Howard and the Garden City," American Planning Association Journal 64, no. 2 (Spring 1998): 125–130.

9 Frank Podmore, Modern Spiritualism, a History and a Criticism (London: Methuen, 1903).

10 Ebenezer Howard, Medium and Daybreak, April 16, 1880, no. 524, vol. XI, Hertfordshire Archives and Local Studies Ref.: HCA, EHo, F.9.

11 Moss-Eccardt, Ebenezer Howard, 6; and Stanley Buder, Visionaries and Planners: The Garden City Movement and the Modern Community (New York: Oxford University Press, 1990), 5–6.

12 Alfred Baker, Sir Isaac Pitman, 1813-1897 (London: I. Pittman, 1919), 125.

13 Robert Beevers, The Garden City Utopia: A Critical Biography of Ebenezer Howard (New York: St. Martin's Press, 1988), 4–6.

14 Dugald Macfadyen, Sir Ebenezer Howard and the Town Planning Movement (Manchester: Manchester University Press, 1970 [1933]), 10.

15 Due to numerous marriages, Cora Lavinia Scott Hatch Daniels Tappan Richmond (1840–1923) was known by various names. See H.D. Barrett, Life Work of Cora L. V. Richmond (Chicago: Hack & Anderson, 1895); Mary Bednarowki, "Spiritualism in Wisconsin in the Nineteenth Century," The Wisconsin Magazine of History 59, no. 1 (Autumn 1975): 2–19; and R. Laurence Moore, "The Spiritualist Medium: A Study of Female Professionalism in Victorian America," American Quarterly 27, no. 2 (May 1975): 200–221.

16 Macfadyen, Sir Ebenezer Howard, 10; Buder, Visionaries and Planners, 218, n. 7; Barrett, Life Work of Cora, 693–694.

17 Howard, Medium and Daybreak.

18 Ebenezer Howard, "Spiritual Influences and Social Progress," Light: A Journal of Physical, Occult and Mystical Research (April 23, 1910): 195–209, 208.

19 Buder, Visionaries and Planners, 62.

20 Macfadyen, Sir Ebenezer Howard, 88; Beevers, The Garden City Utopia, 119–121; Meacham, Regaining Paradise, 128-142.

21 Beevers, The Garden City Utopia, 37, 43, 83.

22 Howard, "Spiritual Influences."

23 Ebenezer Howard, "The Friendship of Religion and Science (c.1906)" Hertfordshire Archives and Local Studies Ref.: DE/Ho/F3/40/1, p. 9; Richard Noakes, "'Instruments to Lay Hold of Spirits': Technologizing the Bodies of Victorian Spiritualism," in Bodies/Machines (Oxford: Berg, 2002), 125–163: Steven Connor, "The Machine in the Ghost: Spiritualism Technology and the 'Direct Voice'," in Ghosts: Deconstruction, Psychoanalysis, History, ed. Peter Buse and Andrew Stott (New York: St. Martin's Press, 1999), 203–225; and Lawrence Rainey, "Taking Dictation: Collage Poetics, Pathology and Poetics," Modernism/Modernity 5, no. 2 (1998): 123–153.

24 Ebenezer Howard, *To-Morrow: A Peaceful Path to Real Reform* (London: Swan Sonnenschein, 1898). Reprinted with commentary by Peter Hall, Dennis Hardy and Colin Ward (London: Routledge, 2003); and Ebenezer Howard, *Garden Cities of To-Morrow*, ed. Frederic Osborn (Cambridge, MA: MIT Press, 1965 [1902]).

25 Hall, Hardy and Ward, in Ebenezer, *To-Morrow: A Peaceful Path*, 31.

26 David Erdman, ed., *The Complete Poetry and Prose of William Blake* (Berkeley and Los Angeles: University of California Press, 1982), 95f; 909f. Blake's poem became a popular Church of England hymn. Nancy Goslee, "'In England's green & pleasant Land': The Building of Vision in Blake's Stanzas from *Milton*," *Studies in Romanticism* 13, no. 2 (Spring, 1974): 105–125.

27 Strauss, *Persecution*, 14.

28 Peter Ackroyd, *Blake* (London: Vintage, 1999).

29 William Blake, *Milton a Poem*, ed. Robert Essick and Joseph Viscomi, in *The Illuminated Books of William Blake*, vol. 5, ed. David Bindman (Princeton: Princeton University Press, William Blake Trust, 1993), 213f.

30 Robert Howse, "Reading between the Lines: Exotericism, Exotericism, and the Philosophical Rhetoric of Leo Strauss," *Philosophy and Rhetoric* 32, no. 1 (1999): 60–77, 69.

31 Howard, *To-Morrow: A Peaceful Path*, 7.

32 Hall, Hardy and Ward, in Ebenezer, *To-Morrow: A Peaceful Path*, 23.

33 Andrew Jackson Davis, *A Stellar Key to the Summerland* (New York: Banner of Light Branch Office, 1858): 80.

34 Ebenezer Howard, "Spiritualism: Lecture II," Paper read by Ebenezer Howard before the Holborn literary and debating society, Thursday, May 8, 1880, Hertfordshire Archives and Local Studies Ref.: D/EHo/F3/43, p.15.

35 Noakes, "Instruments to Lay Hold of Spirits," 150.

36 Jill Galvan, *The Sympathetic Medium: Feminine Channelling, The Occult, and Communication Technologies, 1859-1919* (Ithaca, NY: Cornell University Press, 2010), 3.

37 James Burns, "The Philosophy of the Spirit-Circle," *Medium and Daybreak* 1 (1870): 308; and H.S. "Magneto-Electricity and the Spirit-Circle," *Medium and Daybreak* 2 (1872): 303.

38 Emma Hardinge (Britten), "Rules to be Observed for the Spirit Circle," *Human Nature* 1 (1868): 156–157.

39 Galvan, *The Sympathetic Medium*, 11. See also http://brianaltonenmph.com/6-history-of-medicine-and-pharmacy/hudson-valley-medical-history/the-fowler-estate/andrew-jackson-davis/.

40 Howard, *To-Morrow: A Peaceful Path*, 9–10.

41 "Group of Slumless Smokeless Cities," Howard, *To-Morrow, A Peaceful Path*, Diagram no. 7.

42 Strauss, *Persecution*, 73.

43 Theosopho and Ellora (Gideon Ouseley), *Palingenesia: or, The Earth's new Birth* (Glasgow: Hay Nisbet & Co., 1884).

44 Hay Nisbet should have no comma as he was a leading spiritualist and publisher. The date is not 1894 but 1884.

45 No author, review of *Palingenesia*, in *The Theosophist* (September, 1885) 309–310.

46 "Plan of a Heptapolis, or system of Seven Cities, with their Seven Churches, and the Suburbs or Country around them with their Canals, Roads, etc., leading to the adjoining Heptapoles," in *Palingenesia*, Vol. II, Plate XIII.

47 Cora L.V. Richmond, *Psychopathy: Or, Spirit Healing a Series of Lessons on the Relations of the Spirit to Its Own Organism, and the Interrelation of Human Beings with*

Reference to Health, Disease and Healing by the Spirit of Benjamin Rush Through the Mediumship of Cora L. V. Richmond (Rogers Park, IL: William Richmond, 1890), Plate 6. The Library of Congress indexed Richmond's book under the authorship of Dr. Rush.

48 Christoph Luthy, "Bruno's Area Democriti and the Origins of Atomist Imagery," *Bruniana & Campanelliana: Ricerche rilosofiche e materiali storico-testuali*, 4 (1998) 59–92; and Giordano Bruno, *Corpus Iconographicum, le incisioni nelle opera a stampa*, Catalogo, ed. Mino Gabirele (Milan: Adelphi, 2001), 260–266.

49 Helena Blavatsky, *Isis Unveiled, A Master-Key to the Mysteries of Ancient and Modern Science and Theology* (New York: J. W. Bouton, 1877) vol. II, 264–265, 452–453.

50 Neil Lehman, "The Life of John Murray Spear: Spiritualism and Reform in Antebellum America." (PhD diss., Ohio State University, 1973.)

51 Simon Crosby Hewitt, "Architecture of the Future – Designs for Homes of Harmony, Transmitted from the Spirit World," *Millennial Gazette* (London), ed. Robert Owen, July 1, 1956, 3–11.

52 John Buescher, *The Remarkable Life of John Murray Spear; Agitator for the Spirit Land* (Notre Dame, IN: University of Notre Dame Press, 2006), 167–168.

53 Deborah Cronin, *Kiantone, Chautauqua County's Mystical Valley* (Bloomington, IN: Authorhouse, 2006), 60.

54 Alonzo. E. Newton, ed., *The Educator, Being Suggestions Theoretical and Practical, Designed to Promote Man-Culture and Integral Reform, with View to the Ultimate Establishment of a Divine Social State on Earth, Comprised in a Series of Revealments from Organized Associations in the Spirit-Life, through John Murray Spear* (Boston, MA: Office of Practical Spiritualists, Fountain House, 1857), 347; Roger Macklis, "Magnetic Healing, Quackery, and the Debate about the Health Effects of Electromagnetic Fields," *Annals of Internal Medicine* 118, no. 5 (March 1, 1993): 376–383; and Simon Crosby Hewitt, *Messages from the Superior State* (Boston, MA: Bela Marsh, 1853): 124.

55 Howard, *To-Morrow, A Peaceful Path*, 130–131.

56 Howard, "Spiritual Influences," 195–209, 195.

57 Ebenezer Howard, "The Friendship of Religion and Science (c.1906)," Hertfordshire Archives and Local Studies Ref.: DE/Ho/F3/40/1, p. 9.

58 Howard, *To-Morrow, A Peaceful Path*, 114, 140.

59 Arthur Melzer, "Esotericism and the Critique of Historicism," *The American Political Science Review* 100, no. 2 (May, 2006): 279–295, 285, 292.

4

ON VIRTUE AND THOMAS JEFFERSON

Indra Kagis McEwen

The word "virtue" is Roman in origin, but what the Romans called *virtus*, though admirable certainly, had little to do with what is now conventionally understood as ethical behavior. Also Roman, admirable and by post-colonial standards arguably unethical is, in Vitruvius, the fountainhead of orthodox classicism in western architecture. Prevailing interest shaped what Romans called *virtus*, and it is my contention that, throughout history, certain convergences have occurred between the interests embedded in claims for "virtue" and the aims of those who have adhered to certain traditions in architecture. Indeed, the first of such convergences occurs between the *virtus* Vitruvius himself admired and the aims of his *De architectura* written in about 25 BCE, for Augustus Caesar, the first Roman emperor.

Vitruvius's contemporary Cicero derived *virtus* from *vir*, the Latin word for man, and for a man, said Cicero, courage is the most essential thing, demanding the greatest scorn for pain and death.[1] "Most essential" because the prevailing interest in imperial Rome was conquest, and the Roman claim was that *virtus*, the refusal to accept defeat, was the quality above all others that made Romans conquerors. That Vitruvius knew and subscribed to this view is clear in the fulsome acclamation of Augustus's "invincible *virtus*" with which he begins *de architecutura*: "When your divine mind and power, Imperator Caesar, were seizing command of the world and all your enemies had been crushed by your invincible *virtus*. . . ."[2]

More than a perfunctory nod to the conventions of early Augustan triumphalism, Vitruvius's celebratory tone and, especially, his appreciation of *virtus* derived from first-hand participation in the Roman culture of conquest, deeply-ingrained by years spent working as a military architect in the army of Augustus's adoptive father Julius Caesar during the latter's subjection of Gaul and the civil wars that followed. Right after the acclamation with which he launches his dedication, Vitruvius reminds Augustus of his long-standing devotion to Caesar. It was his knowledge of architecture, he writes, that first brought him to Caesar's attention. It was this, he continues, that bound him to Caesar's *virtus* – not to the man, it must be noted, but to the undefeated general's *virtus*.[3] The alliance between Caesar and Vitruvius – the convergence of architecture and the "virtue" of world conquerors – is part of what underpins *De architectura* and its argument for architecture as the ultimate guarantee of empire.[4]

Personified as a goddess, Roman *Virtus* appeared as an Amazon, in a short tunic with one breast bared, usually armed with a dagger and a spear, similar to representations of the goddess Roma herself.[5] Curiously enough, the figure Romans recognized as Virtue is exactly how *Virtus* appeared (and continues to appear) on the Great Seal of Virginia, designed by a committee Virginian gentlemen in June of 1776, at precisely the moment their friend, Thomas Jefferson (1743–1826), founding father, plantation owner, slaveholder, architect, and future president, was in Philadelphia, drafting the American Declaration of Independence.[6]

The Virginian *Virtus* appears as a revolutionary figure, her left foot resting on the prostrate body of a man dressed like a Roman, with a crown lying on the ground nearby. Underneath, the Latin motto reads *Sic semper tyrannis*, "thus always to tyrants" – words Brutus was believed to have spoken when he stabbed Julius Caesar on the Ides of March in 44 BCE (see Figure 4.1).[7] The dead "Caesar" vanquished here is meant to be understood as the King of England, whose crowned and sceptered image had figured on the seal of the colony in earlier, pre-revolutionary days.[8] After its endorsement as the state seal by the Virginia Convention of 1776, the emblem was, without further delay, emblazoned on regimental flags as well as on state currency.[9]

A slightly more voluptuous, mirror-image of the same *Virtus*, again trampling a fallen tyrant, appears on the obverse of a so-called "Indian Medal" struck in 1780 at the height of the revolutionary war for Thomas Jefferson when he was governor of Virginia, and meant for distribution to Cherokee chiefs who agreed to join the fight against the British.[10]

For Jefferson, overturning the King's rule in America entailed the further rejection of all forms of inherited authority. But this abolition of hereditary aristocracy did not, in his view, mean the dismissal of aristocracy *tout court*. As he wrote to John Adams, the dominance of European-style "pseudo-aristoi" defined by wealth and birth would be replaced in America by the elected

FIGURE 4.1 Seal of the Commonwealth of Virginia

government of what he called "natural" aristocrats, recognition of whose qualitative superiority would, of itself, persuade citizens to vote for them.[11] This natural aristocracy, he wrote, was defined not by lineage but by virtue.

Yet for all that the *Virtus* adopted as the emblem of Virginia in 1776 was military both in Roman origin and current revolutionary intent, the virtue Jefferson prized above all others as the bedrock of the new republic and the key to its perennity was not military but agrarian. "Those who labor the earth are the chosen people of God, . . . whose breasts he has made his peculiar deposit for substantial and genuine virtue," he wrote in his *Notes on the State of Virginia* of 1785.[12] Or again, typically, to James Madison,

> I think our governments will remain virtuous for many centuries as long as they are chiefly agricultural; and this will be as long as there shall be vacant lands in America. When they get piled upon one another in large cities, as in Europe, they will become corrupt as in Europe.[13]

Jefferson did not hold with cities, or for that matter, with commerce and industry – all, as he saw it, potential sources of corruption.[14]

In the end, the agrarian virtue Jefferson prized and the ostensibly military *Virtus* on Virginia's seal were not so very far apart after all, at least in their common aim of forestalling European decadence and the tyranny of its attendant despotisms. As the historian Henry Adams later summed it up, rather acerbically, for Virginians it was axiomatic that Virginia itself "was the typical society of a future Arcadian America. To escape the tyranny of Caesar by perpetuating the simple and isolated lives of their fathers was the sum of their political philosophy."[15]

That the American founders, particularly Jefferson, were steeped in the classics is well known.[16] But thanks to the preservation of Jefferson's voluminous correspondence, it is possible to pinpoint exactly the provenance of the *Virtus* adopted as Virginia's emblem. On July 20, 1776, Jefferson's old friend John Page wrote to him in Philadelphia, asking him to try to find an engraver for the seal in that city. "The Workman Engraver," wrote Page, "may be at a loss for a Virtus . . . but you may refer him to Spence's Polymetis which must be in some library in Philadelphia."[17]

"Spence's Polymetis" is a digest of Roman mythological culture by an English clergyman, one Joseph Spence, published in 1747 in a large, illustrated folio, and cast as a dialogue between a fictitious polymath called Polymetis and his guests at a villa.[18] Jefferson owned a copy of the first edition, possibly as early as 1771, when he noted in a want-list of works of art: "Diana Venetrix (see Spence's Polymetis)."[19]

The compilation of this list was undoubtedly made with a view to the eventual decoration of the house he had begun to build on the top of the mountain he had inherited from his father in 1757.[20] It is possible that the site Jefferson christened "Monticello" was named after the "small hill" on which Palladio set his Villa Rotonda, according to the description in his *Quattro Libri dell'Architettura* of 1570.[21] That Palladio was, famously, "the bible" for Jefferson as architect makes the attribution tempting, even if there is no record that he himself ever owned the Italian edition of the *Quattro Libri*.[22] But the Rotonda's *monticello* was, according to Palladio, *"di ascesa facilissima,"* "very easy to climb," which – as visitors complained – Jefferson's mountain, rising some 500 feet above the river at its base, decidedly was not.[23] Indeed, over the years, he seems to have taken deliberate measures to make its ascent ever more tortuous.[24] Moreover, the choice of a mountaintop for his new residence was at odds with prevailing local custom, which dictated the convenience of low-lying riverside sites for plantation houses.[25] Its inaccessibility made Monticello – both the first and the second houses Jefferson built there – painfully laborious to construct and, for much of the time, very inconvenient to inhabit.[26]

Palladio governed Jefferson's architectural choices; Palladio and the issue of virtue, which, as it happens, also had a Palladian component. Each of the four books of the first Italian edition is preceded by the same frontispiece, also reproduced in Fréart de Chambray's French translation of 1650 and Isaac Ware's English one of 1738, which may have been the book that initiated Jefferson's love affair with Palladio.[27] In this frontispiece, allegorical personifications of geometry and architecture point up at the majestic female figure that dominates the page: Regina Virtus (see Figure 4.2).

FIGURE 4.2 Frontispiece, Palladio, *The Four Books of Architecture*, translated by Isaac Ware, London 1738

This queen, with her scepter and book, does not look anything like the *Virtus* on Virginia's seal, of course. And beyond naming her, Palladio does not explain what he means by her, nor why she looks the way she does.[28] It would, no doubt, have been obvious to his sixteenth century readers. But without going into what Palladio intended by his emblem nor attempting to second guess how Jefferson himself might have understood it, it would be difficult to avoid being struck by the convergence between Jefferson's preoccupation with virtue and his admiration for the "chaste architecture" of which Palladio was, for him, the incomparable avatar.[29] The architecture of Palladio was known through books, of course. Although Jefferson lived in France from 1784 to 1789 and visited northern Italy during that time, he never actually saw a building by Palladio.

If Palladio failed to elaborate on the meaning of his "Virtus," Joseph Spence is less cryptic. The first mention of *virtus* in his *Polymetis* appears a few pages after the account of Diana Venetrix that ignited the young Jefferson's desire to acquire her statue. At issue here is not virtue as such, but nobility. Quoting the Roman satirist Juvenal, Spence writes, "What signify pedigrees . . . and a croud [sic] of old broken statues of our ancestors, if we ourselves are debauched and indolent?" *Nobilitas sola est atque unica virtus:* "Virtue alone is true nobility."[30]

"The Romans," Spence writes in a later chapter, were "of so military a turn, they generally gave Fortitude the name of Virtus," referencing his assertion with the Cicero citation that appears at the beginning of this essay.[31] As already noted, it was this *Fortitudo/Virtus* that gave the Virginians the image for their seal. Spence then launches into a five-page discussion, which opens with the following. "The many difficulties that attend following the dictates of the goddess Virtue . . . were strongly expressed in that very just and very antient [sic] emblem, of a person climbing up a vast, steep, rocky mountain. . . ."

"There can be no virtue without choice," he goes on, introducing an account of the "choice of Hercules" in which the mythical demigod chooses the steep path proposed by *Virtus* over the easy, level road *Voluptas* invites him to take. Among the many sources invoked, one passage from Silius Italicus' epic *Punica* is especially arresting. *Virtus* herself speaks: *Casta mihi domus et celso stant colle penates . . .*

> Chaste is my house, a dwelling set upon a lofty hill; a steep track leads there by a rocky ascent. Hard at first is the toil you must endure. . . . If you seek to enter, you must exert yourself. . . . Soon you will gain the summit and look down upon the race of men below.[32]

The difficult ascent to the chaste house at the top of a lofty hill, presented figuratively as the path to the abode of Virtue, might just as easily describe, literally, the hard climb to Monticello, with the latter – against this background – becoming rhetorically interchangeable with the former. To put it another way, if the path to virtue could be described as a climb to a chaste dwelling at the top of a mountain, then surely, by the same token (for one, who like Jefferson was perfectly aware of the hoary metaphor), the hard climb to Monticello itself became ascent to life on a higher moral plane: something even guests apparently ignorant of the trope acknowledged.[33] "Our own dear Monticello," wrote the man known as its "sage," "where has nature spread so rich a mantle under the eye? . . . With what majesty do we there ride above the storms!"[34]

Moreover, the figure of tortuous ascent to the house of Virtue also throws light on a decidedly odd feature of the second house Jefferson built from 1796 on – the house that still stands. This much-enlarged mansion of thirty-three rooms, with its Doric porticoes and gracious reception rooms, has no proper staircase. Anna Maria Thornton, who recorded a visit to Monticello in 1802 and wrote of the fatigue of ascending the hill, quickly discovered that the fatigue of ascent did not end with arrival at the house. "Exhausted and quite unwell," Mrs. Thornton asked to be shown their bedroom, complaining later in her diary, "We had to mount a little ladder of a staircase, about two feet wide and very steep."[35] In a house where, it has been noted, almost every other part was designed for convenience and efficiency, the steep, dark stairs are a puzzle.[36] One recurring suggestion is that in Jefferson's republican household, the elimination of a proper staircase was meant to do away with the traditional stage for rituals of rank and power that grand staircases provided in the residences of European aristocracy.[37] In the egalitarian American democracy a "natural aristocrat" met his guests eye to eye, on the same level. But did ideology demand that the cramped stairs actually provided be positively hazardous?

The stairs in question lead not only to the bedroom floors, but further up to the dome room at the top of the house. Lit by circular *oeil-de-boeuf* windows in each of its octagonal facets as well as by an oculus, the dome room was, according to one visitor, "the most beautiful room in the house."[38] Yet the room remained empty, and still does. In Jefferson's days it provided a perfect, panoptical viewpoint for keeping watch over activities in the plantation below, as indeed armed with a spyglass, its owner made a habit of doing.[39] Hard to reach, but with a vantage that made it worth the effort, the dome room became the very epitome of Monticello itself: *casta domus*, the chaste abode of Virtue, whose best expression in agriculture Jefferson not only preached but also claimed as his own. "I am become . . . a real farmer," he wrote with pride in 1795, "measuring my fields, following my ploughs, helping the haymakers, and never knowing a day which has not done something for futurity."[40]

Whatever else it was, Monticello was a farmhouse, and in Jeffersonian terms that alone made it virtuous. But farming also connects Monticello to the houses for which Palladio is best known. Designed in the mid-sixteenth century for the mainland estates of the Venetian patriciate, and meant to respond to its members' agricultural requirements as well as to accommodate the pleasures of *villegiatura*, Palladio's villas were more than just farmhouses of course, but farming was unquestionably their principal *raison-d'être*.[41] It was in recognition of its agricultural avocation that the Palladian villa-type, mediated through eighteenth century English Palladianism, was adopted for the plantation houses of the landed aristocracy in the colonial American South even before Jefferson began his career as a builder.[42] Jefferson perfected the tradition, and through adherence to the principles laid down by the master, built a farmhouse that might consequently be called doubly virtuous. Its chaste Palladian expression gave agrarian virtue the force of incontestable truth.

The first design for Monticello, with two-story porticoes front and back, is more textbook Palladio than the second, surviving iteration.[43] The Parisian models Jefferson came to admire during his stay in France, while still Palladian, further informed this second house. As a result, not only is it much larger but also less rigid, more elegant than the first. But no matter how large the new thirty-three-room mansion, it was – here as elsewhere in Virginia – only a part of the plantation's extensive array of buildings. The "dependencies" that augmented the complex included kitchen, laundry, stable, carriage house, storerooms, icehouse, pantry, smokehouse, and privy.[44] Slave quarters were located farthest from the main house, and at Monticello included a blacksmith shop and nailery, where slave boys manufactured iron nails meant for sale.[45] With its many separate buildings, the plantation complex could be readily expanded or altered, if the need arose. As travelogues by contemporary foreign visitors consistently recorded, a Virginia plantation resembled a small village.[46]

America, Jefferson wrote in 1809, was "the sole depository of the sacred fire of freedom and self-government."[47] Ever fearful of the potentially deleterious effect of foreign influence on the purity of this unique republic, he had, twenty-five years earlier, voiced with vehemence his opposition to European immigration. Emigrants would, for the most part, be from absolute monarchies, he wrote and will bring with them the principles of the governments they leave, imbibed in their early youth. . . . These . . . they will transmit to their children. In proportion to their numbers, they will share with us the legislation. They will infuse into it their spirit, warp and bias its direction, and render it a heterogeneous, incoherent, distracted mass.[48]

An analogous fear of contamination was a driving force behind the foundation of the University of Virginia, built between 1817 and 1825 outside Charlottesville, at the base of Jefferson's mountain, from whose summit he supervised construction.[49] Until "Mr. Jefferson's University" opened, the sons of the southern elite generally went north to study. As Jefferson saw it, this meant exposure to corrupting urban values of commerce and industry, which constituted an unacceptable threat to the agrarian virtue that, for him, was the cornerstone of the republic.[50] "I am not a friend to placing growing men in populous cities," he wrote in 1807.[51] Study in northern colleges also, of course, meant exposure to opponents of slavery.

"I consider the common plan . . . of making one large & expensive building as unfortunately erroneous," Jefferson wrote when his university was still in its earliest planning stages. Far better a series of small buildings, "arranged around an open square of grass and trees [which] would make it . . . an academical village, instead of a large & common den of noise, of filth & of fetid air."[52] This "academical village" would, in effect, be modeled on a Virginia plantation – indeed, to a large extent, on Monticello itself.[53] What setting more perfectly suited than this for the cultivation of agrarian virtue?

The core of the University of Virginia remains essentially as Jefferson designed it, with a Rotunda at the head of two ranges of five two-story pavilions, with single-story dormitory buildings fronted by covered colonnades between them, arranged on either side of a terraced field of grass, known as the Lawn. The genesis of the plan was assuredly a plantation-village, as noted. In execution, however, the general layout of this "village" looks uncannily like Marly, the retreat Louis XIV built near Versailles in the late seventeenth century, where the king's house overlooked a double range of twelve small two-story guest pavilions, linked by trellises and flanking a large garden with a *parterre d'eau* in the middle. Jefferson had visited the chateau in 1786 when he was in Paris.

The similarity between the two has often been noted, with some commentators baulking at the suggestion of an absolutist precedent for the University on ideological grounds, "as if Jefferson could consciously make a monarch's pleasure retreat his pattern."[54] But the aristocratic model makes perfect sense if we consider that the University of Virginia was meant not for the diversion of old world "pseudo-aristoi," but for the nurture of a new, virtuous breed of men: the "natural" aristocrats and future leaders of the American republic. From this point of view, it is possible to see Jefferson's university as the appropriation and *reform* of its monarchical antecedent in a sophisticated republican replique to the whole decadent tradition Marly stood for – an institution from which, through their education, students would emerge as the "real" aristocrats: America's answer to the false ones of the old regime.

Part of that education was the carefully wrought architecture of the university itself, which Jefferson meant to provide "chaste models" for students of architecture to learn from.[55] These models were, of course, mainly Palladian, although the orders used for the façades of five of the pavilions were drawn from Fréart de Chambray's *Parallèle de l'architecture antique avec la moderne*.[56] The Pantheon-derived Rotunda, originally the library, which dominates the Lawn, was based on the Pantheon as drawn by Palladio. The 152 columns of the unifying Tuscan colonnade are also from Palladio, as are the colossal orders fronting the five pavilions not based on Fréart. Drawing on Alberti, it was Palladio who wrote that a house is like a small city, which accurately describes both his own villas and the plantation-village that was Mr. Jefferson's University.[57] It was above all Palladio who, as it were, redeemed Marly and made its Virginian iteration a vessel of republican virtue, from whose architecture, "would flow an education in taste, values and ideals."[58]

At least that is the conventional view. But, to return to the theme laid out at the opening of this essay, what interest was served by Jeffersonian claims for virtue – in Virginia, during Jefferson's own lifetime?

Thomas Jefferson was a Virginia planter, whose position and prosperity, like that of his southern peers, were upheld by slavery. The agrarian virtue he claimed as the ultimate bulwark against European decadence was defined by the interest of the slave-owning planter class. When he was elected America's third president in 1800, it was not because voters recognized his "natural aristocracy." It was because of the so-called "three-fifths rule" conceded to the southern states in exchange for their ratification of the American constitution in 1789.[59]

Slaves, of course, had no vote, but the three-fifths rule allowed that for every five slaves owned, their enfranchised owner could claim three votes. A planter possessing one hundred slaves would be considered as having sixty votes; Jefferson, who typically owned two hundred slaves at any given time, would have had one hundred and twenty.[60] Without the three-fifths rule, Thomas Jefferson would not have won the 1800 election. Without the advantage given to him and to southern interests by the three-fifths rule, slavery and the agrarian virtue claimed for plantation imperialism would never have extended its "empire of liberty" westward, as they eventually did, to Louisiana, Missouri, Kentucky and Tennessee.[61]

In April 1864, thirty-eight years after Jefferson's death, the United States Senate passed the Thirteenth Amendment to the constitution which, by making slavery illegal, nullified the three-fifths rule and the "slave power" that went with it. A year later, Abraham Lincoln, author of the amendment, was shot at Ford's Theatre in Washington DC by a southern actor, John Wilkes Booth. "*Sic semper tyrannis*," Booth cried, casting himself as Brutus to Lincoln's Caesar with words taken from Seal of Virginia that also cast him as the implacable hand of Virtue herself.[62] "The South is avenged!"

Notes

1 Cicero, *Tusculanae disputationes* 2.43; and Myles A. McDonnell, *Roman Manliness: Virtus and the Roman Republic* (Cambridge, UK and New York: Cambridge University Press, 2006).

2 Vitruvius, *De architectura* 1, pref.1. Translation by the author.

3 Vitruvius, *De architectura* 1, pref.2; see also Indra K. McEwen, "Virtù-vious: Roman Architecture, Renaissance Virtue," *Cahiers des études anciennes* XLVIII (2011): 255–283 (258).

4 Indra K. McEwen, *Vitruvius: Writing the Body of Architecture* (Cambridge, MA and London: MIT Press, 2003). For an examination of *virtù* as the renaissance itera-tion of Roman *virtus* and its relevance to the architectural thought of the day, see McEwen, "Virtù-vious."

5 McDonnell, *Roman Manliness*, 142–149.

6 Lyon G. Tyler, "The Seal of Virginia," *William and Mary Quarterly* 3, no. 2 (October, 1884): 81–96; Edward S. Evans, *The Seals of Virginia* (Richmond, VA: Virginia State Library, 1911); and David Hackett Fischer, *Liberty and Freedom: a Visual History of America's Founding Ideas* (New York: Oxford University Press, 2005), 62–67.

7 Nicholas Cole, "Republicanism, Caesarism and Political Change," in *A Companion to Julius Caesar*, ed. Miriam Griffin (Chichester, UK and Malden, MA: Wiley-Blackwell, 2009), 418–430 (421); and Maria Wyke, *Caesar in the USA* (Berkeley: University of California Press, 2012), 1.

8 Tyler, "The Seal of Virginia," 83.

9 Fischer, *Liberty and Freedom*, 66.

10 Ibid., 63.

11 Thomas Jefferson to John Adams, October 28, 1813, in Merrill D. Peterson, ed., *Thomas Jefferson: Writings* (New York: Literary Classics of the United States, 2011), 1304-1310. Cf. Richard A. Samuelson, "Consistent in Creation: Thomas Jefferson, Natural Aristocracy and the Problem of Knowledge," in *Light and Liberty: Thomas Jefferson and the Power of Knowledge*, ed. Robert M.S. McDonald (Charlottesville, VA: University of Virginia Press, 2012), 75-95.

12 Thomas Jefferson, Notes on the State of Virginia Query XIX in Peterson, *Jefferson: Writings*, 290.

13 Thomas Jefferson to James Madison, December 20, 1787, in Peterson, *Jefferson: Writings*, 918.

14 Everett E. Edwards, ed., *Jefferson and Agriculture: a Sourcebook* (Washington, DC: U.S. Department of Agriculture, 1943); and Douglas L. Wilson, "The American *Agricola*: Jefferson's Agrarianism and the Classical Tradition," *The South Atlantic Quarterly* 80 (Summer, 1981): 339–354.

15 Cited by Wilson, "The American *Agricola*," 344.

16 Inter alia, Carl J. Richard, *The Founders and the Classics: Greece, Rome, and the American Enlightenment* (Cambridge, MA: Harvard University Press, 1994).

17 Julian P. Boyd et al., eds., *Papers of Thomas Jefferson* (Princeton, NJ: Princeton University Press, 1950–), vol. l, 169–170.

18 Joseph Spence, *Polymetis: or, an Enquiry concerning the Agreement between the Roman Poets and the Remains of the Antient Artists* (London: R. Dodsley, 1747).

19 William Bainter O'Neal, *Jefferson's Fine Arts Library: His Selections for the University of Virginia Together with His Own Architectural Books* (Charlottesville, VA: University Press of Virginia, 1976), 327–330. For Diana Venetrix ("Diana the Huntress"), Spence, *Polymetis*, 100.

20 On the building history of Monticello, see Jack McLaughlin, *Jefferson and Monticello: The Biography of a Builder* (New York: H. Holt, 1988).

21 Andrea Palladio, *Quattro Libri dell'Architettura* (Venice: Domenico de'Franceschi, 1570), vol. II.18.

22 "Palladio is the bible:" Isaac Coles to John Hartwell Cocke, February 23, 1816, cited by, among many others, McLaughlin, *Jefferson and Monticello*, 54; Jefferson's editions of Palladio: O'Neal, *Jefferson's Fine Arts Library*, 247–277; and Warren J. Cox, "Palladio and Libraries in Eighteenth-century America," in *Palladio and his Legacy: A Transatlantic Journey*, ed. Charles Hind and Irena Murray (Venice: Marsilio, 2010), 114–119.

23 Visitors' complaints about the difficulty of ascent, inter alia, George Tucknor in 1819, in Merrill D. Peterson, ed., *Visitors to Monticello* (Charlottesville, VA: University Press of Virginia, 1989), 61. For a full description of the climb, see Andrea Wulf, *Founding Gardeners: The Revolutionary Generation, Nature and the Shaping of the American Nation* (New York: Knopf, 2011), 178–182.

24 Ibid.

25 McLaughlin, *Jefferson and Monticello*, 35.

26 Ibid., and passim.

27 Jefferson acquired the French edition when he was in France (O'Neal, *Jefferson's Fine Arts Library*, 268). Other evidence suggests that the Isaac Ware edition was part of his first library which perished when his family home at Shadwell burned down in 1770 (McLaughlin, *Jefferson and Monticello*, 38). On Jefferson's Palladianism, inter alia, Robert Tavernor, *Palladio and Palladianism* (New York: Thames and Hudson, 1991), 188–209; and Charles E. Brownell, "The Architectural Achievement of Thomas Jefferson," in *The Making of Virginia Architecture*, ed. Charles E. Brownell (Richmond, VA: Virginia Museum of Fine Arts, 1992), 46–51.

28 According to a recent study, the figure's iconographical attributes (throne, book, scepter, chain) suggest that Regina Virtus is Justice, long considered queen of the virtues. Thus, Regina Virtus is not "Virtue, the Queen," but "Queen of the Virtues": Allen Ellenius, "Political Emblematics," in *The Emblem in Scandinavia and the Baltic*, ed. Simon McKeown and Mara R. Wade (Glasgow: Centre for Emblem Studies, 2006), 75–102 (80–81).

29 Chastity, for Jefferson, was something of a touchstone for excellence in architecture. Typically, to his house joiner James Dinsmore regarding his project for the University of Virginia: "[The pavilions] are to be of various forms, models of chaste architecture, as examples for the school of architecture to be formed on." Thomas Jefferson to James Dinsmore, April 13, 1817, Papers of Thomas Jefferson, University of Virginia Library, http://etext.lib.virginia.edu/jefferson.

30 Spence, *Polymetis*, 109; and Juvenal, *Satires*, VIII, 20.

31 Spence, *Polymetis*, 139.

32 Ibid., 14; and Silius Italicus, *Punica*, trans. with emendations J.D. Duff (Cambridge, MA: Harvard University Press, 1934), vol. II, book 15, 101–107.

33 Margaret Bayard Smith, leaving Monticello after her visit in 1813: "Mr. Smith got (into the carriage), the door shut and we drove from the habitation of philosophy and virtue. How rapidly we seem to descend that mountain which had seemed so tedious in its ascent." See Peterson, *Visitors*, 54.

34 Thomas Jefferson to Maria Cosway, October 12, 1786, in Peterson, *Jefferson: Writings*, 870.

35 Anna Thornton, "A Querellous Guest from Washington" (from Anna Thornton's Journal), in Peterson, *Visitors*, 33–34. Cf. McLaughlin, *Jefferson and Monticello*, 5.

36 Ibid.

37 Ibid., 6–7; and Ralph G. Giordano, *The Architectural Ideology of Thomas Jefferson* (Jefferson, NC: McFarland, 2012), 166.

38 Margaret Bayard Smith in Peterson, *Visitors*, 49.

39 Lucia Stanton, "Thomas Jefferson and the Land: The View from Monticello," in *Siting Jefferson: Contemporary Artists Interpret Thomas Jefferson's Legacy*, ed. Jill Hartz (Charlottesville, VA: University of Virginia Press, 2003), 33–37 (33); and Lucia Stanton, *"Those Who Labor for My Happiness": Slavery at Thomas Jefferson's Monticello* (Charlottesville, VA: University of Virginia Press, 2012), 84–86.

40 Thomas Jefferson to Maria Cosway, September 8, 1795, in Boyd et al., *Papers of Thomas Jefferson*, vol. 28, 455. Cf. Stanton, "Thomas Jefferson and the Land," 37.

41 Denis Cosgrove, *The Palladian Landscape* (Leicester: Leicester University Press, 1993), 52–54.

42 Lionello Puppi, "Palladio, Palladianism and Palladianists," in *Palladian Studies in America*, vol. 1, ed. Mario di Valmarana, trans. Joyce Vassallo Storey (Charlottesville, VA: University of Virginia Press, 1984), 5–17; Tavernor, *Palladio and Palladianism*, 182–187; James Ackerman, "Palladio and his Legacy in America," in *Palladio and His Legacy*, ed. Charles Hind and Irena Murray (Venice: Marsillio, 2010), 2–7; and Calder Loth, "Palladio's Legacy to America," in *Palladio and His Legacy*, 42–151.

43 Giordano, *The Architectural Ideology*, 45–51.

44 McLaughlin, *Jefferson and Monticello*, 26–28.

45 Ibid., 109–111.

46 Richard Guy Wilson, "Jefferson's Lawn: Perceptions, Interpretations, Meanings," in *Thomas Jefferson's Academical Village: the Creation of an Architectural Masterpiece*, ed. Richard Guy Wilson (Charlottesville, VA: Bayly Art Museum of the University of Virginia, 1993), 47–73 (68).

47 Thomas Jefferson to the citizens of Washington City, upon leaving at the end of his second term as president, cited by Brian Steele, "'The Yeomanry of the United States are not the Canaille of Paris': Thomas Jefferson, American Exceptionalism and the Spirit of Democracy," in *Light and Liberty*, 21.

48 Thomas Jefferson, Notes on the State of Virginia, Query VIII, in Peterson, *Jefferson: Writings*, 211.

49 Garry Wills, *Mr. Jefferson's University* (Washington, DC: National Geographic Society, 2002); Mary N. Woods, "Thomas Jefferson and the University of Virginia: Planning the Academic Village," *Journal of the Society of Architectural Historians*, 44, no. 3 (October, 1985): 266–283; and Wilson, *Thomas Jefferson's Academical Village*.

50 John Meacham, *Thomas Jefferson: The Art of Power* (New York: Random House, 2012), 469; and Wills, *Mr. Jefferson's University*, 199, 131–132.

51 Thomas Jefferson to Dr. Caspar Wistar, June 21, 1807, in Peterson, *Jefferson: Writings*, 1181.

52 Thomas Jefferson to the Trustees for the Lottery of East Tennessee College, May 6, 1810, cited by Woods, "Thomas Jefferson and the University of Virginia," 269.

53 Wilson, "Jefferson's Lawn," 68; and Wills, *Mr. Jefferson's University*, 71–77.

54 Ibid., 71. See also Wilson, "Jefferson's Lawn," 64.
55 Woods, "Thomas Jefferson and the University of Virginia," 168.
56 Roland Fréart de Chambray, Parallèle de l'architecture antique avec la moderne (Paris: Edme Martin, 1650); and Giordano, *The Architectural Ideology*, 184–219.
57 Palladio, *Quattro Libri*, vol. II. 46.
58 Wilson, "Jefferson's Lawn," 72.
59 Garry Wills, *"Negro President": Jefferson and the Slave Power* (Boston and New York: Mariner Book, 2005), 1–13 and 50–61.
60 Two hundred slaves: Meacham, *Thomas Jefferson: The Art of Power*, 48. In the course of his lifetime he owned a total of 600 slaves.
61 "Plantation imperialism," see Wills, *"Negro President,"* 9. "Empire of liberty," Thomas Jefferson to representatives of the Territory of Indiana, December 28, 1805: "By enlarging the empire of liberty, we multiply its auxiliaries, and provide new sources of renovation, should its principles at any time degenerate." Cited by Wulf, *Founding Gardeners*, 59.
62 Albert Furtwangler, *Assassination on Stage: Brutus, Hamlet and the Death of Lincoln* (Urbana, IL: University of Illinois Press, 1991); and Maria Wyke, *Caesar: A Life in Western Culture* (Chicago: The University of Chicago Press, 2008), 221–226.

Interlude A
The Architect's Fall

Santiago de Orduña

I fall

Am I Lucifer? Adam? Am I Sisyphus?

I fall and as I fall, I repeat the Universal Story of Falls

a universal love claims me

As I fall, I hold a briefcase. In it, I find a deck of cards with instructions:
"The goal of this game is to return alive to the Temple of Love (you have
13 lives and 52 points). If in need, pick a card . . . Good luck"

I pick a card: *golden wings*

I suddenly have a heavy pair of wings on my back. I flap them, but to no avail.

I notice a name engraved on the briefcase:

FRANCESCO PÉREZ - DAEDALUS

I sink into the earth as if sinking into a dream

I land on a large rotunda surrounded by Corinthian columns. Near the
center is a perfect hole inside which a Solomonic column rises projecting a
black light into a motionless sun in the sky. Around the pit is the inscription:

COINCIDENTIA OPPOSITORUM

At a distance, in opposite directions, I perceive two truncated pyramids. One
has a frontal staircase covered in blood, at its top there is a terrace with two

chapels, one blue, the other red, crowned by digital boards displaying the time,

(0:00)

the weather,

(CLEAR)

and future events,

(. . . WE ARE ON THE THRESH HOLD OF A NEW ERA . . .)
On top of the opposite structure is a glass castle with an alabaster balcony. A beautiful, naked, woman waves a handkerchief at me . . .

. . . *déjà vu* . . .

I am thirsty and search for water, but suddenly feel a stab in the heart. I touch my chest, there is no wound. I turn towards the woman who now holds a bow. A great desire for her awakens in me. I rush towards her through tortuous passages, fallen idols, broken obelisks and walls with indecipherable inscriptions, but the broken paths always return to their origin.

I pick a card:

"In the Age of Gods,

men only conceive the Will of the Universe . . .

Do as you must . . . "

I decide to go towards the tower of sacrifices. A broad avenue flanked by statues of heroes leads to the pyramidal temple. I climb the stairs and arrive at a terrace. There, five people who look exactly like me are waiting. Video cameras catch my every move. Inside the twin chapels, gods watch everything on HD-TV. I open my briefcase and pick a card: hummingbird masks, curly wig, sacrificial flint, mp3 player with Mahler's fifth (lose 4 lives). . . . I distribute the artifacts among other players. Everything is ready, the music, the motionless sun, the sacrificers. I lie face up on the altar, they hold me tight; they are all myself: I take the flint . . .

left-handed hummingbird
smoking-mirror
old-god
bird-snake god . . .
(nothing keeps me from saving the universe)
(5 extra lives)

I awaken on the alabaster balcony in the arms of my beloved. Her eyes reflect an infinite light. Her smile is indescribably warm. She speaks with no words. Clear water springs from her breasts. I drink, ecstatically, until my soul rests . . .

we are complete
time stands still

I feel a drop on my forehead. Drums sound in the distance. I open my eyes and see the sun at the zenith. The air turns red, and the star finally resumes its journey. The shadow of an eagle crosses the plaza and sinks into the well. The ruins cast shadows on the ground. On top of the temple, the digital board displays:

(. . . A NEW ERA BEGINS . . .)

I hear the voice of my beloved mourning at a distance and suddenly remembered her names: *Penelope, Carlota, Polya, Malitzin, Magdalene, Eloise.* . . . Her voice fades while telling me that I have to find meaning in . . .

Architecture

I am close to the central pit, but, where once stood the rotunda now stands an elongated court flanked by polished slopes oriented with the New Sun. I pick a pair of cards: "leather underpants (5 lives)", "sneakers with retractable wheels" (7 points). I find myself wearing pre-Columbian ball-game clothing and skates. I hear a whistle. A black hole suddenly falls on the esplanade bouncing heavily towards me. I move quickly. The "thing" seems attracted by me. I keep on running until I turn back and wait for it. I hit it with my hip and toss it. I hear a crowd cheering. The ball reaches the central well. There is a silence, the "singularity" rolls slowly along the edge of the *mundus*. It is then absorbed by the world's navel. From the depth comes an aqueous burp . . .

. . . *Ommmmmm* . . .

I turn around and look towards the castle, only to find a glass skyscraper disappearing in the clouds. On the opposite direction now stands an avenue that fades in the distance. Limits have been abolished. I open my briefcase and find a letter

You have revealed a world generated by soulless ideas. Be sure to erect the
foundational stone in the correct place and choose the right path before it's too late.
To do it you must build a mytho-poetic mechanism as an embodiment of love, hence
provoking the erection of the menhir.

Follow your heart, I will always be waiting for you in the Temple of Love.

Yours:

Eloise

(this message will self-destruct in 20 seconds)

The well is now blocked by a black granite stone. I feel impatient. Whoever is playing god seems quite irresponsible. I take another card: "Victorinox knife " I pinch my index finger with it. A large drop of blood appears with which I draw a mysterious sign on the stone. There is lighting in the sky, and after a few seconds the stone begins to emerge from the ground and floats and spins in the air. It has the monstrous form of a goddess from whose severed neck flow two jets of blood shaped as snake heads facing each other with open jaws. The monolith begins to descend hiding the sign under itself. Suddenly, everything around me becomes wire-frame digital structures with no textured surfaces. I start losing substance; my body begins to fade . . .

The central well is now covered by a transparent dome, like the iris of an enormous buried eye that watches quietly. Through it I see a large void and a lamp in the shape of the solar system suspended at its center. I take the knife and sink it into the glassy surface . . .

pop

I fall
I flow towards the origin of things
scattered in the horizon, I can see the human tribes seeking
for the silent Word
the cenotaph of the gods,
the broken stone,
the fire stone,
the water stone,
the alabaster storm,
¡the mystery of the children of clay¡

I keep falling
attracted, perhaps, by a universal love which claims me
Who am I?
Altazor? Cuauhtemoc? Baumgarten?
In my hand I hold a leather suitcase
my thirst is infinite . . .

PART II
Worldmaking

5

MADE IN USAGE

Architecture in Furetière's *Dictionnaire universel*

Caroline Dionne

> Man stands out [from other living beings] in both respects – in the construction of social practice, and in being given to pure knowledge, seeing and thinking. He is the creature who has the *logos*: he has language, he has distance from the things that immediately press upon him, he is free to choose what is good and to know what is true – and he can even laugh.
>
> *Hans-Georg Gadamer*[1]

In the opening pages of *Le roman bourgeois*, seventeenth-century writer Antoine Furetière (Figure 5.1) concisely sketches the appropriate architectural backdrop for his narrative, a tale involving several "authentic" bourgeois characters of the Parisian context of his time.[2] The author's aim is emphatically stated: the setting of his novel shall be mobile, travelling through several neighborhoods of the city. He also wants it to be as truthful as possible and chooses Place Maubert, "the most bourgeois square in Paris", as the initial location.[3] But, Furetière insists, he will not engage in architectural description.

The book opens with a rather elaborate preterition through which Furetière announces his intention *not to* provide descriptive accounts of architecture. A common figure of speech, the preterition works as follows: a speaker feigns to avoid a certain topic while nonetheless mentioning it. For example, a political candidate could use the preterition as follows: "I will not speak here about my opponent's extramarital affairs." Through this rhetorical device, a sensitive topic is simultaneously occulted from conversation

Figure 5.1 Antoine Furetière, engraving by Gérard Edelinck ca. 1688. In
Antoine Furetière, *Dictionaire universel, contenant generalement tous
les mots françois tant vieux que modernes, & les termes de toutes les
sciences et des arts,* . . . (A La Haye etc: Chez Arnout & Reinier
Leers, 1690)

and brought into focus. In the case of Furetière's tale, and consistent with a
literary approach that has been referred to as *antiromanesque*, the trope partakes to the satire, producing the comical effect sought: it is primarily used to
make the reader laugh. But the rhetorical stratagem serves other, less obvert
purposes: it reinforces the realistic quality of the author's narrated account
while mocking, and criticizing, the grandiloquent and exaggerated tone
found in seventeenth century French romances.[4]

Furtière's non-description thus unfolds over several pages through which
the architectural locations meant to house the narrative – the main edifices,
squares or neighborhoods – are mentioned by name but never described.

Furthermore, in order to make even clearer his point that literary architectural description is highly problematic, Furetière mimicks what a fictitious (or at least unidentified) writer would have written. In a passage concerning a key location for the unfolding of the tale, the Parisian Church of Saint-Joseph des Carmes, Furtière writes: "A less sincere author, in his attempt to bring architecture into play and produce grand effect, could very well take the liberty of replacing the actual church with a description of a famous Greek temple."[5] Such ill-informed process – replacing a modern building with the description of an ancient one, changing the shape of a public square or altering the elements and proportions of a building's facade – Furetière insists, would cause unwanted harm to the field of architecture, and, we may deduce, to the reader's sensibility.

Furetière's satire of a hypothetical counterpart – the figure of the insincere writer – is meant to strengthen his own position: he chooses not to depict an idealized, embellished and most importantly untruthful version of the architectural space of the bourgeoisie. Unlike this other writer who "may well fill his descriptions with words such as metopes, triglyphes, volutes, stylobates, and other unknown terms found in the texts of a Vitruvius or a Vignola to claim expertise in the field of architecture," Furetière will refrain from interjecting architectural descriptions with words that he deems unintelligible to the reader.[6] The author of *Le roman bourgeois* does not wish to aggrandize the architectural backdrop for his tale, nor will he distort or disguise its design. Contrariwise, in order for the context of the narrative to become tangible for the reader, Furetière primarily relies on the latter's actual experience of the locations and edifices mentioned, as they exist in reality, in and around the city of Paris. In addition, the reader is invited to summon his own aptitude for imagination and build more elaborate architectural settings at will: " I will not tell you how the church is, although it is rather famous. Those who so desire can go see it, or else build it in their imagination as they shall please."[7] The sole fact of *naming* a given location is, for Furetière, sufficient to trigger the reader's imagination and set the action into its proper setting. The spatiality of Furetière's narrative thus almost entirely rests on the reader's pre-existing experience of architecture.

The lengthy passage ends with Furetière nevertheless revealing *something* about the church of the Carmes: "I will only mention that it is the center of the bourgeoisie, and that it is highly attended because of the license to speak that this place provides."[8] The architectural merit of the building, central to the unfolding of the first part of Furetière's novel, is therefore tied to the role and potential of architecture to frame the interactions of the Parisian bourgeoisie and, most importantly, to foster voluble social gatherings. Architectural space can be summoned and, ultimately, play a role in literary fiction, as the locus of social gathering and conversation.

Furetière's reliance on the readers' pre-existing experience of architecture and faculty for imagination implies that the kind of architectural knowledge readily accessible through everyday experience prevails over object-oriented description. This knowledge formation relies, as we shall see, on *usage* understood as a collective mode of production of spaces and words. In that sense, Furetière's use of the preterition at the beginning of *Le roman bourgeois* may be understood to serve another purpose: it underlines and problematizes the relationship of architectural knowledge – and of all knowledge – to words, to language.[9] Furetière's treatment of architectural description as this highly sensitive topic, as this subject matter not to be mentioned but nonetheless brought forth, begs the question of the importance of architecture in his wider system of knowledge, a position that we will attempt to reveal by examining his lexicographical work.

Furetière's language-as-lived

The question of knowledge – of universal knowledge – is central to Furetière's entire corpus. Clearly stated in the author/bookseller's warning to the reader that precedes *Le roman bourgeois*, the purpose of his literary production is not only to entertain, as the subtitle of the book "A Comical Work" would suggest, but, essentially, to educate.[10] In this case, education is achieved by providing the reader with the widest possible collection of moral and intellectual attributes, staged in exchanges of words (in conversation but also through accounts of transacted written documents). According to Furetière, indecent or ridiculous actions, unveiled through the specific obliqueness proper to the satire, bear the potential to summon their opposite – morally proper and elevated deeds – thus providing the reader with a universal account of human morality that may guide him towards ethical action and the acquisition of a farther reaching knowledge.[11] The novel shall thus educate in the utmost vital field of ethics, and guide the conduct of one's life with others.

Naturally, it is therefore in questions pertaining to language, understood as the foundation of social life, that Furetière's intent to educate, to provide a general, universal understanding of things, found its most fertile ground.[12] Furetière's *Dictionnaire universel, contenant généralement tous les mots françois, tant vieux que modernes, et les termes de toutes les sciences et des arts* was published posthumously in 1690, under the protection of a foreign prince. The lexicographer had died a few years earlier, after dedicating the last fifteen years of his life to a meticulous process of compilation of the French language.

Furetière's understanding of language and classification conflicted with that of many of his contemporaries: he partook actively in the famous Quarrel of the dictionaries, overtly attacking several members of the French Academy for their position regarding the French language.[13] For those members of the Academy, a proper French dictionary was meant to account first and foremost for the elevated language spoken at court. The purpose of the Academicians' compendium was thus to fix and formalize the limits of the "beautiful language" of the aristocracy that had, for them, reached its apogee: its scope was essentially prescriptive and grammatical.[14]

Furetière exposed his understanding of language at length in his *Factums*, a series of leaflets written and self-published over the years to defend his position against the Academy.[15] There, in contrast with the academicians' views, he posits language as an open, evolving arrangement. For him, the French language of his time, like all languages, cannot be systematized and restricted to a fixed – aristocratic – whole. In Furetière's view, languages are given shape progressively, and undergo constant change.[16] Consequently, the process of ordering a given language implied in the lexicographic endeavor is bound to account for this capricious quality, begging the following question: how can the dictionary, as a finite selection of words and definitions, be productive of true, universal knowledge?

The answer may lie in part with Furetière's enfranchisement of the general public, understood as both beholder and maker of language. Further exposing his view, Furetière writes: "any given language always primarily belongs to those who speak it, that is, to the general public."[17] He then adds: "These books [dictionaries] are not meant to fabricate words, but to account for, and explain their *usage*"[18] Hence, Furetière's task in compiling the dictionary entries is to account for the widest possible levels of discourse, modes of speaking, and for the entire spectrum of words *in use*, understood as crucial accounts of the language's vitality.

The *Dictionnaire* defines the word "usage" as "exercise or habit."[19] Furetière adds: "Several sciences and many arts are better learned through usage, through practice, than through theory."[20] To "use," to "exercise" or to "habituate oneself" are thus crucial to the formation of scientific and artistic knowledge.[21] As we shall see, this process-oriented type of knowledge formation bears a foundational character in Furetière's understanding of universal knowledge.

Architectural knowledge in the *Dictionnaire universel*

As attested by its extended title, Furetière's *Dictionnaire* gives specific importance to scientific and artistic terminology: it includes the widest possible collection of terms pertaining to all sciences and mechanical arts, to the production of artifacts, inventions and machines, as well as to the definition of their corresponding trades. It is notably Furetière's insistence on including such terminology in his dictionary project that led to the famous dispute where he opposed several members of the French Academy. Despite the harsh consequences tied to his views – his eviction for the Academy, the loss of his royal protection and position at court – Furetière unceasingly sustained the necessity to include these definitions in his compendium.

Furetière favored a simple structure for his dictionary: words appear one after the other in an unbroken flow, organized alphabetically according to their first letter, much like in the case of today's lexicons. The reader enters the book at any given point, following a specific query. From there, a system of cross-references may allow one to travel from word to word, moving across the book's scope. This structure implies that words pertaining to the arts and sciences are not grouped thematically, but scattered through the entire compilation, seen by Furetière as binding elements. Terms belonging to astronomy, medicine, geometry or architecture sit next to each other and to day-to-day words, from the most vulgar to the utmost polite. It is in part this interweaving, conjoined with the active participation of the reader, that contributes, in Furetière's view, to a fertile production of knowledge. As stated in the *Factums*, Furetière's lexicographic process is, unlike the Academicians', primarily guided by epistemological, philosophical concerns. All scientific and artistic terms, as well as words pertaining to the human trades, Furetière writes using an architectural analogy, "are the mortar that holds together the entire edifice of language."[22] Removing these words would prevent the reader of the *Dictionnaire* to access a crucial type of knowledge, leaving him with, to extend Furetière's analogy, a pile of unbound stones.

In the vast realm of human knowledge accounted for through his encyclopedic endeavor, architecture is thus cited amongst the most important order-revealing fields of knowledge, after mathematics and geometry, between optics and pyrotechnics, along with what would today appear as esoteric or unscientific realms such as astrology, falconry or fishing (see Figure 5.2). In his definition of the architect, Furetière announces the scope of the trade: "One needs to know many things to be a good architect"[23] The term "architecture" is first defined as the field of theoretical knowledge pertaining to building, "the art or science of building."[24] A second meaning follows: architecture is the means available to actually transcribe this theoretical knowledge into a work, that is, "the manner in which to build and the ornaments to use."[25] Furetière relies here on a comprehensive series of both ancient and modern architects and theoreticians and, much like in the *Le roman bourgeois*,

DICTIONAIRE
UNIVERSEL,

Contenant generalement tous les

MOTS FRANÇOIS

tant vieux que modernes, & les Termes de toutes les

SCIENCES ET DES ARTS,

SÇAVOIR

La Philofophie, Logique, & Phyfique, la Medecine, ou Anatomie, Pathologie, Terapeutique, Chirurgie, Pharmacopée, Chymie, Botanique, ou l'Hiftoire naturelle des Plantes, & célle des Animaux, Mineraux, Metaux & Pierreries, & les noms des Drogues artificielles:

La Jurifprudence Civile & Canonique, Feodale & Municipale, & fur tout celle des Ordonnances:

Les Mathematiques, la Geometrie, l'Arithmetique, & l'Algebre; la Trigonometrie, Geodefie, ou l'Arpentage, & les Sections coniques; l'Aftronomie, l'Aftrologie, la Gnomonique, la Geographie; la Mufique, tant en theorie qu'en pratique, les Inftrumens à vent & à cordes; l'Optique, Catoptrique, Dioptrique, & Perfpective; l'Architecture civile & militaire, la Pyrotechnie, Tactique, & Statique:

Les Arts, la Rhetorique, la Poëfie, la Grammaire, la Peinture, Sculpture, &c. la Marine, le Manege, l'Art de faire des armes, le Blafon, la Venerie, Fauconnerie, la Pefche, l'Agriculture, ou Maifon Ruftique, & la plus-part des Arts mechaniques:

Plufieurs termes de Relations d'Orient & d'Occident, la qualité des Poids, Mefures & Monnoyes; les Etymologies des mots, l'invention des chofes, & l'Origine de plufieurs Proverbes, & leur relation à ceux des autres Langues:

Et enfin les noms des Auteurs qui ont traitté des matieres qui regardent les mots, expliquez avec quelques Hiftoires, Curiofitez naturelles, & Sentences morales, qui feront rapportées pour donner des exemples de phrafes & de conftructions.

Le tout extrait des plus excellens Auteurs anciens & modernes.

Recueilli & compilé par feu

Meffire ANTOINE FURETIERE,

Abbé de Chalivoy, de l'Academie Françoife.

TOME PREMIER.

Figure 5.2 Frontispiece of the 1690 edition of Antoine Furetière's *Dictionaire universel* (Galica, Bibliothèque Nationale de France)

the reader is invited to acquaint himself directly with existing works and treatises to form his own understanding of the field.[26]

The definition provided for architecture ends with a third signification, tied to a substitute usage of the word and connected to how architecture is assessed, or received: "The term architecture is also used in regards to a building's value, it can be attributed to parts of buildings, seldom to entire edifices."[27] This implies that not all architecture can qualify as good – or true – architecture but, more importantly, that assessment processes lay in the communality or popularity of a given expression – its accepted usage – as in, for instance: "The portal of the Louvre is a fine piece of architecture."[28]

Like in the case of all definitions found in the *Dictionnaire*, Furetière appears to follow the principles of persuasive argumentation and presents the meanings of a given word according to three co-dependent levels of knowledge, akin to Aristotle's tripartite division of science: the theoretical, the practical and the poïetic.[29] The first signification points towards theoretical knowledge: it presents the logical or reasonable meaning of the word "architecture." With the second level, Furetière ascertains the authority of his definition and secures his impartiality in the eye of the reader by relying heavily on the work of knowledgeable authors: the *Dictionnaire* radiates towards an extensive body of existing architectural treatises and buildings. Philibert de l'Orme's famous *Trompe* at Anet, praised by Furetière for its awe-producing quality, "as it seems to be supported by nothing," is but one example of how architecture can embody the practical knowledge of the architect, his cunning intelligence or know-how.[30] Thirdly, Furetière's means to account for the poïetic level of knowledge is to provide a colloquial expression, bringing forth an alternate usage of the word that invokes the reader's personal experience, who most probably has heard or uttered the expression and seen the building in question.[31] Usage can therefore be seen as a specific mode of knowledge formation. Albeit different in scope from the combined theoretical knowledge and practical know-how of the architect or, to borrow Alberto Pérez-Gómez terminology, his *techne-poiesis*, usage nevertheless participates to the production of architecture.[32] Architecture is completed as it is being used.

Accordingly, it can be argued that the definition of architecture as a field of knowledge goes beyond the three previously mentioned significations given for the word. Its scope extends as the dictionary is used, that is, as the reader actively engages with the work and navigates between words. More than a hundred occurrences of the term "architecture" appear in Furetière dictionary, and definitions are provided for an extremely wide selection of architectural components, from "abaque" to "zoophore," including the same "triglyphe," "metope" and "stylobate" that Furetière had deemed unfitting to appear in *Le roman bourgeois*. An elaborate architectural terminology thus finds its *voie royale* in the *Dictionnaire*, precisely because once the terms are defined, used and understood by the general public, they may enter common usage and become crucial vehicles towards universal knowledge.

Usage, architecture and social life

For Furetière, the value of a scientific, artistic or literary work is assessed through the consent of the general public, an approbation that "shall be earned through pain and reason."[33] Not only is it good to obtain the public's agreement in conjunction with the approbation of the Prince, but ultimately: "the origin of truth and the order of justice lay in the universality of the [public] vote."[34] In the early enlightenment context of the late seventeenth century, Furetière's valuing of the judgment of the general public remains perplexing. If, for him, the vote of the public does not yet stand apart or overrule the consent of the King, it is nonetheless given explicit authority. Could this position announce the formation of a bourgeois public sphere or the development, in the legal and political context of the eighteenth century, of the notion of a public's right?[35]

In light of our previous observations, we would nuance this claim. If Furetière's general public is given a decisive power to rule, engaged in an active relationship with artistic, scientific or, in the case that interests us here, architectural production, this relation remains grounded, like all matters pertaining to human life, in language. Usage is defined through the social practice of space, as men converse and debate amongst each other. Furetière's public's vote is therefore cast collectively and indirectly: it is the expression of social life revealed through usage. In that sense, it does not yet represent the democratic voice of a fully formed political body.

From the structure, content and scope of the definitions provided in the *Dictionnaire*, we can infer that architecture, as an order-revealing form of knowledge, remains for Furetière contingent to the poetic making of its audience. As shown in *Le roman bourgeois*, the space of this encounter permeates the ordinary life of men: architectural knowledge is formed through everyday experience and good architecture fosters conversation.

Like in the case of all arts and sciences, the meaning of architecture can only be made effective through language, as it is being used, that is, ingrained with and embedded in conversations. Much like Furetière's understanding of language as "alive," architecture belongs to those who use it, as it is built collectively and progressively, from within. By positing usage as semantically creative, Furetière's work reveals how architecture remains, in the late Renaissance, bound to epistemological questions and embedded in an everyday life governed by the polysemy of language, an architecture understood as the proper expression of social life and as the site of ethical choices made through conversation. This architecture is also the site of the satire, of unveiling the true by mimicking the false, and of understanding through laughter.

The final version of this paper was completed in the context of the Canadian Center for Architecture (CCA) Visiting Scholars Program.

Notes

1 Hans-Georg Gadamer, *Praise of Theory* (New Haven; London: Yale University Press, 1998), 58.
2 Born in the very context of the bourgeoisie satirically exposed in *Le roman bourgeois*, Antoine Furetière (1619–1688) progressively ascended the social hierarchy. His practice as a writer was secured by obtaining the religious title of Abbey, a nomination in Richelieu's recently founded French Academy and a royal privilege that led to the publication of a partial version of his future dictionary (*Essais d'un dictionnaire universel*, 1684). In the context of the *Grand siècle*, his literary works received limited attention. Furetière was, however, well known for his lexicographic production, and notably for his central participation in the Quarrel of the dictionaries. Extensive biographical accounts can be found in Alain Rey, *Antoine Furetière: Un précurseur des Lumières sous Louis XIV* (Paris: Libr. A. Fayard, 2006). I am grateful to Maarten Delbeke for first bringing Furetière to my attention and sharing his insight on the topic.
3 Antoine Furetière, *Le roman bourgeois* [1666], ed. Marine Roy-Garibal (Paris: GF Flammarion, 2001), 75.
4 Usually associated with twentieth century avant-garde literary movements, the anti-romanesque approach finds its roots, as Ugo Dionne has pointedly shown, in much earlier literary practices. Dionne has stressed the ambiguous "modernity" of the seventeenth century *antiroman*, and more specifically how such an approach not only operates an internal critique of the genre itself but contributes to the historical development of the modern novel, playing in France a role analogous to that of Defoe, Fielding and Richardson in England. See Ugo Dionne, "Le paradoxe d'Hercule ou comment le roman vient aux antiromanciers." *Études françaises* 42 (2009): 141–167. Marine Roy-Garibal has also stressed the experimental character of literary productions by Antoine Furetière, Charles Sorel and Paul Scarron in the context of the seventeenth century and emphasized their intent to convey a critique of the abundantly practiced and popular heroic romance of the time (especially those of Georges and Madeleine de Scudéry). Roy-Garibal also comments on Furetière's use of to preterition as typical of the approach. Marine Roy-Garibal, "La crise du romanesque," in Antoine Furetière, *Le roman bourgeois* [1666], ed. Marine Roy-Garibal (Paris: GF Flammarion, 2001), 350–351.
5 Furetière, *Le roman bourgeois*, 77.
6 Ibid.
7 Ibid., 78.
8 Ibid.
9 On the problematic relationship of knowledge to language, see Hans-Georg Gadamer, "Language and Understanding" (1970), *Theory, Culture & Society* 23 (2006): 13–27 and *Truth and Method* (London; New York: Continuum, 2004).

10 Furetière, *Le roman bourgeois*, 67.
11 Ibid., 67–70.
12 Processes of compilation permeate Furetière's entire corpus and in this regard, *Le roman bourgeois* can be seen as a field of experimentation towards his lexicographic production. On this connection, see Marine Roy-Garibal, "Présentation" in Furetière, *Le roman bourgeois*, 49–56.
13 A detailed account of Furetière's involvement in the Quarrel can be found in Alain Rey, *Antoine Furetière*, 83–126.
14 See François Ost, *Furetière: la démocratisation de la langue*, (Paris: Michalon, 2008), 49–56.
15 Trained as a jurist, Furetière's main defensive strategy in regards to his dictionary project took the form of a series of *Factum*, in which the lexicographer engages his oratory skills to expose the facts in his defense and break his opponents' argumentation. In the corpus of Furetière's work, these form a third level of literary expression. See Antoine Furetière, *Recueil des factums d'Antoine Furetière de l'Académie française: contre quelques-uns de cette Académie. Suivi des preuves et pieces historiques données dans l'édition de 1694 par CH. Asselineau* (Paris: Poulet-Malassis et De Broise, 1858). Translations are mine.
16 Furetière, *Recueil des factums*, I, 16.
17 Ibid., I, 66.
18 Ibid., I, 10. Italics are mine.
19 Antoine Furetière, *Dictionaire universel, contenant generalement tous les mots françois tant vieux que modernes, & les termes de toutes les sciences et des arts, . . .* (A La Haye etc: Chez Arnout & Reinier Leers, 1690), 2155.
20 Ibid.
21 Furetière, *Dictionaire universel*, 1880.
22 Furetière, *Recueil des factums* I, 12–14.
23 Furetière, *Dictionaire universel*, 128.
24 Ibid.
25 Ibid.
26 See Furetière, *Dictionaire universel*, 128.
27 Ibid.
28 Ibid.
29 Philippe Beck identifies several locations in Aristotle's corpus where this firm distinction between three "forms" of science appears, notably in the *Metaphysics*, the *Nicomachean Ethics* and the *Topics*. See Philippe Beck, "Logiques de l'impossibilité" in Aristote, *Poétique* (Paris: Gallimard, 1996), 8.
30 See Furetière, *Dictionaire universel*, 2071.
31 The term poïetic, from the Greek *poiesis*, "to make" is found in both Plato and Aristotle. In Plato's *Symposium*, *poiesis* is connected to love (by *Agathon*) and associated with man's strive for immortality which takes three forms: (1) natural *poiesis* through sexual procreation, (2) *poiesis* in the city through the attainment of heroic fame and finally, and (3) *poiesis* in the soul through the cultivation of virtue and knowledge. The two latter seem central to Furetière's understanding of usage. See Plato, *Symposium* 208c–d, 209c–d, in *Selected Dialogues of Plato*, trans. Benjamin Jowett (New York: Modern Library, 2001).
    In *Built upon Love*, Pérez-Gómez shows how similar spatial intervals exist between "a work of architecture and the observer/participant and between the architect and his work of *techne- poiesis*," and pointedly traces the historical origin of these intervals to "eros," to love, to a mode of making connections between things driven by a longing for knowledge and wholeness. See *Built ipon Love:*

Architectural Longing after Ethics and Aesthetics (Cambridge, MA; London: MIT Press, 2006), 34.

32 On the relationship of theory to practice and the techno-poetic dimension of architectural making in the context of the late Renaissance, see Alberto Pérez-Gómez, *Architecture and the Crisis of Modern Science* (Cambridge, MA: MIT Press, 1983), especially Chapters 5–7.

33 Furetière, *Recueil des factums*, I, 311.

34 Ibid., II, 48.

35 Jürgen Habermas has connected the appearance of a "bourgeois public sphere" in the context of the eighteenth century to specific spatial configurations that were not yet actively practiced in Furetière's lifetime. See Jürgen Habermas, *The Structural Transformation of the Public Sphere: An Inquiry Into a Category of Bourgeois Society* (Cambridge, MA; London: MIT Press, 1991). Also, closely examining Furetière's production as a jurist, François Ost characterizes Furetière's lexicographic approach as eminently modern and prefiguring the development, in the eighteenth century legal context, of the democratic notion of a public's right. See Ost, *Furetière*.

6

BEYOND EXPRESSION

Lily Chi

In the early 1990s, the Office for Metropolitan Architecture (OMA) was commissioned to design a plan for doubling the size of the city of Hanoi. Rather than tamper with the existing fabric, the OMA proposal leaps over the Red River to establish a new district twenty-five kilometers from the city center. Hanoi New Town is an archipelago of fantastic island-districts that build on the city's fabled relationship to water: an intriguing dreamscape and a provocative vision of cosmopolitan life as might be imagined by the author of *Delirious New York*.[1]

As victim of an Asian financial crisis, OMA's plan was not implemented but its twin-city configuration presaged a common, if less visionary logic of development in many cities all over the world today. In Hanoi, the "36-street" district has been designated a preservation area, and plans are to remove all manufacturing and automobiles from this market quarter; in their place, boutiques selling the city's culture and history to international visitors, and on the expanding peripheries, corporate parks, gated communities, and leisure compounds. This is a common pattern of development in so-called "new markets" all over the world as governments open their economies and resources to global finance, and their histories to leisure industries and corporate branding.

Understandably, global capital's apparent alternatives of "museum city" and "generic city" are not universally embraced, and there is widespread, resurgent interest in Regionalism in various forms. Far from the nuanced arguments of the original authors of Critical Regionalism,[2] the rallying cries for architectures of "Identity, Place and Human Experience" against the homogenizing forces of globalization project great optimism through a narrow lens.[3] "The time is now for an architecture of resistance," notes one proponent, "a spirited architecture of place . . . that belongs to the soil within which it is sited, and which belongs to its people too."[4] Architecture can reclaim, or appropriate the local, even invent "new identities" through "careful borrowing of elements from rich architectural traditions" to create "the 'new local.'"[5] Other regionalist trends graft identity and sustainability issues, calling for place-specific architectures arising out of concern for local environmental, material, and human ecologies.

Anxieties of homogenization, ungroundedness, and cultural identification are not unique to twenty-first-century globalization, nor are critiques of Regionalism as an approach.[6] As Alberto Pérez-Gómez, Dalibor Vesely and others have argued, questions about architecture's ability to contribute to cultural location, continuity, and coherence need to be posed within a broader horizon of knowledge structures and practices that underlie and prefigure the dilemmas of the contemporary discipline.[7]

In the spirit of such thinking, this essay explores an underlying premise of Regionalist ambitions: the idea of architecture as expression of site. I would like to begin with context of concerns for which the specific site, or program of a building, came to be posed not as one concern amongst others in design work, but as *the* generative factor for formal invention. In considering the quest for legible form as a "worksite" − a paradigmatic response to a defining dilemma of modern architectural work − rather than a design intention, I will point out two critical blind spots in the navigation of this terrain and, in a postscript, touch upon what an expanded notion of site might comprise.

Provisional grounds: architecture as expression

While architects have long been concerned with conditions of site, the idea that design should create a unique *expression* of a particular site is a relatively recent preoccupation. Vitruvius devoted chapters of *De architectura* to site considerations for ensuring the health, propriety, and operative needs of cities, buildings and theaters, but discussions of appropriate ordering and ordinance fell under entirely different principles. Site figures in these latter discussions in the need to adapt such principles − symmetry, for example − to local conditions of appearance. This understanding of site persisted well into the eighteenth century in European architectural writing. Formal references and design procedures varied greatly in the course of this history, but the guiding principles of design and the discourses thereof were attuned to a different scale of context. Whether embedded in the constructive geometries by which Gothic builders literally drew out an architecture, or played out in geometric figurations that structured building in the Vitruvian tradition, design aimed at situating the local, the particular, within a more important "macro" site: the harmonically proportioned geometric universe of classical and Biblical teaching.

The idea that the designer should "adapt his Building to the Situation," or site, was a departure of the early eighteenth century, as David Leatherbarrow noted in his study of Robert Morris.[8] Even for Morris, however, this adaptation was not a matter of individuated expression, but one of *differentiation* guided by three descriptive tropes – variously depicted perceptual qualities associated with the proportioning and ornamentation of Vitruvius' three Orders. The systematic elaboration of this idea was the theory of architectural character, first introduced in the French Academy and subsequently published by Germain Boffrand in 1743. Emerging from a commingling of texts on classical rhetoric and, to a lesser extent, on physiognomy, the idea that "an edifice should present a character fitting to its destination" became widely accepted in the late eighteenth century. As disseminated by Boffrand and fellow academician Jacques-François Blondel, character theory was effectively a reformulation of key Vitruvian principles – harmony, proportionality and the use of the Orders – into a theory of architectural expression. Most adherents assumed Boffrand's premise about how "character" would be rendered in architectural terms: the Orders served as ready-made formal tropes, three *genres* of appearance and perceptual effect. The judicious choice and adaptation of these genres to specific sites and programs would render legible the entire range of possibilities in the eighteenth century's changing social and urban landscape.[9]

The terms of character theory were, however, intrinsically open-ended. In due course, all terms in the formulation came to be rethought: from the formal basis for architectural character, to premises about the "spectator" in or of architectural works, to the very "destinations" or programs that comprised a civil society.[10] In leaving behind the Vitruvian Orders as a basis for architectural character, in drawing on premises of corporeal sensing and ideation to explore entirely unprecedented formal inventions, Etienne-Louis Boullée's projects in *Essai sur l'Art* perhaps comes closest to contemporary notions of design as a search for individuated expression.

Despite this divergence on what exactly constituted architectural "character," architects converged in their anxieties. "Such is the degeneracy of fashion," lamented Boffrand, "that at times what ought to be at the top has been placed at the bottom."[11] Boffrand's complaints can still be heard a half-century later: "There are no certain principles in architectural composition; each architect has his *esprit*, his own specific way of arranging proportions. . . . Thus, the diverse qualities, the constitutive proportions of a beautiful building . . . are but arbitrary qualities?"[12] Readers of Pérez-Gómez's scholarship will recognize in Charles-François Viel's rhetorical question the long shadow cast by Claude Perrault. If the principles of harmonic proportion that had long guided architectural invention and collective apprehension have no basis beyond custom, what then? Is architectural work left to the wiles of individual fancy and the vagaries of relativism? Boullée summarized the angst of the period in one plaintive question: "Is architecture merely fantastic art belonging to the realm of pure invention or are its basic principles derived from Nature?"[13]

Writers on architectural character diverged greatly on Boullée's second question, but were resolute on the first. The significance of these varying theories of architectural character for the eighteenth century's crisis of grounds lies not so much in the emergence of a coherent new idea of Nature, but in their very structure. The formulation that design should express the character of a building program or site effectively replaces Vitruvian tradition's *extrinsic* schema of harmony – between micro and macro, between the ordinance of buildings and bodies, both heavenly and corporeal – with a more modest, *intrinsic* "harmony:" that between a building program or site, an architecture that gives visual expression to that program/site, and a sentient "spectator." The space opened up between these three terms is a dialogical structure, a linguistic space: a finite, delimited public realm in which architecture acquires legibility, and creative invention and critical discourse find a local, provisional ground.[14]

In other words, the idea that site or program could serve as a referent for architectural form emerged in a context where premises about the grounds for architectural ideation, and concordantly, for creative invention, could no longer be assumed but must be actively sought in the work of design itself. One can see in this predicament a common thread between apparently antinomic design doctrines since the eighteenth century, from Form follows Function to the various historicist and semiotic approaches that ensued therefrom. Regionalism in its various guises is but one expression of a broader "burden" of creative invention in modern contexts: to wager and posit within the work itself the terms for its legibility and grounding.

Naturalizing expression

Defining the quest for legible, expressive form as a modern problematic – a worksite rather than a specific design intention – surfaces new sympathies between seemingly distant design methods and agendas, but also one important point of difference. For many eighteenth century architects, "taste" guided the interpretation of site and program into visual form (through proportions, geometry, figurative elements . . .). Taste, in turn, was defined as consensus amongst the most "enlightened" men about the parameters for appropriate form. This explicit reliance on the opinions of men, and the ambiguous measure of *appropriate* – as opposed to *correct* – form made character theory a historically short-lived idea.

In the dawn of a new, post-Revolutionary France, Jean-Nicholas-Louis Durand's reformulation of architectural character reflects a slightly different tack:

> if one composes an edifice in a manner fitting to the usage to which one destines it, will that not perceptively differentiate it from another edifice destined for another usage? Will it not naturally have a character and, furthermore, its own character?[15]

With correct reasoning and method, self-evident, readable architecture automatically follows. In developing his compositional method, Durand was of course not concerned with architectural expression. Legible, expressive form is not a matter for deliberation – not a matter of choice, interpretation, or judgment – but the direct outcome of correctly applied principles and procedures. This aspiration for a method of work out of which a "natural" expression arises – one that could bypass the finitude and fallibility of human judgment and individual wills – articulates an enduring trope in modern efforts to define a theory of design without recourse to transcendent givens.

A particularly illuminating illustration of this trope in contemporary architecture is given in an early and influential argument for "morphogenesis" as a design method. For Sanford Kwinter, Lindy Roy's "Delta Spa" project in Botswana exemplifies a "different design methodology," one that begins with a clearing of the decks of tradition, on the one hand and of willful form-making on the other.[16] Working with clear analytical parameters and computational tools, design becomes a tapping of Nature's own volatile, dynamic forces, as exemplified by the African landscape and its peoples. Generative software is key to this mimetic aspiration: the architect does not make forms; s/he sets up processes of interaction and parameters for their unfolding. The results of the two algebraic processes that generate the work may be compared to "pheromonal wakes of termite swarms," African space–time, African music, with each of these being alternatively understood as an "animal event," a "dance of genesis, of life," "African genesis in general," "feminine forces," the "feminine weave of temporalities," and even "the classical Chinese tradition." Morphogenetic design in this project aspires, in short, to the very principles of originary harmony between site, beings, and dwellings. "Site" in this case is not a physical given, not a cultural given, but the principles of emergence of both: with strategic use of computational tools, the designer may simulate nature's own processes of form-giving – that which generates human and animal, the geological and the biological.

Such aspirations retrace a pervasive theme in nineteenth- and twentieth-century art and architecture, from the search for models in physical and biological processes to surrealist automatism: the dream-wish for the ultimate performance of authentic invention, one that could be finally free of the taint of "willfulness" and artifice, whether cultural or individual, but would nonetheless result in natural, directly signified, meaning.

Theories of Natural, machinic or automatic processes of formation have their own dilemmas, however. In the asymptote towards pure, unmediated becoming, human agency remains at work somewhere in the generative process: designing the set-up, making selections and editorial choices along the way. What role does this interpretive agent have, and to what critical criteria would that agency submit? To the extent that this question goes unanswered, such agency goes underground, sublimated by method and procedure. Premises and preconceptions sink to an unexamined subterrane. The narrative in "African Genesis," for example, recalls a number of common tropes in nineteenth- and early twentieth-century literature in its conflation of geological formations, climatic processes, animal behaviors, and diverse cultures and peoples past and present as exemplars of Becoming, and in its romanticizing of this composite Other, Africa, into a figure of prelapsarian harmony and originary innocence. The schema of natural versus acculturated ("genetic" versus "willful"), popular in early twentieth-century art, finds its mirror image in the "savage"/"modern" or uncivilized/civilized dualism used by colonizing nations to present their economic and political agendas as "civilizing" missions. This idealization of pre-modern harmony seems benign on the surface, but in fact reiterates a framework of imagination with a dark history. In naturalizing premises about the grounds and limits of expressive/legible form, in seeking recourse from cultural constructions, opinion, or individual judgment, theories of automatic or emergent form – whether derived from rational method or a-rational procedures – risk critical blindness when such premises resurface in unexpected ways.

Instrumentalizing expression

While the specter of groundlessness remains a predicament of design work, architecture's location in contemporary contexts compels reconsideration of the parameters by which the site of architectural work is defined.

In Enlightenment France, "speaking architecture" promised a new approach to urban and civic coherence. Whether drawing on Aristotelian notions of sympathetic comportment, or on new sensorial theories of understanding, writers on architectural character hoped to inspire virtuous conduct in the spectator. Similar aspirations towards liberatory forms of individual and collective experience characterize the early twentieth-century avant-garde's efforts to seek out new grounds for visual expression in art and architecture. "In our architecture, as in our whole life," wrote El Lissitsky in 1929,

> we are striving to create a social order, that is to say, to raise the instinctual into consciousness. . . . It is not enough to be a modern man; it is necessary for the architect to possess a complete mastery of the expressive means of architecture.[17]

Architecture's affect can also be useful, however, and early modern revolutionaries and social reformers recognized this potential. Jean-Baptiste Say, the economist and businessman behind the famous Law of Markets, or Say's Law, gave architecture a formative role in his utopian fiction *Olbie, ou essai sur le moyens de réformer les moeurs d'une nation* (1800). Olbie was a readable moral landscape, its architecture a vehicle of instruction:

> If the attentions of society towards its members were everywhere in sight, everywhere also they read their duties toward it. The language of monuments makes itself understood by all men, for it addresses itself to the heart and imagination. The monuments of the Olbiens rarely recounted purely political duties, because political duties are abstract, based more on reason than on feeling. . . . It was not only in the cities that monuments spoke to the people; they were also to be found in other frequented places, in the middle of promenades and along the main roads.[18]

Different from mid-eighteenth-century formulations of architecture as dramatic staging for virtuous comportment, Olbie's sensible landscape operated alongside other ubiquitous forms of persuasion to cultivate *internalized* behaviors. For Say, who read Rousseau and Locke, Olbie was a work in time: if the father had to be taught proper morals, for the child it would become second nature.

The instrumentalization of expressive monuments is decidedly less utopian in the context of late capitalism. For corporations and city governments seeking a competitive edge in the global market, the "Bilbao Effect" – the extraordinary role played by Frank Gehry's Guggenheim design in reversing the fortunes of a depressed industrial town – has become paradigmatic. In the experience economy, singular, novel design has emerged as a powerful instrument for generating capital and investment.[19] At the same time, the common ground opened up by engaging architectures and spaces have been pressed into economic service in the form of thematized environments for consumption, or for selling. Both kinds of architectural "products," as they are un-ironically called in the industry, aim not only at passive spectatorship but, different from the docile citizenry in Olbie, at pacified consumption – that of novelty on the one hand, and of familiarity on the other. The commodification of architecture – and by implication, of occupants, designers, builders, and workers – plays out behind the architect's back, inscribed into frameworks and practices well beyond the designer's worksite.

The ideal of architecture giving relevant expression and therefore coherence to a social, cultural context is complicated by other dynamics and invisibilities. Evidence points, for instance, to increasing ephemerality in everyday environments the world over – and not just that given in technology, media and consumer products. In post-industrial economies, for example, migrancy has become a permanent life experience for an increasing number of people in all walks of life: from corporate heads, to professionals, to laborers. Theorist Arjun Appadurai and others have called for new analytical terms to comprehend these trans-territorial imaginations of world and of location: it is not that physical, regional or national territories are no longer relevant but that these describe only one dimension of such imaginings.[20] There are also invisibilities *within* this migrancy. In Hanoi, for instance, "informal" workers contribute one-sixth of the city's gross domestic product (GDP), making up nearly half of the city's workers. Their contribution is informal because neither their work nor their very presence is officially recognized. Rural migrant workers literally do not count as citizens of the city, even as their vital role in the city's welfare, its maintenance, its physical nourishment and even its economics is commonly known. This is the case in much of the world's centers of commerce, from Mumbai to Nairobi, to the fringes of North American cities.

Love of the city

What kind of potentials lay in the place in which we were standing. What can it mean to think about and design architecture beside da-me architecture?[21]

At the center of our research has been the fostering of an expanded modality of architectural practice.[22]

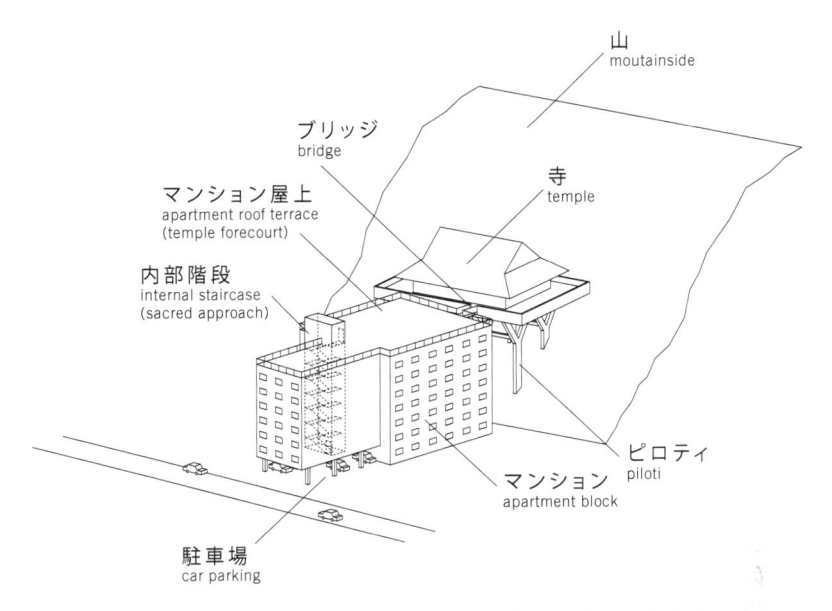

山
moutainside

ブリッジ
bridge

マンション屋上
apartment roof terrace
(temple forecourt)

寺
temple

内部階段
internal staircase
(sacred approach)

ピロティ
piloti

マンション
apartment block

駐車場
car parking

Figure 6.1 Atelier Bow-Wow, apartment mountain temple, analytical drawing
from *Made in Tokyo* (2001); courtesy of Atelier Bow-Wow

Atelier Bow-Wow's *Made in Tokyo* documents selections in what others
might call a generic urbanscape: a driving school on the roof of a big box
supermarket, colonnaded tennis courts inserted into the leftover center of
an expressway off-ramp, a hilltop temple grafted to an apartment block. . . .
"We decided to call these 'da-me architecture' (no-good architecture), with
all our love and disdain," writes Yoshiharu Tsukamoto:

> Most of them are anonymous buildings, not beautiful, and not
> accepted in architectural culture to date. . . . However, if you look
> closely . . . in terms of observing the reality of Tokyo through build-
> ing form, they seem to us to be better than anything designed by
> architects.[23]

Curious or no good as they may be for architects accustomed to the "self-
standing completeness" of architecture as icon, these "mongrel" buildings
reflect how urban coherence is experienced by city dwellers. "Everyday life
is made up of traversing various buildings," notes Tsukamoto, "living space
is constituted by connections between various adjacent environmental conditions rather than by any single building."[24]

The tactics of co-location by entrepreneurial Tokyoites – spatial borrowings, parasitic adaptations and symbiotic "interlappings" of program, structure or surface – hint at the marvelous logics and spatial inventiveness hiding in plain sight in the everyday city. Indeed, examples like the Apartment Mountain Temple (Figure 6.1), wherein the staircase and flat roof in the one are the ritual ascent and forecourt in the other, testify to a more complex and agile perceptual practice – one in which form is not a static, self-identical substance, but emerges in relation to circumstance and engagement. As for the user, so for the tactical builder – the physical city is a malleable substrate for creative adaptation and improvisation. Through this and other meticulous field studies, through their multifaceted design practice, Atelier Bow-Wow reveals and engages the city as a living, dynamic, and irreducibly heterogeneous context shaped by diverse agents and agency. Speculations on "void metabolism," "urban ecology," "micro-public space," or "behaviorology" are efforts to articulate these other forms of agency, and to reposition design as an engagement with latencies, with "stages in waiting" and dramas *in media res* (Figure 6.2).

Teddy Cruz, too, finds critical grounds and motive in the quotidian urban: in his case, the neglected suburbs and shantytowns wherein the service and factory workers of global commerce reside. Here, on the borderlands between San Diego and Tijuana, Cruz gives witness to unseen logics and formations entailed in supplying, sustaining and servicing affluent America. South of the border, American factories congregate in low-tax, and low-wage "special economic zones"; around them, expanses of informal worker settlements. On the US side, zoning regulations and finance policies literally prescribe and preform the built environment: "catch-22s" that privilege big developments and exclusionary land uses, resulting in evacuated public

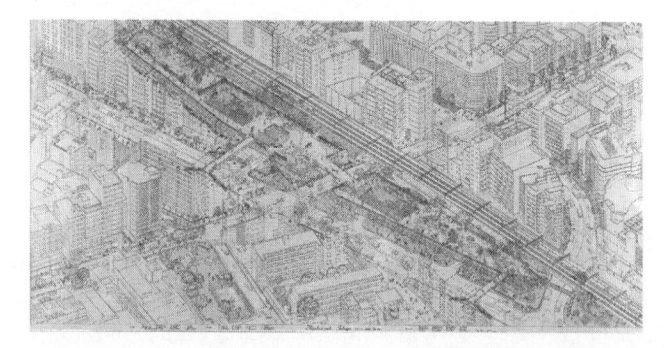

Figure 6.2 Atelier Bow-Wow, renovation of Miyashita Park, Tokyo (2011); courtesy of Atelier Bow-Wow

realms. Across this territory, a steady northward flow of goods and services belie the rhetoric of border security. A reverse flow removes the discards of American gentrification: bungalows slated for demolition to make room for luxury condominiums in San Diego head towards the shantytowns for inventive re-use.

Cruz finds great creativity in these "sites of scarcity." In Tijuana's settlements, and in San Diego's older first-ring suburbs where immigrants from Latin America, Africa and Asia have settled, rich and complex practices of building, adaptation, entrepreneurship and communality flourish. Well below the radar of southern California's vast tracts of single-family zoning, for example, an "alternative zoning" has taken root: a vibrant bottom-up urbanism of parking lot social spaces, second businesses in garages, informal flea markets and street vendors in vacant lots, and a Buddhist temple in a converted bungalow. These "plug-in" programs and architectures "pixilate" the monotonous and vacant sprawl produced by traditional zoning in the area (Figures 6.3a and 6.3b).

For Cruz, both the disparities produced and maintained by dominant socio-economic structures, and the informal practices of sociality and livelihood that counter them bear profound lessons for contemporary architecture. Rejecting fetishistic images of the informal, Cruz sees the tactical procedures therein as "urban operations" that, in allowing for local transgressions of imposed political and economic logics, and in offering models for rethinking conventional terms of planning and development, can initiate "trickle-up" institutional and political transformations on the whole

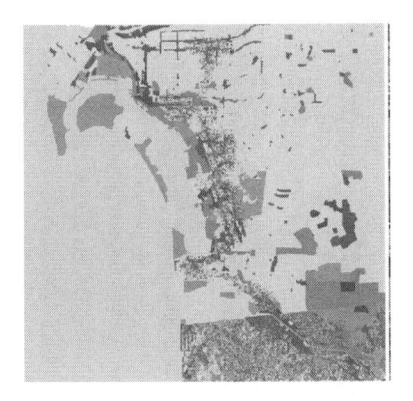

Figure 6.3 Estudio Teddy Cruz, analysis of land use near US–Mexico border: (a) 'pixilation' of official zoning by informal uses in southern California (left) and (b) and in the suburb of San Ysidro (right); courtesy of Teddy Cruz

system (Figures 6.4a and 6.4b). For Cruz, these are the springboards of truly experimental architectural and urban work:

> Ultimately, it does not matter whether contemporary architecture wraps itself in the latest morphogenetic membrane, pseudo-neo-classical propositions or LEED-certified photovoltaic panels if all of these approaches continue to camouflage the most pressing problems of urbanization today. As architects, we can be responsible for imagining counter-spatial procedures, political, and economic structures that can produce new modes of sociability and civic culture.[25]

Atelier Bow Wow and Teddy Cruz ground their practices in a love of the city – its creative intelligence, but also its invisibilities and injustices. For both, the city is a wellspring of critical provocations and creative vitality for an interest in civic architecture. Their respective projects offer two takes on an expanded concept of site, and by implication, an expanded worksite for architecture.

In drawing this discussion to a close, I would like to trace the outline of such a worksite. In this "macro" site, the technological, economic, and socio-political pre-figurations of a context would rank alongside physical and cultural location for critical inquiry. What logics and agendas are already at work in circumscribing, delimiting, or prefiguring a work of design? What is the architect's and building's role, complicity and effect in the movement of money, power, ideas and material resources? How might design be already instrumentalized by these contexts, and what opportunities are

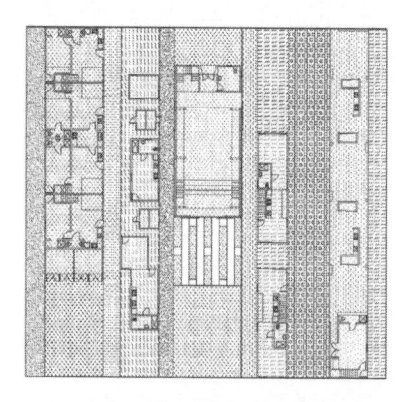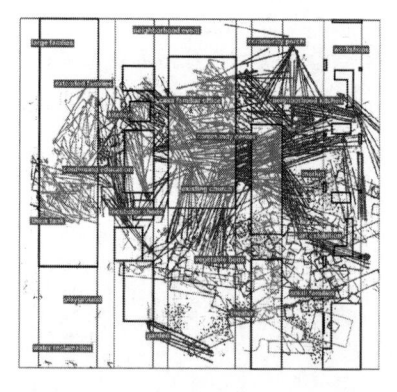

Figure 6.4 Estudio Teddy Cruz, Living Rooms at the Border project: (a) static plan (left), and (b) dynamic plan constructed over Barry Le Va's 1968 drawing Three Activities (right); courtesy of Teddy Cruz

there for counter-construction? To that end, an expanded worksite would be nourished by research and inquiries into negative histories – or histories of anti-models – as well as histories of possibility. This, so that we can see their intertwinement, and better recognize ourselves in them.[26]

In a worksite drawn beyond formal terms, furthermore, architecture's "agency" would emerge as a question for critical analysis and creative intervention. Design would entail deliberation on not just appropriate form, but on appropriate action and measure. In looking beyond expressive form to modalities of effect and enablement, we might come to see that there is no such thing as a "generic" city. Moreover, if architecture is technologically, economically, politically, and culturally pre-figured and disseminated in arenas beyond the building site, how could these arenas be opened to Daedalian cunning?[27]

Finally, while I write of contemporary challenges, I am mindful that this argument for an expanded worksite is not novel. In the opening chapter to *De architectura*, Vitruvius, who was not one for abstract ambitions, set out a long list of learning pertinent to architects. Beyond skill in drawing, he wrote, the architect must be knowledgeable in geometry, history, philosophy, music, medicine, jurisprudence, astronomy, and the theory of the heavens. Acknowledging the list's expansiveness, Vitruvius insisted on an understanding of principles in these areas. Such learning is "indispensable" so that the architect may not be found wanting when "[s/]he is required to pass judgment."

Notes

1 Rem Koolhaas, *Delirious New York* (New York: Oxford University Press, 1978).
2 Rem Koolhaas, "The Generic City," *Domus* 791 (March 1997), 3–12.
3 Kenneth Frampton, "Towards a Critical Regionalism: Six Points for an Architecture of Resistance," in *The Anti-Aesthetic*, ed. Hal Foster (Seattle: Bay Press, 1983); and Alexander Tzonis and Liane Lefaivre, "The Grid and the Pathway," *Architecture in Greece* 5 (1981).
4 Paul Brislin, "Identity, Place and Human Experience," *Architectural Design* 82, no. 6 (November/December 2012): 13.
5 Farrokh Derakshani, "Appropriating, Reclaiming and Inventing Identity through Architecture," *Architectural Design* 82, no. 6 (November/December 2012): 31.
6 See, for instance, Hajime Yatsuka, "Internationalism Versus Regionalism," in *At the End of the Century: One Hundred Years of Architecture*, ed. Richard Koshalek and Elizabeth Smith (Los Angeles: Museum of Contemporary Art, 1998); Alan Colquhoun, "The Concept of Regionalism," in *Postcolonial Space(s)* (New York: Princeton University Press, 1997); and Keith L. Eggener, "Placing Resistance: A Critique of Critical Regionalism," *Journal of Architectural Education* 55, no. 4 (May 2002).
7 Alberto Pérez-Gómez, *Architecture and the Crisis of Modern Science* (Cambridge, MA: MIT Press, 1983). See also Dalibor Vesely, "Architecture and the Conflict of

Representation," *AA Files* 8 (Spring 1985): 21–39; and Dalibor Vesely, *Architecture in the Age of Divided Representation* (Cambridge, MA: MIT Press, 2004).

8   David Leatherbarrow, "Architecture and Situation: A Study of the Architectural Writings of Robert Morris," *Journal of the Society of Architectural Historians* 44, no. 1 (March 1985), 48–59.

9   See, for example, Jacques-François Blondel, *Cours d'architecture* (1771), vol. I, 373–374, 389–90, vol. II, xxv–xxvi, xli, xlv, 229–231; and Jacques-François Blondel, *Discours sur la nécessité de l'étude de l'architecture* (1764). See also Antoine-Chrysostôme Quatremère de Quincy's definitions of *caractère* in *Dictionnaire d'architecture* (1788–1825) and *Dictionnaire historique d'architecture* (1832), and his arguments on modern architecture in *Sur l'idéal dans les arts du dessin* (1805), *Considérations morales sur la destination des ouvrages de l'art* (1815), *De l'invention et de l'innovation dans les ouvrages des beaux-arts* (after 1816), and his *Essai sur la nature, le but et les moyens de l'imitation dans les beaux-arts* (1823); and Lily Chi, "On the Use of Architecture: the Destination of Buildings Revisited," in *Chora: Intervals in the Philosophy of Architecture*, ed. Alberto Pérez-Gómez and Stephen Parcell (Montreal: McGill-Queen's University Press, 1996), vol. 2, 17–36.

10 Compare ideas of character in: Germain Boffrand, *Livre d'architecture* (1743); Blondel, *Cours d'architecture* (1771); Jean-Louis Viel de Saint-Maux, *Letters sur l'architecture* (1787); Étienne-Louis Boullée, *Architecture, essai sur l'art*; Nicolas Le Camus de Mézières, *Le Génie de l'architecture* (1780); and Antoine Chrysostome Quatremère de Quincy, revised entry on *caractère*, *Dictionnaire historique d'architecture* (1832).

11 Germain Boffrand, *Book of Architecture*, trans. David Britt, ed. Caroline van Eck (Aldershot, England and Burlington, VT: Ashgate, 2002), 5.

12 Charles-François Viel, *Des anciennes etudes de l'architecture* (Paris: 1807), 5.

13 On the specter of relativism, see also Boffrand, *Livre d'architecture*, 3–9; and Blondel, *Cours d'architecture*, vol. I, 463, on decadence see vol. III, and *Discours sur la nécessité de l'étude de l'architecture*. On the problem of grounds for judgment, see Quatremère de Quincy, "Architecture" in *Encyclopédie méthodique* (1788), *Considérations morales*, *De l'invention et de l'innovation*, *De l'emploi des sujets d'histoire modern dans la poésie et de leur abus dans la peinture* (1825), and *Essai sur la nature*.

14 Quatremère de Quincy's lucid definition of "necessity" in *Considérations morales* is particularly illuminating. Reflecting upon the different ways in which two things can be said to be "necessarily" related, Quatremère concluded that the only form of necessity that can be created by mortal beings is the apparent harmony between the form of a thing, its *destination*, and the beholder. As in his 1932 definition of *caractère*, meaningful creative work is here defined not in an intrinsically universal principle, but as the result of an internal correspondence between a work and its programmatic situation – an integrity that opens up a finite, common ground for critical discussion. Meaning in the arts, in other words, rests on the accomplishment of a linguistic circuit – a language community.

15 Jean-Nicolas-Louis Durand, *Nouveau Précis* (Paris, 1813), 19.

16 Sanford Kwinter, "African Genesis," *Assemblage* 36 (August 1998).

17 El Lissitsky, "Ideological superstructure," in *Programs and Manifestoes of 20th-century Architecture* (Cambridge, MA: MIT Press, 1964), 121–122.

18 Jean-Baptiste Say, *Olbie, ou essai sur le moyens de réformer les moeurs d'une nation*, 1800. (Paris: Deterville, Treuttel et Wurtz, 1800), 612; trans. adapted from Roy Swanson, *Utopian Studies* 12, no. 1 (2001): 104–105.

19 See, for example, Richard Florida's highly influential *The Rise of the Creative Class* (New York: Basic Books, 2002); and Brian Lonsway, *Making Leisure Work: Architecture and the Experience Economy* (London: Routledge, 2009).

20 Arjun Appadurai, *Modernity at Large* (Minneapolis: University of Minnesota Press, 1996).

21 Momoyo Kaijima, Junzo Kuroda and Yoshiharu Tsukamoto (Atelier Bow-Wow), *Made in Tokyo* (Tokyo: Kaijima Institute Publishing Co., Ltd, 2001).

22 Teddy Cruz, "On Returning Duchamp's Urinal to the Bathroom," *Arquine* 55 (Spring 2011): 96; the title quotes artist-performer Tania Bruguera.

23 Yoshiharu Tsukamoto, "What is Made in Tokyo?" *Architectural Design* 73, no. 5 (September/October 2003): 40–41.

24 Ibid., 43.

25 Cruz, "On Returning Duchamp's Urinal," 96.

26 The projects of nineteenth-century colonialism and nationalism, for instance, play a formative and constitutive role in some of the most prominent concepts of modern intellectual and creative history and yet these remain the most consistently repressed aspects of contemporary critical discourse. Notions of tradition as counterpoint to the modern, of the cultural Other as models of purity or primitivism, and even the concept of Regionalism find their roots in this history.

27 Alberto Pérez-Gómez, "The Myth of Daedalus," *AA Files* 10 (Autumn 1985): 49–52.

7

ON WATER AND OTHER FLUIDS

A bloody account of urban circulation

Louise Pelletier

In 1628, English physician William Harvey (1578–1657) introduced one of the most celebrated contributions to physiology: the notion of the full circulation of blood in living beings. His treatise, *On the Motion of the Heart and Blood in Animals* (*De Motu Cordis et Sanguinis*) gave an account of the double circulation of the blood and the motions of the heart.[1] Combining observations, experiments, and measurements, Harvey looked at the heart not as a spiritual seat of the soul, but as a pump that could be analyzed in mechanical terms. Harvey argued that the pulsation of the arteries depends upon the contraction of the left ventricle, while the right ventricle propels the blood into the pulmonary artery. Blood is pumped around the body by the heart, and once it comes back, it is circulated in a closed system through the lungs before being returned to the main circuit.

Harvey investigated among other things the effect of ligatures on blood flow and established that a tight tourniquet fasten on the triceps would interrupt blood flow from the arteries and the veins, causing the forearm to turn cool and pale from lack of blood, while above the ligature it becomes warm and swollen. By loosening the tourniquet slightly, blood flow is restored only from the arteries because they are deeper than the veins. Consequently, the opposite effect occurs in the lower part of the arm that becomes engorged with blood, turning warm and swollen. This experiment also made the veins more visible as they were distended with blood. By pushing on the veins down the arm, Harvey noticed that the flow was interrupted at various intervals by little bumps (identified by his teacher Hieronymus Fabricius as valves). But when he pushed upwards, the flow was not interrupted (Figure 7.1).

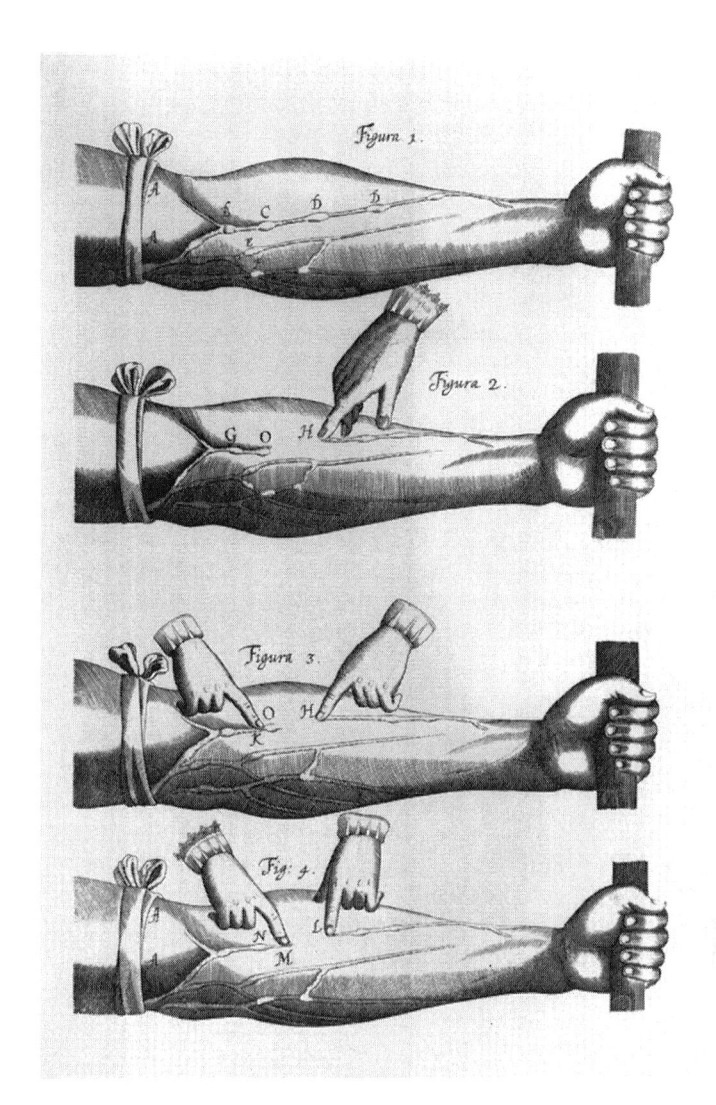

Figure 7.1 William Harvey, *De Motu Cordis et Sanguinis* (1628), plate showing the effect of ligatures on blood flow

He noticed the same effect in various veins of the body, except those of the neck where blood flows downwards – towards the heart – rather than upwards. Harvey concluded that valves allow blood to flow in one direction only – that is toward the heart.

In *H2O and the Waters of Forgetfulness*, Ivan Illich explains how Harvey's discovery of blood circulation transformed our understanding of the human body, but it also influenced our perception of society and the city as living organisms. Around the middle of the eighteenth century, the notions of wealth and money were "spoken of as though they were liquids" and began to circulate. Social hierarchy came to be imagined in terms of connections as a system of conduits. "Liquidity is a dominant metaphor after the French revolution; ideas, newspaper, information, gossips and – after 1880 – traffic, air and power circulate."[2] If toward the end of the seventeenth century, the removal of fecal matter from the corridors of the Palace of Versailles and the streets of Paris was at best a weekly procedure, during the Enlightenment, cities became perceived as evil-smelling places that could no longer be tolerated.[3] In fact, until the middle of the eighteenth century, it was common practice to throw bodily wastes into open spaces such as the Cemetery of the Innocents in Paris. The city gradually became understood as a body through which water ought to circulate without interruption in order to wash it from its impurity, its wastes. Thus, the circulation of air and water became an architectural concern long before the remodeling of Paris by Baron Haussmann in the nineteenth century.

Flowing beneath the pavement

Pierre Patte (1723–1814), a French architect under the reign of Louis XV, is credited for having been the first to design a modern sewer system for Paris to manage not only drinking water, but also rain and wastewater. Accordingly, he devoted an entire chapter of one of his treatises on what he calls "the corrupted distribution of cities" – "Considérations sur la distribution vicieuse des Villes," in which he expresses the virtues of air and water circulation, but where he also speculates on the working of the guts of the city.[4] His interest in the subterranean domain is made explicit from the very beginning, since the title page of his treatise dedicated to *The Most Important Objects of Architecture* depicts different monuments, ornaments and a public square, but most importantly, an arch on the bottom left of the image that leads to the underground, and incidentally, announces the first chapter of the book (Figure 7.2).

Patte began his reflections on circulation by acknowledging the role of tradition in first choosing the site of a city by referring to Vitruvius who recommended checking the liver of animals to see if they were healthy.[5] Patte stresses the importance of knowing the composition of soil in order to determine its fertility, but also its propensity to earthquakes. Yet, he deplores that founders never seem to pay attention to these considerations, as they are

Figure 7.2 Pierre Patte, *Mémoires sur les objets les plus importants de l'architecture* (1769), detail of the frontispiece

more concerned with political reasons, taking possession of a strategic route; the confluent of two rivers; a strategic commercial position.[6]

Patte asserts that never before has a city been laid out with the purpose of insuring "the well being of its inhabitants, of preserving their life, health, goods, and for insuring the safety of the air and their homes."[7] In any big city, what is most striking, he complains, is to see from all parts flowing excrements and wastes in open streams before continuing into the sewage system, and exhaling in its path all sorts of nauseous smells. Furthermore, the blood from slaughterhouses runs in the middle of the street; entire neighborhoods reek of waste from latrines; hospitals and cemeteries perpetuate epidemics and exhale the germs of sickness and death in the houses. Elsewhere, he says, one can notice that rivers that cross the cities and whose water serves to quench the thirst of its inhabitants are also receptacles of the cesspools and of all the refuse. When it rains, water washes off the roofs transforming the streets into rivers of mud. In short, cities are the embodiment of filthiness, infection and disease. Moreover, cities are often the prey of other calamities such as engulfing fires, floods and earthquakes. The purpose of his book, therefore, is to imagine how to take advantage of the elements, to control them for the benefit of men and to ensure the healthiness of cities and the happiness of its inhabitants.[8]

In order to attain such ideals, it is foremost important to ensure that cities be as compact as possible, and the trades and crafts that create smell and noise such as tanneries, tripe shops, blacksmiths, edge-tool makers, laundress, hostelry for public transportation, etc., should be placed beyond the edge of cities in suburbs. He advises that slaughterhouses as well as their stables also should be relegated to the outskirts of cities to prevent herds of cattle crossing the streets causing embarrassment for all.[9] This is indeed the beginning of industrial urban sprawl. According to Patte, a twenty-five foot wide channel would surround the suburbs and would communicate with the river crossing the city at its entrance and exit so as to ensure air circulation. We should place hospitals and cemeteries beyond the suburbs on elevated and well-aired location to prevent the spread of diseases, he warns, and forbid the construction of houses on bridges as they are found in Paris, because they stop the flow of air on rivers that serve to clean the city. Ventilation and ease of circulation between different areas is set as a priority.[10]

The cleanliness of a city should be one of its principal ornaments, Patte argues. However, experience shows that it is never the case; no matter how much effort and money is invested, large cities continue to exhale bad smell coming from polluted water from various industries or trades, hospital, cemeteries, latrines, etc. Before solving the problem of how to purge cities from their harmful smells, however, it is necessary to understand the manner in which the transportation of water is administered; and only by combining water and sewage conduits can we expect to find a solution, he writes, again echoing the dual circulation system first introduced by Harvey.[11]

Patte analyzes different transportation systems made of lead pipes, wood and even clay conduits placed two feet below ground. Given their perpetual failure, he comes to the conclusion that the entire system has to be redesigned from scratch. He suggests an underground aqueduct six feet wide by seven feet high, placed five feet under street level. Two iron pipes located at four feet from the bottom of the aqueduct on little shelves of about fourteen inches would take the water from various reservoirs to the public fountains and houses without risking being crushed by horse carriages (Figure 7.3). That water would serve for everyday use, for bathing (an early mention of such domestic activity) or to drink. The system would also connect individual latrines to the cesspool and use rainwater to clean the system.[12] Sewage would drain to the bottom of the cesspool into another aqueduct parallel to the river gathering sewage from all streets, itself draining into the river outside the city. As in a living organism where the oxygenated blood runs side

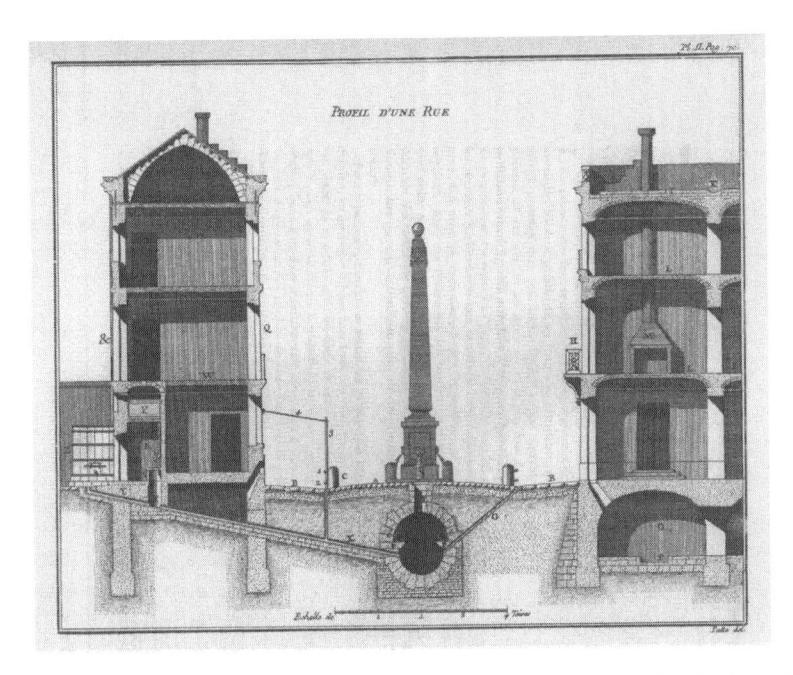

Figure 7.3 Plate 2 from Patte's *Mémoires* showing the appropriate distribution of a street

by side with the vitiated blood, fresh water runs together with sewage in a complex system of fluid discharges.

In addition to this circulation of water and waste, Patte insisted on the importance of air circulation for human health. He gives the example of a fan invented by Stephen Hales to renew the air of Newgate prison that improved noticeably the health of prisoners.[13] Patte also criticizes the "relatively recent" tradition in Europe of burying the dead within city walls, or even inside churches as this custom was most harmful to the health of the inhabitants. Patte devised an inspired system to get rid of diseased bodies that was as ingenious as his dual aqueduct system. His invention involved a new ritual for burying the dead. The coffin would be placed in a chapel on the street side with an operable trapdoor opening on a vault beneath it that would allow for the removal of the body:

> At a present time – like two in the morning – a cart pulled by horses, covered with a mortuary sheet, would come from the parish cemetery to remove the bodies from the crypt; the gravediggers with one

> lantern each and a priest in confidence who would be in charge of the cemetery would accompany the convoy. This priest would have a key to the exterior door of the crypt. . . .[14]

After removing the bodies, the priest would register them and would make sure that they be buried with the proper decorum in a cemetery outside the city walls, located approximately one mile from the city limits, in a well ventilated location. Walls of at least twenty feet would surround them: "in this way, vapors would rise into the atmosphere, and couldn't infect the air."[15] To put Patte's ideas in context, a law was passed in 1765 making cemeteries illegal inside the city, but it would take almost fifty years for remote cemeteries to be widely accepted. Even though the Cimetière du Père Lachaise was officially inaugurated in 1804, it is only after the remains of Héloïse and Abélard were transferred there, together with those of Molière and La Fontaine, that it began to enjoy some recognition.

In time, Patte speculates, families would build their funerary monuments that they would decorate with sculptures and medallions with portraits and obelisks, so that such places could very well become the most curious places in a city by the importance of their monuments and their works of art. In Patte's view, it would be a great advantage not only from a health standpoint, but also in regard to social and religious issues. What is most interesting, however, is that the disposal of bodies – like that of excrement – would then become hidden from sight (removed in the middle of the night) in order to purify the air but also the unsightly activity. It signals a detachment – Illich might say a denial – of death.

A century later, Patte's insight about the role of water and air circulation to ensure the health of a city would help transform Paris under the direction of Baron Haussmann. Circulation became synonymous not only with the health of an urban agglomeration, but in French it also refers to the flow of vehicles: traffic (*circulation routière*). It could be argued that the paradigm of health and circulation that came about between the seventeenth and eighteenth centuries and that led to the need to relegate some functions away from urban centers, transformed into an obsession with transportation (and a different approach to consumption) in the early twentieth century. Moreover, it brought about the plague of urban sprawl.[16]

Water as commodity

Today, one would imagine that we have mastered all issues regarding water circulation and related matter. Yet, according to the "Global Annual Assessment of Sanitation and Drinking-Water," a UN commissioned report, access to drinking water remains an important issue for many communities around the world as one billion individuals are said to be without access to any reliable source of drinking water and more than two and a half billion people cannot rely on a sanitation system.[17] The problem, however, is rarely due to a lack of technological means. Water has become a commodity and, as such, its consumption has become an economic as much as a political issue. According to Transparency International, a non-governmental organization (NGO) that monitors political corruption in international development, in many countries, water has become the source of transboundary disputes and terrorism, corruption and political instability.[18] Some communities rely on bottled water, which only compounds the problem with the environmental impact related to the accumulation of plastic garbage and other technological waste. Again, the problem of water circulation has been transformed into a problem of water transportation and consumption. But circulation as a concept may still offer some alternatives for improving the health of some communities.

Nowadays, circulation (as traffic) plays an important role in city planning. No longer restricted to the movement of air and water, urban planning is now primarily concerned with the movement of vehicles and people, and the commercial transport and exchange of goods.[19] Thus, circulation is no longer synonymous with the happy flow of a balanced organism. In its association with traffic, it implies that what circulates (water) has become a commodity. In *H2O*, Illich argues that in contemporary cities, water has been devoid of its original sense of purity, "its mystical power to wash off spiritual blemish." Water has been reduced to "the new stuff, on whose purification human survival now depends," "a resource that is scarce and that calls for technical management," a cleaning fluid "that has lost the ability to mirror the water of dreams."[20] As water became a commodity in the twentieth century, the city was reduced to circulation and stopped being a "place," or at least devalued "places" – buildings can no longer occupy the old bridges, and the cities of the dead, which were necessary as the foundation for the cities of the living, were severed from the inhabited quarters. The issue then is to find a new way to create significant places in the complex network of circulation that has become the contemporary city. One example comes to mind.

Fluidity of information

In the city of Medellín in Colombia, the development of a network of forty-six libraries in the city and the surroundings (known as the *Red de Bibliotecas*) and a complex system of public transit has radically transformed one of the most dangerous cities in the world, with an extremely high level of crime, into an urban development re-appropriated by the citizens. In the past decade, an enlightened municipal government provided the resources to develop a dual system of cable cars and metro lines that now links the slums that surround the city to the center, but most importantly, every cable system is connected to a new cultural center (at the heart of those communities) that includes primarily a library, meeting places, daycare and other facilities that create a sense of community.

Medellìn, the City of Eternal Spring – formerly known as "Murder Capital of the World" because of drug lord Pablo Escobar's activities during the second half of the twentieth century, has a population of more than three million inhabitants (including the surrounding illegal settlements).[21] The building boom that transformed the city since the turn of the millennium can be attributed in part to Mayors Sergio Fajardo (2003–2007) and Alonso Salazar (2008–2011). Convinced that architecture and urban design can initiate major social transformations, they launched a series of architectural competitions to develop cultural nodes in strategic locations in an attempt to revive civic responsibility and a sense of community. They invested all their efforts in restructuring the most desolate areas of the city to integrate them in the urban fabric. Combining infrastructure and innovative community programs, the municipal government intended to use architecture as a means to fight poverty. The general strategy involved direct interventions in the urban ghettos, called *Las communas*, in an attempt not only to cater to the basic needs of the population, but also to develop meaningful meeting places. It began with the construction of cable cars (Metrocables) to give easy access to the most remote areas. A trip that could take up to an hour and a half by foot now takes seven minutes with the Metrocable! Every station then became the anchoring point for public places and new housing developments; and finally, the construction of a library and community services accessible to all.

Two of the most discussed projects were developed by Colombian architect, Giancarlo Mazzanti, who won the public competitions in 2005 for the libraries in La Ladera, and the Parque Biblioteca España, in Santo Domingo Savio barrio – one of the most violent areas of Latin America.[22] Built in 2007, the 5,500 square meter program is divided in three volumes that evoke three huge rocks roughly cut (Figure 7.4). Each is occupied by specific functions: a cultural center with an auditorium, a library with reading rooms (Figure 7.5), and a training center with classrooms. It also includes a daycare center. Although it has been criticized for its architectural detailing and the bluntness of its architectonic massing, the Biblioteca España is probably the project that had the most direct impact on social change. Through training and education, the project intends to provide new opportunities to the population and help them fight poverty, one of the primary causes of violence and social injustice.

Figure 7.4 Parque Biblioteca España by Colombian architect, Giancarlo Mazzanti in Medellín Colombia, view from a cable car (photo by author)

Figure 7.5 Library of the Parque Biblioteca España (photo by author)

In addition to the decrease in crime rate, the number of jobs has increased by 300 percent in the Barrio San Domingo and three banks have opened along the Metrocable route that leads to the cable car (Linea K).[23] Children offer architectural tours of their barrio to tourists getting off the gondolas, thus confirming the sense of pride created by the project. To this day, five library-parks have been developed: La Ladera, Belén, La Quintana, Santo Domingo and San Javier.[24] They have become symbols of urban and social transformations in Medellìn, contributing to the integration and participation of the entire population.

In his *Mémoires* dedicated to the most important objects of architecture, Pierre Patte had insisted on the importance of clean water and devised a complex system of distribution toward public fountains and public squares to help maintain the health not only of the inhabitants, but of the city itself as a live organism. It could be argued that like the water fountains of the *Ancien Régime* that provided vital infrastructure to sustain the life of entire communities, the democratization of knowledge and education in the library-parks of Medellìn, through their common ethical concern for the public good, have had a regenerative role on the community.

Notes

1 William Harvey, *Exercitatio Anatomica de Motu Cordis et Sanguinis in Animalibus* (Frankfurt: Guilielmi Fitzeri, 1628). Blood circulation was first described by Ibn al-Nafis in his *Commentary on Anatomy* in Avicenna's Canon (1242).
2 Ivan Illich, *H2O and the Waters of Forgetfulness* (Berkeley: Heydays Books, 1985), 43–44.
3 Ibid., 46.
4 Pierre Patte, "Considérations sur la distribution vicieuse des Villes, & sur les moyens de rectifier les inconvéniens auxquels elles sont sujettes," in *Mémoires sur les objects les plus importants de l'architecture* (Paris: Chez Rozet, 1769).
5 Vitruvius, *De architectura*, Book 1, chapter 4.
6 Patte, *Mémoires*, 5.
7 Ibid., 5.
8 Ibid., 5–7.
9 Ibid., 9.
10 Ibid., 10–13.
11 Ibid., 28.
12 Ibid. In plate 1, P indicates a latrine connected to the main system O; in plate 2, S is the seat, T is the pit and X, the pipe leading to the aqueduct; V is a small reservoir above the latrine which can be filled with rainwater from the roof; Y provides additional water from the courtyard.
13 Ibid., 38–39. This concern with the health of prisoners is somewhat paradoxical since Newgate was the largest short-term criminal prison in London that housed most of the highwaymen before execution at the Tyburn gallows.
14 Ibid., 43.

15 Ibid., 43–45. Ten years after the publication of his treatise, the *Cimetière de Innocents* closed in Paris, according to the law of 1765 that made cemeteries illegal inside the city. However, only after the decree of June 1804 that prohibited interment within city perimeters did the practice of suburban cemeteries become more widely spread.

16 This could be the subject of another article, or better yet, of another book – and Carolyn Steel addressed the issue in a masterful way in her own book, *Hungry City: How Food Shapes Our Lives* (London: Vantage Books, 2008).

17 "Global Annual Assessment of Sanitation and Drinking-Water (GLAAS)," World Health Organization, accessed January 6, 2014, http://whqlibdoc.who.int/publications/2008/9789241597166_eng.pdf.

18 "Transparency International," accessed January 6, 2014, www.transparency.org.

19 The word traffic in English comes from c.1500, and meant "trade, commerce," from the French *trafique* (mid-fifteenth century), which in turn came from the Italian *traffico* (early fourteenth century), from *trafficare* "carry on trade." "Klein suggests ultimate derivation of the Italian word from Arabic *tafriq* 'distribution,' meaning 'people and vehicles coming and going' first recorded 1825. The verb is from the 1540s (and preserves the original commercial sense)." In comparison, circulation comes from the Latin "circulationem (nom. circulatio), noun of action from pp. stem of circulare 'to form a circle,' from circulus 'small ring.' Used of blood first by William Harvey, 1620s." Online Etymology Dictionary, accessed March 11, 2012, www.etymonline.com.

20 Illich, *H2O*, 75–76.

21 The capital of drug trafficking in the early 1990s, the crime rate for violent crimes was over 25,000/year. Pablo Escobar was killed in 1993.

22 Estimated at about four million dollars, part of the construction was financed by Spain.

23 "The Gondola Project," accessed February 20, 2012, www.gondolaproject.com.

24 Conceived in 2007 by Javier Vera.

8

EARTH OR WORLD?

Aerial image and the prosthetic imagination

Lawrence Bird

The image is one mode by which architecture appeals to us. The image has long been bound to the conditions of architecture's creation, its presence and its performance. But images today are fraught. They easily become commodities, objects of exchange, fetishes substituted for what they ostensibly present to us. They are increasingly swept up in a rapid, international traffic in which each image is devalued in the sense Walter Benjamin articulated as early as the 1920s.[1]

That trade is made possible by technical frameworks such as media technologies and infrastructures. It seems obvious to understand such systems as instances of what Heidegger referred to as the *gestell*: the technical enframing of human life. There is nothing, however, obvious about the essay from which Heidegger's term is drawn, "The Question Concerning Technology." Referring to technological enframing, Heidegger cites Hölderlin's poem *Patmos*:

> But where danger is, grows
> The saving power also.[2]

Heidegger suggests that just as art is not about aesthetics, so the essence of technology is nothing merely technological. For Bernard Stiegler, this means that *gestell* is not simply about instrumentalization or the achievement of an end. Instead it stems from and is one aspect of the unfolding of our humanity. In this essay, I will draw on Stiegler's reading of Heidegger to consider images harvested from Google Earth, probably the most ubiquitous imaging resource available today. My intention is to address the following questions: Is the devaluation of the image, its reduction to a mere product – and the corollary of that process, the impoverishment of our ability to compel and enchant – inevitable? Or is there evidence from within the territory of the technologized image that some kind of redemption might be found there – that in some sense a saving power grows where danger is?

Rendering image

Heidegger made a distinction between the conditions of "earth" and "world." The former was considered as a bare well of material, and the latter as that material gathered, shaped, and rendered meaningful through our work. The technological system discussed in this paper perhaps unintentionally acknowledges that distinction in its very name: Google Earth. This online mapping resource is the most accessible and widespread of Geographic Information Systems (GIS). Earth presents for public consumption an exhaustive documentation of global geography and inhabited space. As such, it seems to fulfill one of the promises of the Enlightenment: a complete and seamless mapping of the world, a mapping made possible through the triumph of technology. Charles Waldheim has used the term "representational domestication" to describe the modern aerial image's reduction of the landscape to an object of surveillance, control, and consumption.[3] Google Earth's most ambitious attempt to fulfill that project would seem to deny any possibility of imaginative consideration of our being in the world. But that is not the case. The work of several artists, including Doug Rickard, Jon Rafman, Edward Burtynsky and Mischka Henner, suggests that one can find in those images the potential for interpretation and criticism.[4]

The work I present below, while dovetailing with such explorations, has a different focus: it considers the rifts that appear within digital images themselves as a result of their technologization. This chapter is a first attempt to tease out the anomalies in such systems, and to think about what they might mean for those who, like architects, try to make earths into worlds. The images I will look at are those of the landscape of the Canadian prairies, where I currently make my home. There has long been a resonance between our technological manipulation of that landscape and our manipulation of the image generally. One irony in the history of electronic imaging is that the first all-electronic television drew on an agricultural precedent. The so-called "image dissector" of the 1920s was inspired by the realization of a farm boy that the movement of one man, a horse and a plow across the landscape inscribed a pattern on the surface of the earth. That epiphany provided the principle for the electronic conversion of images (two-dimensional) into signals (one-dimensional) and back again.[5] The term "image dissection" can describe just as well our digitization of images today, their decomposition into pixels and ultimately bits. Progressive scans across a flat surface, each pass harvesting or sowing another fragment of image, are still the basis of most digital displays. The discussion that follows will demonstrate that this resonance between our modern management of the earth and our manipulation of its image runs quite deep.

Not mere instruments

Rather, as Stiegler asserts, such forms of technical manipulation matter profoundly to our condition as human beings.[6] He insists that our humanity is, and has always been, negotiated with technical objects and processes outside of ourselves. Mankind is in fact defined by the use of tools, that is, of prosthetics. Drawing on anthropological sources, Stiegler argues that human beings are engaged in an instrumental maieutic.[7] By this he means an interplay in which our creation of tools in anticipation of need on the one hand, and the formation of human cognition in response to this creation on the other, results in a drawing forth of the human being. Our works create the conditions that surround our own development. Today's mechanized planet is only the latest manifestation of this phenomenon. What might be different now is that our prosthetics today can seem all-encompassing. Google Earth's ostensibly complete mapping is a graphic demonstration of that.

In the circumstances Stiegler describes, it is meaningless to imagine a condition of man's original independence, in which he did not always lack something whose substitution through technics he anticipated. Instead, lack becomes man's very definition and, therefore, his fulfillment. Today we experience this as the circumstance in which our actualization is the same thing as our derealization. This is not a post-human but an acutely human condition. It binds us with complex technical prosthetics existing somewhere between the conditions of living and non-living objects. Stiegler proposes that these constitute in fact, after the two genres of animate and inanimate beings, a third kind: organized inorganic beings. These, like us, demonstrate perfectibility and a movement toward complexity and indeterminateness. It doesn't need to be pointed out to us that this genre of being can include architecture and landscape architecture.

Stiegler warns of, or heralds, the contemporary manifestation of this condition with his words describing a modern man's "disappearance in the movement of a becoming that is no longer his own."[8] We move forward into the future not alone but accompanied by technical creations, which are other than us, part of us yet alien. This is Stiegler's understanding of Heidegger's saving danger. In this condition we cease to be merely the designers of our works but instead become their operators, or perhaps more precisely their stalkers. We follow along in wake of our work, as the farmer behind the plow. This is my condition as I navigate Google Earth, harvesting images in which I find meaning.

Before we turn to the evidence we might glean directly from those images, we need to understand that Google Earth forms one specific type of prosthetic complex: a prosthetics of perception. In allowing us to see, and perhaps even to begin to act, on the other side of the world, it obviously extends our own sight to incorporate the mechanical eye of a satellite. So doing, it extends our body there too. Maurice Merleau-Ponty briefly addresses prosthetic perception in the *Phenomenology of Perception*, where he makes that case that the edge of the body is not merely our physical boundary, our skin. Rather, it lies beyond us, where we act; or even as far as the eye can see.[9] As he explains:

> The blind man's stick has ceased to be an object for him, and is no longer perceived for itself; its point has become an area of sensitivity, extending the scope and active radius of touch, and providing a parallel to sight. . . . To get used to a hat, a car or a stick is to be transplanted into them, or conversely, to incorporate them into the bulk of our own body.[10]

While these words are often interpreted as referring to physical extensions of the body, a kind of materialization of sight, the point is that the realms of visual perception and hapticity bleed into each other as we incorporate devices into our perceptive apparatus. Merleau-Ponty himself, in his later writing, imagined the incorporation of even the new information technologies into this understanding of perception. In 1959 he wrote the following working notes in anticipation of the task he saw for himself with regard to this area of knowledge:

> Show . . .
> that information theory applied to perception, and operationalism applied to behaviour – is in fact, confusedly glimpsed at, the idea of meaning as a view of the organism, the idea of the flesh . . .
> that the perception-message analogy (coding and decoding) is valid, but on the condition that one discerns a) the *flesh* beneath the discriminating behaviours b) speech and its 'comprehensible' diacritical systems beneath the information.[11]

In other words, the processes of coding and decoding imply their own kind of chiasm. Merleau-Ponty's mention of speech here is worth putting in context. In *The Visible and the Invisible*, as though in anticipation of the work others were later to pursue in semiotics, Merleau-Ponty made the first forays into territory he would be not have time to fully explore himself. He asserted that the relationship between signs and things is an analogue of the subject/object relationship: "As there is a reversibility of the seeing and the visible, and as at the point where the two metamorphoses cross perception is born, so also there is a reversibility of the speech and what it signifies. . . ."[12] These lines suggest that even signal and informatic response, on which the operation of a computer is based, as well as sign and signified (and in the case we are examining here, earth to its image), imply a condition of flesh in Merleau-Ponty's terms. Thus perhaps it is not incidental that Google Earth has built into its interface a kinesthetic response: we don't merely see, we fly like bodies through the air, we accelerate and decelerate as though we had mass. While seeming to take us out of our own bodies, this tool also paradoxically drags them along with us to the other side of the world. As we will see, rather than distancing us from images through vision, it implicitly embeds us in images and in the landscape they represent. This is far from a Cartesian space, but to be convinced of this we have to find evidence within the phenomenon itself.

A pixilated prairie

The upper half of Figure 8.1 shows the prairie landscape as viewed in Google Earth. The square-mile grid of prairie fields on display here is a result of modern systems of demarcating the world, dividing and owning land, and growing and distributing crops. This system for organizing the prairie dates from the nineteenth century, but it has a strange resonance with today's imaging technologies. On seeing these images, we might even say that the prairie surface seems pixilated. In fact, it is. A pixel is a picture element, a component of a whole image broken down into cells of identical size (generally consistent and organized by a grid within a given image) and with a single defined color. Complex, rich, and whole images are broken down into minimal elements manageable by a digital infrastructure. The same is true of the contemporary prairie. Native plants are replaced by domesticated, monocultural and genetically modified crops. Laid out in a grid of exactly one mile square, these cells render crops up to transportation networks, which carry the crops to markets across the globe. Both the imaging systems and agricultural systems, in Heidegger's terms, expedite their object, by unlocking it, exposing it, and directing it toward an end. It is perhaps no surprise to see this strange congruence between the treatment of

Figure 8.1 Aerial views of prairie landscape: upper image, courtesy Google
Earth, USDA Farm Service Agency; lower image courtesy Google
Earth, © 2012 Digital Globe

the landscape and the treatment of its image made so apparent in an environment like Google Earth, where two parallel systems for reduction of things – landscapes on the one hand and images on the other – to mere objects confront and map onto each other.

But the prairie landscape resists total instrumentalization. The lower half of Figure 8.1 displays a tangle of loops, oxbows, and curves that disrupt the grid. These disruptions demonstrate the effect of water undermining the agricultural grid. This disruption is not only spatial but also temporal: the riparian tangle represents a time frame of seasonal and episodically cataclysmic cycles. Every few years, thousands of square miles of farmland are inundated by floods. Over time the course of rivers alters dramatically, snaking across the landscape in an ever-changing evolution, and leaving the traces of past inundations and watercourses as rifts in the grid. This process occurs over cycles of time of long and short duration, in contrast to the grid, which aspires to act "out of time," trying but failing to preserve one pattern forever.

We might note in these images a simple dichotomy between artificial and natural, and as designers we might find inspiration in the wet and cyclical processes that oppose the hard and straight edge of the grid. That might imply a similarly curvaceous, liquid, or perhaps even gaseous architecture, one that escapes all controls. But dichotomies like this are too simple. Things are more complicated than that today.

Time and disruption

Media resources – from components of a computer, to digital networks – have their own relationships to time, which cannot be reduced to a simple modern rationalization of the flow of life. Media-based objects are created in time (almost "just in time" – they do not exist until rendered active by a central processing unit); they can evolve over time (like a wiki). They carry information which is potentially eternal, but which can decay over time with their media substrate (disk or tape), or can be zeroed-out in an instant. Media systems all have clocks, and record their activity over time in logs and archives. Google Earth can be understood as one such archive, and one that records not just changes in the physical environment but also developments in the imaging systems recording that environment. Google Earth's Time Slider function, for example, reveals the evolving resolutions and extents of aerial imagery taken in different years. An example of this shift appears at the top of Figure 8.2. Because different places came under the eye of a satellite at different points in recent history, the mapping of the prairie landscape is uneven.

These various engagements with time are instances of that paradoxical complexity and indeterminacy that Stiegler asserted are characteristic of complex technical systems. The last mentioned – digital archives – can be understood as instances of what he refers to as the intertwining of anthropogenesis and technogenesis, in which human memory is displaced into an epiphylogenetic history, a historical record outside of our species. This is central to his thesis that technics is time: that our historical becoming is

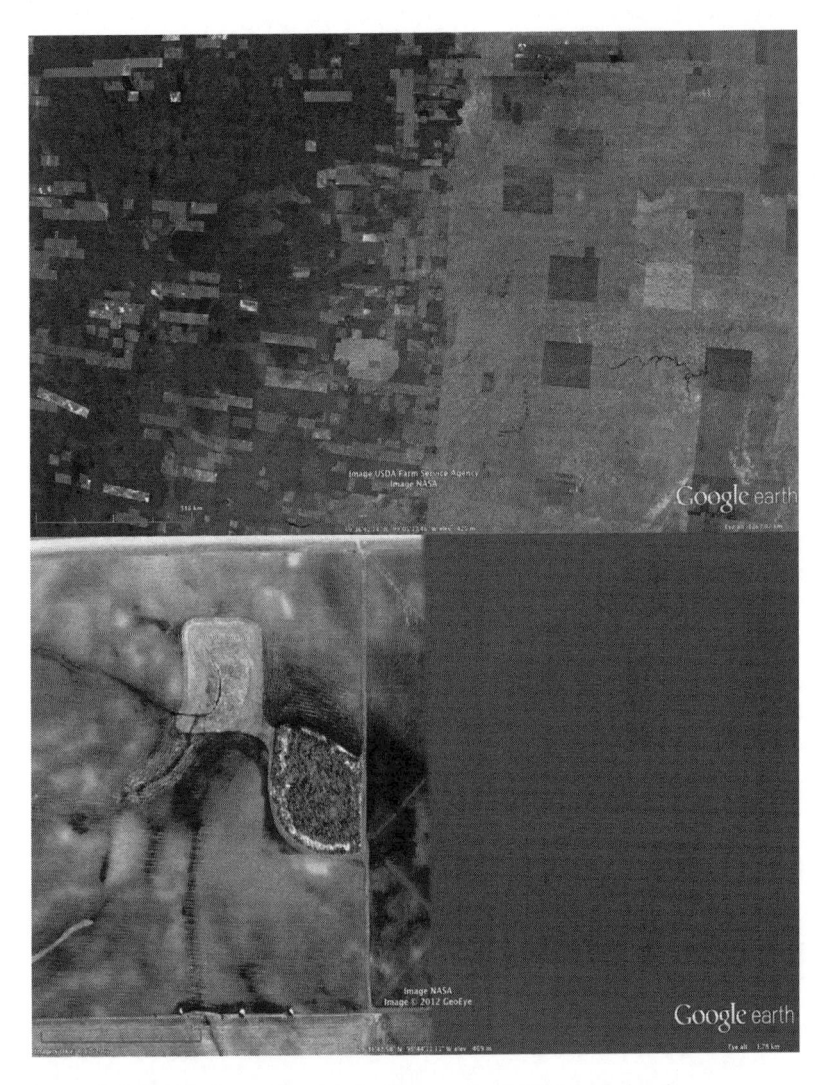

Figure 8.2 Aerial views of prairie landscape, near US/Canada border: upper
image, courtesy Google Earth, USDA Farm Service Agency and
NASA; lower image courtesy Google Earth and NASA, © 2012
GeoEye

inseparable from our engagement with technical instruments. In the case of
the Google Earth's archive of time, this history and the disparities of image
reflecting it can involve disparities in technological development, in financial
or political power, in the relationship of the territory to those controlling

the imaging system and those curating its content.[13] In the upper half of Figure 8.2, for example, the most notable feature is the border between the United States and Canada (north is to the left). The origins of such anomalies are complex; my interest here is in the fact that they exist at all, that this epiphylogenetic history is lumpy and uneven, shot through with contradictions and disparities.

One such disparity can be seen in the lower half of Figure 8.2, a detail of the upper image.[14] On the left side of Figure 8.2, a plowed field displays the furrows left by agricultural machinery as its operator negotiates between the square-mile grid and the natural processes and emergent forms native to the prairie. We recognize in it a specific and concrete landscape, a landscape marked by the working of the plow. This is one kind of technical engagement with the earth. To the right of the same image we can see a field of another kind: a portion of a satellite tile, one of much lower resolution than the source of the image to the left. This is another form of technical engagement with the earth. In it we can read a different prairie: a digital field that stands as landscape in its own right, with its own boundaries, topography, areas of density and intensity. We know – we recognize this in its array of brown and green digital artifacts – that this landscape has been created by a complex system of mechanical and electronic devices. This apparatus of prosthetic perception is visibly imperfect. Perceiving these two fields we are, perhaps despite ourselves, both compelled and discomfited by their juxtaposition, by their simultaneous foreignness from yet assimilation to each other. In light of Stiegler's and Merleau-Ponty's arguments, that resonance is comprehensible. This is a prosthetic perception entangled with a complex and non-linear (and politically-inflected) engagement of time. It implies a reversibility of landscape and image in which distinct but related forms of plowing and harvest can be understood as one flesh, if a flesh divided. If architecture can be seen as an analogous working of the land (and materials), this might imply an engagement of its image, and distortions of that image, in the creative process as one means of transcending the purely utilitarian condition of building.

Seams in the map

At times the temporal displacement between images can be just a matter of hours, and this can be enough to disrupt a homogeneous reading of geographic space. In Figure 8.3 we see two examples of this. In the upper half of the image, a succession of zooms draws us into the edge between two satellite tiles. Each of these images is spliced together by Google's machinery from two tiles. One of these was captured while a cloud overlaid the prairie

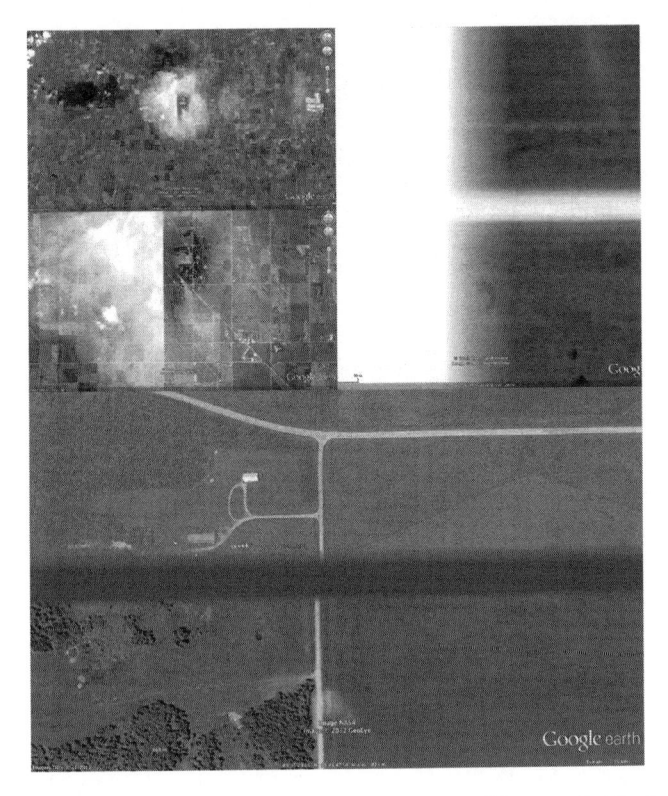

Figure 8.3 Aerial views of prairie landscape, environs of Stonewall, Manitoba: upper images, courtesy Google Earth, © Cnes/Spot Image and Digital Globe; lower image courtesy Google Earth and NASA, © 2012 GeoEye

town of Stonewall; the other was captured after the cloud had moved on. We perceive in one image two contradictory worlds: both an opaque white cloud, and the clearly seen prairie. As one continues to zoom in, the line between the two worlds fluctuates between the sharpness of a knife and the indeterminacy of fog. If one continues until just before the image transforms into Street View, the whiteness of the cloud generates a hieroglyph-like display of artifacts: has the image been transformed into text? On what hidden code have we stumbled as we wander through this fog? What script has begun to be played out here? The fusion of two times has created a heterogeneous space whose artifacts seem to speak, if accidentally, of conditions at the heart of the digital generation of images. Other displacements and accidents provoke similar speculation. We see one of these in the lower half of Figure 8.3. In this image the line between satellite tiles takes on its own material and spatial qualities, becoming an opaque swath between the beginning and end of a road. What shifts and displacements does this anomaly imply? What, might we imagine, lies in the shrouded space between upper and lower images? What occurs out of sight along the road between them, shifted just slightly to one side somewhere along the way?

These images provoke a kind of narrative interpretation, introducing the potential for fiction and imagination into an ostensibly objective documentation of geography. If, as Paul Ricoeur has claimed, narrative is what sews up the rifts opened up within us by our experience of time, we might see in these images a narrative force provoked by the gaps in Stiegler's epiphylogenetic history, the record of time captured and created in part through technical devices.[15] These devices seem to struggle and fail alongside us in our impossible attempt to process temporal experience. Out of this failure emerge the rifts in heterogeneous invented spaces into which we can imagine stories. The fictive dimension of representation confirmed by these images – that all images have a narrative aspect, that no image is precisely what it pretends to represent, that all involve transformation of the real rather than its straightforward representation – seems here to implicate time, geographic space, and by extension architectural space, a connection Ricoeur himself has outlined.[16] They become spatial instances of what Ricoeur, drawing on François Dagognet, termed *iconic augmentation*: poetry's capacity to actually add to reality, to carry an ontological weight comparable to that of being.[17]

The opacities from which these fictions are drawn are evidence of the failure of the promise, dating at least since the Enlightenment, of a complete and seamless mapping of the world. The imaging infrastructures of GIS seem to have built into them their own shadow, their own failure. I have already suggested that rifts in the system can be provoked by political circumstances. Perhaps other provocations of this failure are economic. The pressures of capitalism – commerce's never-ending attempt to expand into new territories, displaced from real into virtual space – tend to push new technological products toward the edge of current capacities of processing power. As until-recently-new capacities are repeatedly exhausted by even-newer needs (or perceived needs), the rifts in these images emerge at an ever-displaced breaking point between means and desire. This phenomenon might in itself be related to the condition of inherent human lack asserted by Stiegler. It shares a space with his instrumental maieutic: between our anticipation of need, the creation of tools to fulfill that need, and the formation of our understanding. As that maieutic is the territory within which our being is drawn forth, it is no wonder the images that emerge from this space compel us so: their own rifts speak of analogous wounds within us.

Agencies

But if our compulsion by such images is a result of gaps within us, injuries we have sustained, we are not mere victims here. Beholding images like these, we continually push the limits of what they might convey precisely because we are not their passive consumers. Our imaginations act upon them – and they in turn push back. We can see further evidence of this in the sequence of images in Figure 8.4. These images were recorded after a jump into Ground Level View, that is, when Google Earth starts to react as though we were a body moving over the land. These three images present to us an aerial image mapped over the topography of the earth: that is, the superimposition of one piece of data (the image, captured by a satellite) with another (elevation variations, in all likelihood collected by LIDAR mapping).[18] But rather than representing this piece of geography accurately, we find that as we move over it, both the image and the land it represents break up beneath us. Curlicues whip over aching voids. Structures collapse and melt into smears of barely recognizable photographic fragments. That condition is provoked by the motion of our technologized body (a cyborg) through space; one source of the image's anamorphic distortion is our movement relative to it. This distortion occurs when we begin to act in that space, even if we are ambiguously, and simultaneously, embodied and disembodied there. These are perhaps the most architectural of the images I have shown here, for the same reason: they engage our bodies.

Our agency is implicated in this transformation of the image from a pure sign to a thing, as it begins to exercise its capacity to become something different. The art theorist Georges Didi-Huberman was preoccupied by works which move back and forth between being signs of something else and being

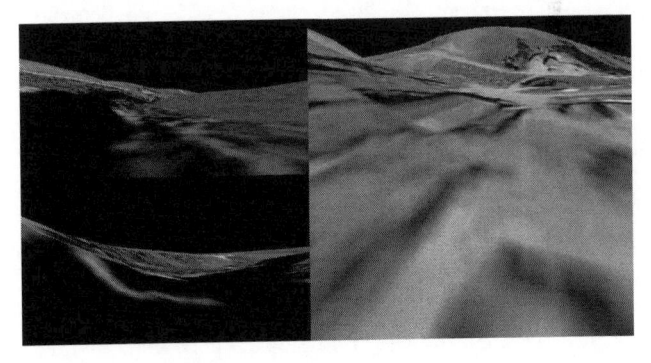

Figure 8.4 Ground-level views of prairie landscape: courtesy Google Earth, © 2012 GeoEye

compelling phenomena in their own right, raw flashes or splashes of color and texture.[19] This distinction between signs and signification, I would propose, is exactly what is implied in the aerial images in Figure 8.4. In each, the signification of meaning breaks down at the very moment in which we begin to engage with the image. Such images cease to be objective representations of the earth. Rather, they become worlds in their own right.

And here lies another form of agency: of the image itself. This is the moment at which a picture becomes not merely something we look at, but rather, something that looks back at us, *ce qui nous regarde*, a thing which we confront rather than observe. W.J.T. Mitchell speaks of something similar, the desiring image, an image that wants.[20] The image is not simply a passive object for our consumption, any more than the prairie is: rather, it lives. We will recall here Stiegler's proposal of a third genre of being, both inorganic and alive. If architecture, similar to these imaging systems and their products, might form such a genre of being, we would hope to identify or instill in it a similar condition of agency: an architecture which regards and confronts us, does not simply contain and serve us.

The introduction of agency to the image overturns any notion of "representational domestication," to return to Waldheim's term. These images are not tamed in the sense of being reduced to instruments; instead, they become wild. Andreas Broeckmann has referred to a transgressive disruption of codes as the wild in media.[21] For Broeckmann that disruption is about excess, and the simultaneous undermining and animation of our technological culture – as explored by artists like Jean Tinguely, Herwig Weiser and JODI. While underlining the irony that much media art depends on a "tamed" technological environment to function at all, even that predicated in discovering "glitches" in that environment, Broeckmann asserts the importance of art that "transgresses these technical functionalities and explores failure, dysfunctionality, misuse, or uncontrollability as categories of aesthetic experience."[22] We have seen that even within as ambitiously encompassing a technological environment as Google Earth, such failures and escapes from control can be everyday occurrences.

I began this chapter by referring to *pixilation*, reading into it the confluence of two modes of manipulation – of land and of image. One irony of the etymology of this term is that the homophonous term *pixilation* dates not to the invention of the pixel in the 1960s, but to the nineteenth century. It was at the time an American term describing a person crazed, bewildered or intoxicated: as though led astray by pixies. The term became popular in the 1930s and 1940s, appearing in numerous popular entertainments; it was later adopted to describe stop-motion animation, a process that makes use of film's dissection of images in time rather than space. Today it is generally accepted as a variant of pixilation, a word that was not invented until the 1960s. Might one propose a fictional, perhaps premonitory, etymology for this term, emerging from both information technology and from folklore, that encompasses both the sense of a digital instrument and the presence of a wild, disruptive force? The images discussed here are native to both of these domains. Despite their emergence from a platform that ostensibly instrumentalizes and commodifies the earth and its image, we can see that these images encompass a space in which imagination, compulsion, enchantment and perhaps even dread can be discovered. We stalkers of technology can seek out these qualities in the rifts between and the artifacts within such images, and imagine into them the fictions that allow us to gather a world or worlds.

Perhaps we might hope to pry open a similar space between today's commodified architecture and its image. How might we explore the reversibility of these two, analogous to the reversibility of landscape and image on displayed above? What anomalies might we provoke in industrial processes of construction based on their own inherent contradictions, the rifts within them? What interplay between optical and haptic experience might we explore? And what hybrid fictional spaces might be created out of this exploration: neither merely built nor merely virtual; never either inanimate or alive, but both? What might our buildings become?

Notes

1 Walter Benjamin, "The Work of Art in the Age of Mechanical Reproduction," in *Illuminations*, ed. Hannah Arendt (London: Fontana, 1968), 214–218.
2 Martin Heidegger, "The Question Concerning Technology," in *The Question Concerning Technology*, trans. William Lovitt (New York: Harper & Row Publishers and Garland Publishing, 1977), 28.
3 Charles Waldheim, "Aerial Representation and the Recovery of Landscape," in *Recovering Landscape: Essays in Contemporary Landscape Architecture*, ed. James Corner (New York: Princeton Architectural Press, 1999), 121.
4 Doug Rickard's and Jon Rafman's works, gleaned from Google Earth Street View, offer a compelling social commentary on abandoned spaces and subjects. See Rickard's series "A New American Picture," accessed December 27, 2013, www.dougrickard.com/photographs/a-new-american-picture/; and Rafman's "9eyes," accessed December 27, 2013, http://9-eyes.com/. Edward Burtynsky's and Mischka Henner's images shot from airplanes, automated drones, and satellites document the damage industrialization has wrought on landscapes. See for example Burtynsky's own website, accessed December 27, 2013, www.edwardburtynsky.com/; and Henner's series "Feedlots," accessed December 27, 2013, http://mishkahenner.com/filter/works/Feedlots.
5 The farm boy was Philo Farnsworth. In 1927 he completed his image dissector, which scanned two-dimensional images and converted them into electronic signals; in 1933 he applied for a patent for an analogous system which projected electrons in progressive rows back and forth on the inside of a vacuum tube.

An electronic transmission of the image had been imagined by others but never successfully completed; Farnsworth's innovation was to break down images electronically, through the use of electrons, rather than mechanically, with mirrors.

6 Bernard Stiegler, *Technics and Time, 1: The Fault of Epimetheus*, trans. Richard Beardsworth and George Collins (Stanford: Stanford University Press, 1998).

7 Specifically André Leroi-Gourhan, philosopher Gilbert Simondon, and historian of technology Bertrand Gille.

8 Stiegler, *Technics and Time*, 133.

9 "What counts for the orientation of the spectacle is not my body as in fact it is, as a thing in objective space, but as a system of possible actions, a virtual body with its phenomenal 'place' defined by its task and situation. My body is wherever there is something to be done." Maurice Merleau-Ponty, *Phenomenology of Perception*, trans. Colin Smith (London & New York: Routledge Classics, 2002), 321.

10 Merleau-Ponty, *Phenomenology of Perception*, 165–166.

11 Maurice Merleau-Ponty and Claude Lefort, *The Visible and the Invisible; Followed by Working Notes* (Evanston, IL: Northwestern University Press, 1968), 200–201.

12 Merleau-Ponty and Lefort, *The Visible and the Invisible*, 154.

13 Such disparities can be intentional, the result of governments censoring certain aerial views. Henner has documented examples in his series "Dutch Landscapes," accessed December 27, 2013, http://mishkahenner.com/filter/works/Dutch-Landscapes.

14 This was captured directly from Google Earth; none of the images in this chapter have been Photoshopped.

15 He makes this argument in Paul Ricoeur, *Time and Narrative*, trans. Kathleen McLaughlin and David Pellauer (Chicago: University of Chicago Press, 1984).

16 See Paul Ricoeur, "Architecture and Narrative," in *Identity and Difference*, catalogue of the Triennale di Milano, XIX Esposizione Internazionale (Milan: Electa, 1996), 64–72.

17 Ricoeur, *Time and Narrative*, 81.

18 LIDAR is a portmanteau of "light" and "radar." A laser is used to scan the ground; the reflected light is analyzed to measure its distance from the laser source; from this elevations can be calculated and contours determined.

19 Georges Didi-Huberman, *Confronting Images: Questioning the Ends of a Certain History of Art* (University Park, PA: Pennsylvania State University Press, 2005).

20 W.J.T. Mitchell, *What Do Pictures Want? The Lives and Loves of Images* (Chicago: The University of Chicago Press, 2004).

21 Andreas Broeckmann, "Playing Wild!" in *Sarai Reader 06: Turbulence*, ed. Monica Narula et al. (Delhi: Centre for the Study of Developing Societies, 2006).

22 "Intimate Politics: An Interview with Andreas Broeckmann," Furtherfield, online interview by the author, last modified October 8, 2011, accessed December 26, 2013, www.furtherfield.org/features/interviews/intimate-politics-interview-andreas-broeckmann.

Interlude B

The door of theory

Marco Frascari

Source: 2009 © Marco Frascari Estate

PART III
Flesh / Eros

9

TOUGH LOVE

A study of the architecture of Pezo von Ellrichshausen

David Leatherbarrow

> Love that has yielded to the right order can no longer be understood as craving and desire because its direction is not determined by any particular object but by the general order of everything that is.[1]
>
> *Hannah Arendt*

In *Built upon Love* Alberto Pérez-Gómez linked together three concepts that can be said to be essential in any architectural work: *project, program* and *promise.* I have called them "concepts," which they are of course, but they can also exist concretely and give durable form and legibility to spatial and social agreements (Figure 9.1). He addressed the interrelationships of these three terms in the second part of the book, where the meanings of the prefix *pro* were described.[2]

Project making, to start with the most obvious case, is essentially *prospective*. *Projectum*, the English word's Latin stem, meant something cast or thrown forward. With respect to architectural drawing, Robin Evans captured this sense of the word very well when he described the construction of a perspective as a *"projective* cast."[3] Alternatively, one can think of the flight of a fisherman's baited hook, sent on its way in the belief that a catch is somewhere "out there," the wide target of the cast. Advance is also indicated by the term's cognates: *projectile, projection, projector,* and so on. Yet, the advances to which Pérez-Gómez refers occur not only in space but time; *pro* indicates temporal *progress* as well as spatial *projection*. Priority can refer to phase or position, something anterior or in front of. *Projects* move forward in weeks, months, and years, just as they advance outwardly in feet or meters. As such,

Figure 9.1 Pezo von Ellrichshausen, Casa Poli, 2002–5, side elevation (photo by author)

a *project* constitutes something like an offering, extended to another person or place, whereby relationships change. Donations of this kind often involve giving ones word – making a *promise* – that in turn inaugurates a *program* of activity or involvement. In architecture, narrowly defined, a *program* is a *proposal* for new ways of living in altered settings and spaces. Still another *pro-* word points to the enactment of a *program* and its *promises*: every *project* unfolds as a *process*, over which architects have no more than partial control. The full realization of a *project*, *program*, or *promise* is also conditioned – maybe

Figure 9.2 Pezo von Ellrichshausen, Casa Poli, 2002–5, window frame (photo by author)

largely so – by the pre-existing structures or order of the world in which it is to find its place and play its role. In the epigraph cited above, the world, "the general order of everything that is," is the target of desires (*projects*) that have, Hannah Arendt says, "yielded to the right order."

"For love of the world" is the answer Arendt gave when asked why she had devoted her entire life to philosophy. So important was the theme that she first thought to use the Latin version of the phrase (*amor mundi*) as the title of the text ultimately published as *The Human Condition*.[4] The world she had in mind was not, of course, the planet earth, not even the natural world; it was all of that plus the human order that had (and has) been discovered and established within it – including all of our buildings, cities, cultural institutions, stories, histories, laws, and so on. Another evidence of her long-standing concern with the adventures of affection is the title and subject of her first book, *Love and Saint Augustine*. The true correlative of desire, she argued, is something lacking in one's life, something or someone wanted as a counterpart. A sense limitation is required for this experience – self-limitation especially, sensed at the edge or boundary of one's abilities or capacity – and something beyond it, some image of richness or abundance, in a person, a place, or some wider quarter of the world (Figure 9.2). Anne Carson, in *Eros: The Bittersweet*, described this liminal situation under three interrelated headings: "Finding the Edge," "Logic at the Edge," and "Losing the Edge."[5] In architecture an analogous relationship exists between the needs of the work and the resources of the world, played out at the building's borders, through elements that enclose and open the interiors, constructed of course, and defined geometrically. Were we to ask the architects whose work I will consider, Mauricio Pezo and Sofia von Ellrichshausen, why their buildings are defined so substantially, precisely, and resolutely, I suspect their answer would be some equivalent to Arendt's *for love of the world*, for they, too, explore the spatial, social, and personal "logic at the edge."

The geometries used by Pezo von Ellrichshausen seem simple, disarmingly so (Figure 9.3). In a time when formal experimentation often seeks novelty above all else, the plans and sections of these buildings appear out of season, at least initially. Yet, if a desire for something spectacular does not prevent us from looking at their work more closely, the designs reveal exceptional refinement, elegance, and inventiveness. Here is my opening question about their work: how can inventiveness occur when plans deploy familiar forms, forms that might seem to result from uncritical borrowing?

The square appears in the plan of many of these buildings, variously resized or adjusted proportionally, by doubling, adding or subtracting a half or the length of the diagonal – nothing new in that. Likewise axial symmetry, seen so often in this work, is an unfashionable but well-known instrument of plan arrangement; although the lines of composition in these layouts generally do not structure spatial passage, the main rooms of the Cien House and the mid-plan stairway of Arco House are exceptions. And finally, the nesting of smaller spaces within proportionate subdivisions of primary forms is an equally recognizable motif of *compartition* – Alberti, whose term I am using, argued for this procedure centuries ago. Assuming that the reuse of familiar techniques is not an end in itself, two explanations suggest themselves: either Pezo von Ellrichshausen intend their geometries to be representational in some way, or they are mechanisms of design technique. Nuanced differentiation shows that there is nothing mechanical about these arrangements.

Figure 9.3 Pezo von Ellrichshausen, Casa Gago, 2011–12, windows of façade (photo by author)

Nor does formal variation appear to be the aim, even if it is in evidence; rather, it is the result of precise attunement to the requirements of inhabitation and the opportunities of the location. If one says these plans are representational, it is because they anticipate and trace patterns of inhabitation, proportioning, one can say, the ratio between what the work lacks and the world supplies. But this kind of specification is only the first indication of their allegiance to the principle of *amor mundi*.

The imitation of praxis (*mimesis tes praxeos*) is the principle that governs plot composition, according to Aristotle's *Poetics*[6] (see Figure 9.4). He was concerned with tragic drama, but the etymological ties between the words plot, plat, and plan suggest there is no mistake in applying his principle to architecture too. Art does not fashion likenesses of people and things, but of their behaviors, how they interact with one another and the world, their "performances," which can be inspiring or disgusting, and everything in between. Action is the key. Again: drama does not imitate people but what they do; more exactly, what they should or should not do, which is why poetry is more true (to what life can be) than history, which only reports

Figure 9.4 Pezo von Ellrichshausen, Casa Cien, 2008–11, kitchen (photo by author)

what has happened. Articulating their own emphasis on performance – but not in the narrow sense of the word that is common in today's talk about high performance buildings – Pezo von Ellrichshausen's buildings define enclosures not geometries, settings prepared to accommodate typical patterns of living, not create interesting plans and profiles. Similarly, lines of symmetry are lines of sight or movement. Further, nested forms cluster co-dependent purposes: cupboards buttress workspaces, for example, and closets support the use of bedrooms. When geometries are disciplined in these ways everyday life unfolds freely. Instead of requiring attention, the forms adopt a reticent stance, rather like a silent witness attending to some unselfconscious act of generosity – not of giving, but of allowing. Quiet but ready, provisioning in their buildings expect to be consulted only when the practices of dining, sleeping, conversing, or working need a little support – limiting their involvement to the anticipations and tracings I mentioned earlier.

Support such as this seems effortless. What is more, these configurations show impressive economy. I do not mean the tight-fisted, sparing sort, but the elegance that results from a sharing of spaces that hold common interest. Proportioning is, after all, a way of giving each person or place the right portion or share, as in a meal. There are a very few corridors in these buildings; typically patios or entry halls combine and condense circulation requirements. Likewise, storage and service spaces are normally packed into wall thicknesses, making the space of the room as generous as possible. And the furniture that is not freestanding and centrally located is also immured into load-bearing depth – seating alcoves, benches, etc. – so that the movements of residing have the fewest constraints, as in the Abba, Gago, and Solo Houses, for example. The seating alcove of Casa Cien can serve as an example of these kinds of settings: a room within a room has been carved out of wall thickness, with its floor raised to seat-height and ceiling lowered to the right proportion, and equipped with all the instruments of domestic comfort and intimacy: concealed bookshelves of unequal depth to the left and right, a fireplace in the deeper niche, seating cushions, and a central window to the side slope. Its compactness allows corresponding openness to the room it adjoins, a much more ample setting, comparatively public, and emblematic of the composition of the whole, but nevertheless engaged with the alcove because the surfaces of both are clad with the same painted timber and their geometries are entirely congruent. One suspects that these economies resulted from painstaking studies of intervals and alignments, worked and reworked until their number and variations were reduced to fullness, fullness of potential. My main point is that the labor of design is not in service of pleasing geometry – certainly not that alone, even though it is pleasing – but the performances and practices the forms accommodate and represent (Figure 9.5).

Figure 9.5 Pezo von Ellrichshausen, Casa Cien, 2008–11, sitting alcove (photo by author)

The part-to-counterpart relationship one sees in the plans of these projects is also apparent in their sections and elevations, but with a difference. What the program is to the plan, topography is to the section and elevation. With the word *topography* I mean land of course (terrain), together with its less weighty other half (climate, atmosphere, densities, and distances), but also the cultural aspects of a place (settlement patterns, histories, and characters).[7] Obviously, content as rich as this exceeds what any single building can supply – the "world" to which Arendt's love and Carson's "reach" referred. Once architecture's essential poverty is observed, elements such as apertures become *instruments of longing*.[8]

Many, though not all, of the sites on which Pezo von Ellrichshausen have built are sloped. In response, their projects adopt either of two siting strategies: rising above the fall of the terrain or cutting into it. This alternative was set out clearly decades ago by Marcel Breuer in *Sun and Shadow*, where he observed in a chapter called "Architecture in the Landscape" that a building is always and inevitably "a man-made thing, a crystallic, constructed thing . . . that should not imitate [the forms of] nature . . . but be a thing in itself."[9] The work's artificiality meant either of two approaches to siting could be adopted: placing the house on columns, above uneven terrain, allowing passage below, or installing it into the land, elaborating its levels, and permitting free movement from inside to outside. Breuer admitted that he sometimes tried to combine these approaches. Pezo von Ellrichshausen have not used columns to raise their buildings above the land, but they do surmount a number of their sites. This strategy can be seen in the Sota, Abba, Guna, and Solo houses, for example. The stone and soil of Casa Guna's site, for example, slopes into the small bay of a lagoon, while the platform on which the rooms have been distributed hovers above, its load-bearing walls drawn within, where they do their work quietly and in shadow (Figure 9.6). Pezo von Ellrichshausen have also taken an approach that is similar to Breuer's second strategy, as can be seen in the Gago, Faro, Cien, Fosc, and Poli houses. Seen from the side, Casa Cien conceals a number of its stacked decks, within and above the site's slope; but a single platform opens at the front to allow an entry stair to descend and extends at the back to expand the guest bedroom. Both siting methods lead to the multiplication of platforms, below, within, and above the building's basic volume.

Another way to think of this is to view the building as a very big stairway with each of its platforms (inside or out) serving the function of a landing, connected to others and the wider milieu by a few intermediate steps, so that the building-stairway continues the approach and extends the departure. Pezo von Ellrichshausen have suggested as much in a comment they offered about the Cien House: "decisive coincidences such as the number of steps

Figure 9.6 Pezo von Ellrichshausen, Casa Guna, 2010–12, side elevation (photo by author)

Figure 9.7 Pezo von Ellrichshausen, Casa Cien, 2008–11, side view (photo by author)

on a hill path nearby, an old cypress . . . , or even the elevation above sea level that defines [the] podium can explain this building's silhouette" (Figure 9.7).[10] Well, at least partly. The stairway sense of the section, its continuity within and extension beyond the building's proper limits, allows the work's involvement with natural and cultural dimensions of the ambient surround, dimensions that are not properly the building's own (Figure 9.8).

Something very similar happens with the apertures of these houses. Perhaps the most vivid case is the Poli House. Here the part-to-counterpart relationship unfolds by means of simply-shaped and sharply-cut openings in the building's massive perimeter walls. It is hardly surprising to find walls as bulky as these in a landscape that suffers earthquakes with discouraging frequency. Yet, when inside this house, resistance to the wider landscape seems to have been the last thing the architects had on their minds, for the perforations in the perimeter welcome the site's light, air, and sound so openly that the work seems best described as a receptacle, an open hand to all the world has to offer. The notion that the inside and outside should be connected is, of course, a commonplace of modern architecture. From the time of Le Corbusier's "every inside is an outside" to contemporary arguments for "flowing space" we have been treated to countless attempts to remove

Figure 9.8 Pezo von Ellrichshausen, Casa Poli, 2002–5, interior (photo by author)

what architecture seems particularly well-suited to provide: elements that divide, partition, and separate settings within the area on which one builds.[11] Seeing the openings in these works as instruments of "flow" means overlooking their very hard edges, their sharp profiles, and their substantial back up, impassive as it is, resolute, and fully committed to *resistance*. The work opens itself to the world because all of its energies are concentrated on maintaining its own definition, not making any claims on what is not its own. Outward reach has not been accomplished because it was never attempted (Figure 9.9). Instead, the building is willing to wait – again like a silent witness – confident that the qualities of the world that will enrich its unpolished surfaces will make their appearance when they choose, according to their own schedule, with a force and direction they decide, according to the building's expectations sometimes, often not, but always giving rhythm and amplitude to the life within its walls. Even though it argues for receptivity, the house does not adopt the restrictions that architecture called minimalist imposes on itself. Posited instead – through the procedures of construction craft as much as design and specification – are spaces and surfaces that resist what cannot be suffered and allow what will be enjoyed.

Rainer Maria Rilke defined love as an agreement that protects and nurtures individualities. It is, he said, just the opposite of a "quick commonality" that results from tearing down all boundaries. As if he were writing

Figure 9.9 Pezo von Ellrichshausen, Casa Poli, 2002–5, interior (photo by author)

about concepts of connection and communication that are common in architecture, Rilke argued that "merging" is in fact senseless; when approximated it results in a "hemming in," a denial of freedom. Differences and distances always exist, unyielding though they seem, tough though they may be. Far from being a problem, toughness of this sort allows for the emergence of a "marvelous side-by-side living."[12] The transactions between the work and the world instituted by the buildings of Pezo von Ellrichshausen advance the same thesis I think: caring for our lives and the environment by quietly and confidently staging their ever-changing interplay (Figure 9.10).

Figure 9.10 Pezo von Ellrichshausen, Casa Poli, 2002–5, exterior view (photo by author)

Notes

1 Hannah Arendt, *Love and Saint Augustine*, ed. Joanna Vecchiarelli Scott and Judith Chelius Stark (Chicago: The University of Chicago Press, 1996), 39.
2 Alberto Pérez-Gómez, *Built upon Love* (Cambridge, MA: MIT, 2006), especially Chapters 8 and 9.
3 Robin Evans, *The Projective Cast: Architecture and Its Three Geometries* (Cambridge, MA: MIT, 2000).
4 Elizabeth Yong-Bruehl, *Hannah Arendt. For Love of the World* (New Haven: Yale University Press, 1982), 324.
5 Anne Carson, *Eros: The Bittersweet* (Princeton: Princeton University Press, 1986), 30–52. The next two chapters, "Archilochos at the Edge" and "Alphabetic Edge," place less stress on the spatial characteristics of this situation, more on its

relationships to verbal expression and experience. The chapter titled "Reach" also addresses the spatiality of border experience, while the chapter called "Gone" elaborates its temporal order.

6 Aristotle, *Poetics* 1448a; for elaboration and commentary, see Ernesto Grassi, *Die Theorie des Schönen in der Antike* (Köln: Dumont, 1980), 125.

7 I have tried to develop these several senses of the term in *Topographical Stories: studies in landscape and architecture* (Philadelphia: University of Pennsylvania Press, 2004), 1–16.

8 Kyra Stromberg has used an equivalent phrase, the window as a "place of longing" (*der Sehnsuchtsort Fenster*), in "The Window in the Picture – The Picture in the Window," *Daidalos* 13 (1984): 59.

9 Marcel Breuer, "Architecture in the Landscape," in *Sun and Shadow* (New York: Dodd, Mean & Company, 1955), 38–41.

10 Maurizio Pezo and Sofia von Ellrichshausen, "Cien House," *Harvard Design Magazine* 34 (Cambridge, MA: Harvard University Press, 2011), 110.

11 As with my brief comments on "compartition," this sense of subdividing the space of the platform derives from Alberti's account of what we now call plan making.

12 Rainer Maria Rilke, *Letters to a Young Poet* (New York: Norton, 1934), 52ff.

10

FLESH OF STONE

Buildings, statues, entangled bodies

Tracey Eve Winton

Gods in Antiquity were bodily things. The Druids worshipped oaks; Egyptians worshipped animals; shapeless stones were venerated by the Greeks, and the Sherpa reverenced Mount Everest as their mother goddess. Hindu avatars and the mass of the Roman temple testify that invisible powers need bodily presence to dwell and act in the world. As conscious persons we identify ourselves with our corporeal flesh, which furnishes us with our finite limits and carnal pleasures. Our awareness, though, involves a world beyond the body's limits. The flesh of the world and of others is sentient and responsive, vulnerable to our words and thoughts, especially to our desirous gaze and touch. I'd like to turn to the *Hypnerotomachia*,[1] to which Alberto Pérez-Gómez first introduced me, and read out a poetic understanding of man's intertwining with architecture.

In the *Hypnerotomachia*'s text and images, published at the height of Renaissance naturalism, embodiment is inseparable from thought's phantasmic imagery. Poliphilo frames his vision of rarefied philosophical and theological ideas concretized in symbols with an ekphrasis of the world coming into physical being through the rising Sun, in the Spring as a time of universal rebirth. He dreams, and within his dream he dreams again: a Neoplatonic symbol for liberating the contemplative soul from bodily needs. Yet in this dream, his body and its organs haunt him in every scene. He missteps and trips over roots, stones, shards, and uneven ground; he suffers from thirst and exhaustion; he endures shame for being scratched and dirty; he sweats; he sighs, he eats; he grows aroused and blushes. In short, he brings his body with him.

Besides his beloved Polia and the creatures who populate his dream's complex settings, Poliphilo describes architectonic objects which at every scale integrate sculptural figures, effigies and statues. In Renaissance architecture, the statue is an architectural element in human form. It's also an iconic image of the intertwining of the mortal self and the enduring universe, and its intermediate position on the spectrum implies a continuum between man and his architecture. In Poliphilo's mythic world, distinctions between flesh and stone initially seem clear enough, but closer inspection yields contaminations, interpenetrations, and crossovers. His story thus foregrounds threshold and passage conditions and thematizes metamorphosis. Our attention seduced and secured by the ornamental articulation of all liminal zones, boundaries that first appeared solid transpire to be permeable, as we map out the migration of physical characteristics, and confusions between bodies and buildings.

Both woodcuts and text present types of heads and bodies, ranging from portraits and icons to the aniconic: tree trunks, nymphs, topiary or mineral statues, free-standing or in bas-relief, classical columns and capitals, obelisks, fountains in human form, funerary masks, hollow armor, grotesques, flat encaustic wall-portraits or fleeting reflections in mirrored surfaces, nuancing the continuum between Poliphilo as perceiving subject and the architectural objects of his desire. In all its variants, the statue – *imago hominis* in architectural matter – is the primary symbol of this space of exchange.

Figure 10.1 Poliphilo in the ruins of the ancient city. The limbless torso of a statue lies juxtaposed with a column capital

Poliphilo's journey takes us through temples, palaces, tombs and gardens evoking Antiquity. Besides artificial human figures and other images of the body, his architecture teems with exquisite materials and ornamental details chosen to demonstrate it bursting with life. Among these are architectural figurations so naturalistic that they lack only breath to live, visibly lifelike relief carvings and sculptures whose coldness to his touch surprises him, and marble statues so carnally alluring they draw his eyes away from living creatures. Architecture and its constituent elements are dynamic, circulatory bodies that seduce, provoke, mimic, confront, contemplate, and make eye contact. His buildings also circulate airs and fluids within; they lactate, urinate, inhale, swallow, incubate and give birth. Whole structures become bodies to be entered, and the corporeality of their inner cavities explored, not without a "digestive process" that entangles and effectively consubstantiates architecture and inhabitant.

Architectural form, though organized by geometry and abstract qualities, is attributed animate features. Poliphilo's vocabulary revives arcane Latin and Greek terms that depict architectural elements as organic tropes and, supported by ornamental statuary and carvings on the buildings' visible surfaces, reveals that buildings have living parts: divine, monstrous, spiritual, human, animal and vegetal. The word he uses for "frieze" – *zoöphor* – is Greek for "that which conveys life." Among the buildings' defining lineaments and ornaments he names dentils (teeth), caulicoles (sprouts), echinus (sea-urchins), ovolo moldings (eggs), capitals (heads), auricles (ears), and astragals (ankle bones). He compares column bases and pedestals to feet, and a column's entasis to pregnancy; building elements swell and protrude like flesh. Following Vitruvius, Poliphilo identifies sexual connotations that the columns carry in the details of the classical orders, but also notices "bisexual" rudentured shafts and unknown hermaphroditic orders mixing Doric (male) and Ionic (female) elements. He recollects the ancient atlantes and caryatids: structural columns taking human form, fluting mimicking women's clothing, and responds to this animate, sexualized architecture with feelings of burning desire.

Ideas in the abstract risk sterility. To propagate desire, and fulfill our highest form of activity, creation, imagination requires the body's sensuality and drives. Foreshadowing the depths of the matrix as flesh, Poliphilo conveys the incarnation of stone at the Great Portal through which he entered:

> The craftsman had painstakingly set off this *historia* against a colored background of coralite stone introduced between the undulating moldings of the altar in the spaces surrounding the figures. Its incarnate coloration diffused itself throughout the translucent stone, imparting to the nude bodies and their limbs the semblance of blushing flesh.[2]

By extension, this intimates that the life force is latent in all of the architecture. Once inside, Poliphilo finds himself in a grotto whose mother-of-pearl revetment suggests his incorporation, enfolded in an architectural oyster-shell.[3] An intimate form of encounter ensues in the pyramid's foundations below where navigating a subterranean labyrinth by feel alone, he runs across a shrine to Venus glowing in the inchoate darkness.[4] The body, in its turn, needs imagination to reciprocate love.

As he explores the debris-heaped terrain around a ruined ancient city, Poliphilo discovers a bronze colossus, lying on the ground, yet intact. This is an architectonic monument, a built form vast enough to inhabit. The colossus is a double, mirroring and merging the hero's dreaming body with the architecture in his vision. In his recumbent, sleeping form, the gigantic statue is primarily bodily. Dreaming, he moans in pain, for ventilation holes bored into the soles of his feet suck in the breeze and make him resound like a musical instrument. Poliphilo clambers over his chest, spelunking his mouth, down his gullet, exploring the cavernous interior:

> I saw intestines, nerves and bone, veins, muscles and flesh, as if I were in a penetrable human body. And wherever I was, each part that you would seen in every natural body had its name engraved in three idioms: Chaldaean, Greek and Latin, as well as what kind of diseases are generated in which, and their causes, remedies and cures.[5]

At the heart Poliphilo reads about Love, and suddenly feels his own unrequited love resurgent. As he breathes a heavy sigh, the entire bronze structure shudders in sympathetic resonance. The colossal figure is not solid, impervious metal, but enfleshed and responsive to his very spirit. Departing, Poliphilo sees a female counterpart, buried in rubble up to her neck. Like himself, the male statue suffers from existential separation, from love that is not able to exchange its life-giving energy and complete the erotic circuit.

Poliphilo's dream-quest is to find and join his Polia. She is the female to his male, the mythos to his logos, the (lost) history to his (melancholic) modernity, the otherness hidden within him and around him. The neologism "hypn-eroto-machia" incorporates the philosopher Empedocles' dual principles of cosmic change: universal Sympathy (the basis of natural magic, related to mimesis and the forces of attraction) and Antipathy (the force behind fragmentation and dissolution): *Eros* and *Machia*, Love and Strife. Poliphilo's dream materializes these through divine figures, the former by Venus–Aphrodite, and the latter by Minerva–Athena in her martial aspect. Polia towers over Poliphilo's narrative like a marble Venus crowned with the head of Minerva, an "Idea" as he calls her, willful and irrational, elusive and sensuous, strange and familiar. She is a matrix overflowing with Nature's unlimited plenitude: a theocracy simultaneously generous and cruel, a paradox brimming with poetic ambiguity, resistant to analytic thought with its rational, divisive categories. The ancient city is a woman whom you love at your peril. To know her at an intellectual distance – a visual distance – can never satisfy him; he hungers for an unmediated, corporeal, tactile encounter. And the architecture he describes thus evidences his yearning to enter her – to become one with her – an intertwining of the self and the world.

A *quattrocento* commonplace characterized an unresponsive lady as being made of stone. In a sonnet, Lorenzo de' Medici calls his mistress "adamantine," hard as diamond.[6] Polia too, not reciprocating Poliphilo's love, is "frozen and stony." To be a body of flesh is to return love, to recirculate the vital energy that links and bonds the world together. Only the embodied imagination, with its capacity for desire, can do so, and thus can participate in world making. To be flesh and thus receptive radiates and circulates erotic energy, not just between lovers, but throughout the universe into which the superabundant creative force overflows.

In every tale in Ovid's *Metamorphoses* love transforms. Yet the metamorphoses in the *Hypnerotomachia* illustrate two kinds of subject–object intercorporeality: one constituted through mutual visibility (Athena–Minerva); and the other through touch (Venus–Aphrodite). With sensitive caresses Pygmalion coaxes hard materials to warm into flesh and by eye contact Medusa petrifies pliant flesh into rock. Both emerge between the lines in enigmatic images to unfold this cosmic process through poetic metaphor.

Poliphilo himself plays Pygmalion, a sculptor, and priest of Aphrodite. In the days when the love goddess had punished hard-hearted women by turning them to stone, Pygmalion builds his own woman, a statue of ivory. She is so beautiful he falls in love with her and asks Aphrodite to intervene. As he adorns the statue, strokes her, kisses her, he feels the hard ivory soften like beeswax under his fingers, sees her blush, and hears her begin to breathe. She comes to life as flesh and blood, an organic creature who in time will bear his child.[7] Similarly, Poliphilo's dream traces his invention of Polia from architectural "Idea" to a living woman with her own voice and story. She, ultimately, will make Poliphilo visible to himself.

Polia instantiates the other process as a type of Athena Polias, virgin goddess of wisdom and the city, who wears Medusa's head on her breastplate. Beautiful Medusa makes love with Poseidon in Athena's temple, and the angry goddess turns her hair to living serpents, cursing her that her eye contact will convert living flesh to stone. To avoid her eyes, Perseus deploys his mirrored shield, and decapitates the pregnant Medusa. Her monstrous offspring are Pegasus and Chrysaor, a golden giant, and in the ruined city

Poliphilo encounters them as monuments: the winged horse and the bronze colossus. Perseus mounted on Pegasus, holding Medusa's severed head, flew past Atlas holding the sky aloft, and transformed him into a mountain. At the city gate, the vast Titan materializes as a massive pyramid of white marble reaching to the heavens, entered through the howling mouth of a marble Medusa's head, her giant snaky tresses serving Poliphilo as stairs.

Though flesh and stone are both stuff of the world and share materialized form, life and the non-living are differentiated by self-aware compassion, the bonding spark of desire linking subject and object. The paradoxical exclusiveness of the world and a body that share properties and qualities engenders the libidinal will to action, the intention to engage. Things of extreme beauty come to life, and monstrous things contaminate their surroundings, by a conversion of the erotic force. This motive force, however, is a mode of relationship, one possible only through the embodied imagination, and as such the ground of meaning. As Pérez-Gómez explains in *Built upon Love*,

> architectural meaning is neither intellectual nor aesthetic in a formal sense, but originates instead in our embodiment and its erotic impulse. . . . The harmony of architecture is always tactile and "material" (referring to the mother of all). Architectural meaning, like erotic knowledge, is a primary experience of the human body and yet takes place in the world, in that pre-reflective ground of existence where reality is first "given."[8]

His work suggests how to understand the *Hypnerotomachia*'s porous distinction of flesh from stone, their reciprocal convertibility, in terms of the tenuous and fragile qualities characteristic of the living body that confront Poliphilo at the goal of his pilgrimage.

Pérez-Gómez begins with Daedalus, mythology's first architect, whose *daidala* were works marked by the mutual adjustment of the components and the integrity of their fit. Some of these awe-inspiring statues were so well composed that they seemed alive, and had to be tied down. In the underlying concept of harmony, connected to proportion, he notes that essential to beauty (*venustas*) is "an arrangement of parts that seduces the . . . observer and creates a significant space of participation. It is important to notice that *harmonia* initially had nothing to do with mathematics; it was a quality of embodiment (perfect adjustment) with the ultimate aim of love."[9] Tracing the origins of harmony to the ideal of things cleaving together in mutual agreement, which we might visualize architecturally in the spatial relation of the tectonic connection or the elements composing a city, he finds harmony later develops into a concordance of distinct elements or sounds, which form an orderly, internally consistent, and unified whole. He notes that for Galen, writing on anatomical structure in the second century, *harmonia* described "the union of two bones by mere apposition: a perfectly adjusted joint."[10] For the physician, the perfect relationship of heterogeneous and symmetrical parts to the whole were evidence of the divine hand, while today we can observe the centrality of embodiment persisting in our word "organization" which indicates the highest and most complex degree of order in a unified structure of specialized elements. While the linking power of Eros brings lovely things to life, this love is evoked, made, inspired by the beauty itself, and ultimately too, the origin and meaning of beauty are in the erotic cleavage of organic jointing. That which has been perfectly made, and thus made with love, verges toward animation. The craftsman seeking in the material its own potentiality, its pre-existing propensity to come alive when sensed, works to embody *phantasia* and passion from *within* it as Nature does in her own processes. The hand of the architect brings "Eros-qualities" to the raw materials, transubstantiating them from separate to composite, bestowing visibility and luminosity, ordering them through geometry, symmetry, proportion, refining through calibration, and elaborating through meticulous detailing, provoking the desirous onlooker to respond.

The background presence of Aphrodite and Athena, the goddesses respectively presiding over the tendency towards flesh and the tendency towards stone, introduces simultaneous desires to collapse the gap between subject and object through the act of touching, and through the eyes, the distance needed to see, to maintain the tension between subject and object. Beauty is integral to the mechanism that circulates erotic energy between lover and beloved, self and other, body and world, inhabitant and architecture. Yet becoming visible is not just "aphrodisiac"; it also depends on the Athena principle: the necessity to maintain the distance of know-how or embodied wisdom, only possible in a tense balance of proximity and separation, a "formula" for the architect's ability with which we could also describe lived space, Plato's *chora*, or the architectonic situation. Architecture as a form of embodied knowledge demands responsive touch. To perceive beauty, though, requires mutual visibility. To act and create in the world, we need the agency and responsibility of individual identity, our mortal experience of separateness, even the pain and terror of impermeable, existential solitude.

Sustaining the tension between pulling apart and joining, the architectural settings of the *Hypnerotomachia* reveal the co-presence of generation and corruption, form rising to visibility as *cosmos*, orderly knowable surface, and dissolving beneath the threshold of perception, its degeneration in time and through neglect and violence into formless *prima materia*. Poliphilo's intimation of his own mortality and thus of his separate self, who

ΠΑΝΤΩΝ ΤΟΚΑΔΙ

Per laquale cofa io non faperei definire, fila diuturna & tanta acre fe-
te pridiana tolerata ad bere trahendo me prouocaffe, ouero il belliffimo
fufcitabulo dello inftruméto. La frigiditate dil quale, inditio mi dede che
la petra mentiua. Circuncirca dunque di quefto placido loco, & per gli
loquaci riuuli fioriuano il Vaticinio, Lilii conuallii, & la floréte Lyfima
chia, & il odorofo Calamo, & la Cedouaria, Apio, & hydrolapato, & di
affai altre appretiate herbe aquicole & nobili fiori, Et il canaliculo pofcia

e

Figure 10.2 The Fountain of the Sleeping Nymph in the Garden of the Senses.
Her breasts run with streams of hot and cold water

appreciates beauty through vision and thinks as a maker, comes in the shape of architecture in a state of disintegration. At the abandoned city, the material corruption of the ruined buildings is spatially juxtaposed with a carved gigantomachy of lacerated, tormented and perishing bodies. The fractured elements render a fatal sensibility of transience, death and injury. A fallen column has lost its capital; minerals tarnish and bloom; masonry fallen out of place is cracked open and rank with weeds. Further on, surrounding the life-affirming Temple of Venus, he finds a study of *machia* in the brute decomposition in the Polyandrion: a vast necropolis of shattered sarcophagi and funerary monuments to separated lovers.

In the Neoplatonic philosophy structuring the *Hypnerotomachia*, the One is a divine unity and superabundant source from which emanates the multiplicity of the phenomenal world. Elements become material and temporal as they devolve or unfold into definition, separateness, and locality. Simultaneously completing the circuit, the Many, are drawn upward through the orders of being by the power of Love enacting the return to the One – re-acquiring harmony and unity through the creative work of the human artifex. The Many serve as "raw materials" to be refined and joined. In their assembled state – architecture – they are representations of the yearning for eternal interconnectedness and ultimate unity conceived through desire by a human subject. The *Hypnerotomachia* hides the Many in plain sight as Poliphilo's wide-ranging polyglot vocabulary from cultural and natural history, naming plants, minerals, birds, legendary heroes, historical buildings, mythical creatures, and architectural elements. In his architecture, this alchemical cycle of *solve et coagula* is incarnated as the dissolution of bonds and the return to the soil of fragmented ruins of statues and buildings, and the rigorous re-composition of the minerals, plants, and iconic images into new totalities.

These opposing powers of Love and Strife, the dual font at which creation drinks, are centrally embodied in the human imagination, in a psychological faculty that Poliphilo encounters in architectonic form at the Palace of Free Will. There he traverses three drawing rooms representing his brain's ventricles, cavities that staged the sensory processes of *sensus communis, phantasia*, and *memoria*. The frontal "common sense" reunites percepts from the five external senses into "virtual realities," and archives these phantasms in the memory. But the *phantasia* (a word that keeps erotic connotations in *fantasy*) can anatomize holistic phantasmic images into elements that then can be reorganized into novel compositions, like a horse with wings, a woman with snakes for hair, a satyr whose features mingle goatish with human, or a building mixing Egyptian, Greek and Roman forms and technical arts.

The sequencing of architectural settings in the primary narrative hints at an identical process. Clustered or individual qualities (semblance, icon, material, figure, proportion, geometry, arrangement and so on) of each architectural object separate out, to be subsequently rejoined with others in new combinations, and increasingly high levels of visible order. Each work of architecture including the pyramid, the bathhouse, and the temple, geometrical complexes of stone and bodily figurations, gets dismembered behind the scenes into phantasmic elements that in successive re-compositions are transformed yet recognizable to the reader. Through the ruin settings, Poliphilo recognizes himself as incomplete, and anxiously desires intercorporeal reconnection with both Polia and the architecture itself. Thus his *phantasia* drives forward the iterative metamorphoses of his idealized physical environs, with his embodied imagination modeled on the perpetual self-creation of the cosmos.

Seeded throughout the text and woodcuts you find two key configurations. One is the solar symbol or patera ☉ that diagrams the circuit bonding the One and the Many. Platonic Being and Becoming manifest as center and circumference, with *chora* or space opening between them like an amphitheater's arena. The other is a knot work motif, gardens of interlacing embodied in living, growing matter, a glyph for the workings of that space in-between, the unity of multiplicity, the ever-incomplete, the linking and joining power of love.

Hypnerotomachia Poliphili, Poliphilo's dream of strife and love and the meaning of his dream lie in the necessary intertwining of the world in its most essential aspect with that which constitutes *humanitas*, a virtue governed by Venus. The culminating iconic image of Book I is a statue of Venus presiding over a garden on the Island of Cythera commemorating Adonis, her late younger lover:

> On the tomb's polished upper surface sat the divine mother sculpted as a woman recently delivered of a child, marvelously executed in priceless tricolored sardonyx marble. She was seated on an antique throne, which did not go beyond the vein of sard, while through incredible invention and artifice her whole Cytherean body had been carved from the milky vein of onyx. She was nearly nude, since only a veil formed from the red vein, left to conceal Nature's secret, was covering part of one thigh. The rest of it cascaded to the floor, then wandered up just beside her left breast, turned aside, encircled her shoulders, and flowed back down towards the water, with astonishing craftsmanship closely following the lineaments of her sacred limbs. The statue manifested her motherly love by cradling Cupid who was nursing at her breast. Both of their cheeks were gracefully tinctured by the rosy vein, along with her right nipple. In this beautiful work, miraculous to contemplate! Nothing was lacking but the vital spirit![11]

Figure 10.3 The Garden of Adonis: Polia and the other nymphs gathered around the statue of Venus nursing Cupid

The body and the other, who is also the world, are paradoxically at the same time one and two. For this reason, the non-dual or mystical experience is quintessentially erotic. The statue of Venus compassionately nurturing her newborn child demonstrates how bodily union intertwines *Eros* with *machia*'s agonizing separateness and difference. At this monument, Poliphilo and the nymphs insert themselves in the circuit of erotomachia by kissing the statue's graceful foot. Juxtaposing visibility and tactility in embodiment, its stratified material binds creamy onyx, the archetypal color of cool, classical marble, with sard the color of living blood, whose visible vein reveals and traces a vital continuum between mother and son, but also between the architecture proper, the statues, and the human figures. In *The Visible and the Invisible*, Maurice Merleau-Ponty characterized this proximate distance in contemporary terms saying " . . . a sort of dehiscence opens my body in two, and because between my body looked at and my body looking, my body touched and my body touching, there is overlapping or encroachment, . . . we may say that the things pass into us, as well as we into the things."[12] The design of this garden, dedicated to evanescent beauty, recognizes embodiment as a moment in time to be seized or lost, with an urgent message to be more than a mirror to love. Listen to the world that speaks; grasp *occasio* by the forelock and act; create in the world, and recirculate the energy that bonds all things.

Notes

1 *Hypnerotomachia Poliphili*, anonymous (Venice: Aldus Manutius, 1499).
2 Ibid, (unpaginated) Chapter V. All translations by the author.
3 Ibid, Chapter VI.
4 Ibid.
5 Ibid, Chapter IV.
6 Lorenzo de' Medici Sonnet XV, in *The Autobiography of Lorenzo de' Medici the Magnificent: A Commentary on My Sonnets*. Translated with an introduction by James Wyatt Cook, together with the text of *Comento de' Miei Sonetti*, reprinted from the critical edition of Tiziano Zanato (Florence: Olschki, 1991). Binghamton, NY: Center for Medieval and Early Renaissance Studies, 1995 (Medieval and Renaissance Texts and Studies 129): 132.
7 Ovid, *The Metamorphoses*, Book X, lines 243–297.
8 Alberto Pérez-Gómez, *Built upon Love: Architectural Longing after Ethics and Aesthetics* (Cambridge, MA: MIT Press 2006), 42.
9 Ibid., 35.
10 Ibid.
11 *Hypnerotomachia*, Chapter XXIV.
12 Maurice Merleau-Ponty, *The Visible and the Invisible; Followed by Working Notes*, trans. Alphonso Lingis (Evanston, IL: Northwestern University Press, 1968), 123.

11

GENIUS AS EROS

Lian Chikako Chang

Opening

One's first reaction to the book is entirely favorable. The type is beautiful and the book handles well. It is only as we turn over the pages that we become aware of something amiss. . . .[1]

C. E. Kellet

Charles Estienne's 1545 anatomical treatise *De dissectione partium corporis humani libri tres* appears bizarre to contemporary eyes.[2] Its woodcuts are anatomic both in a medical sense, in terms of depicting information about the body's parts, and in a sense that has been interpreted as pornographic, in terms of displaying bodies and body parts in a manner intended to arouse sexual feelings.[3] They have often been dismissed as failed scientific representations, particularly in contrast with the more anatomically precise and aesthetically refined images in Vesalius' treatise. For historians of medicine Kenneth Roberts and John Tomlinson, the images are "mannered, even surrealistic," and "quite unconnected with any didactic purpose."[4] For historian Bette Talvacchia, "the result can be hardly less than disturbing, fueled by motives that creep toward the sadistic."[5] More prosaic but just as damning, literary historian Arthur Tilley has described Estienne as an underachiever whose "learning was greater than his science."[6]

The failure of these images, however, is only apparent when judged from the point of view of modern science. In light of Estienne's sixteenth-century humanist context, a different interpretation becomes legible.

Whereas modern anatomy focuses on body parts, often literally removed from their context, and modern pornography focuses a relentless gaze on parts and actions similarly divorced from human experience, the figures in *De dissectione* are emphatically immersed in a context that is at once religious, artistic, philosophical, and erotic. In this essay I will argue that this contextualization, disturbing as it may seem, allows us a glimpse of the erotic role of vision and transformation in Renaissance notions of creativity.

Charles Estienne was born in 1504 into the French Renaissance's most prominent family of printers. His father Henri, brother Robert, and nephew (also named Henri) printed hundreds of translations and commentaries that set standards for French scholarship, typography, and orthography. Their works included influential texts on the Greek, Latin, and French languages; the authoritative New Testament; and the complete works of Plato. While studying classics in Padua in the 1530s Charles became interested in medicine and botany, and he subsequently studied Galenic medicine in Paris as a classmate of Vesalius.[7] As a medical doctor Estienne lectured on anatomy in Paris, as a printer he published over a hundred works, and as a scholar he produced a varied oeuvre including texts on ancient and modern agriculture, clothing, and a road-guide to France.[8] His two monumental projects were an influential eight-hundred page encyclopedia on the ancient and biblical world entitled *Dictionarium historicum, geographicum, poeticum*; and the enigmatic *De dissectione*, in Latin and later in French.[9] Estienne became King Henry II's printer in 1551 and under royal privilege edited and published the complete works of Cicero using the text established by his brother Robert.[10] While Robert was exiled from Catholic France to Calvinist Geneva, Charles ran into financial difficulties and died in 1564, imprisoned for unpaid debts.[11]

In the absence of a patron, Estienne was author and publisher of *De dissectione* throughout its fifteen-year gestation. It was the most expensive work from the famed press of Estienne's stepfather Simon de Colines, and its printing was nearly complete in 1539 when its publication was delayed by a lawsuit between Estienne and surgeon–illustrator Estienne de la Rivière.[12] As such, although published in 1545, two years after Vesalius' *De humani corporis fabrica*, Estienne is considered Vesalius' contemporary or forerunner.

The cultural context surrounding anatomical practices in Estienne's time can be roughly summarized through the following three points: First, as cultural historian Jonathan Sawday describes, the representational tradition of the doctrine of incarnation indicated God's willingness to assume a human form in order to redeem mankind from its sins and corporeal bonds.[13] Incarnation marked the human body as inhabited by a divine grace that could be witnessed and understood. Second, Renaissance man had a newfound faith and fear in his own mind and vision as quasi-divine means to penetrate, understand, and engender change in oneself and the world.[14] This realization elevated sight and the image not only as conveyors of ideas, but as generative and potentially transformative points of contact with order and meaning. Third, the sixteenth-century print revolution, enabled by Gutenberg's invention of moveable type in the previous century and advancements in woodcut techniques, allowed the creation of both the printed bible and the printed and fully illustrated anatomical treatise.

In turn, a more accessible printed bible fueled Protestant emphasis on each individual's encounter with scripture, and particularly the Calvinists' insistence on each person's scrutiny of their inner state. According to Sawday, the Calvinist belief that to understand the human form was to understand God's design brought theological and anatomical interests into alignment.[15] Dissections were often performed on the bodies of executed criminals, which fulfilled the pragmatic need for corpses and aligned with the notion of the anatomy theater as a site for redeeming the criminal body – and, symbolically, fallen mankind – through the sight and knowledge of God's work.[16] It is also relevant that alongside the bible and anatomical treatise, there was a third newly emerging genre of printed material: the pornographic text and image, which historian Lynn Hunt describes as most often being used between 1500 and 1800 in the service of criticizing religious and political authorities.[17]

As an anatomist, scholar, publisher, brother, and uncle of prominent early Calvinists – and as a worldly courtier in contact with the circle of author Pietro Aretino, the Italian writer considered to be the founder of modern literary pornography – Estienne was working at a convergence of these currents in humanist culture.[18]

The three books of *De dissectione*

De dissectione, with sixty-two full-page woodcuts and just over four-hundred pages, comprises three books. Book One introduces anatomy not with dissection, but with a construction of the body, the noblest construction by the noblest of creators, constructed from the bones, cartilage, ligaments, nerves, muscle, veins, arteries, heart, liver, and fat, to the skin, fingernails, and hair. As throughout the treatise, and in accordance with the Renaissance belief in the anatomized body as an active participant in its own dissection and redemption, the figures are depicted alive (Figure 11.1). They are often set outside the city, next to a building or ruin, perhaps emphasizing the liminal state of these bodies – partially made or unmade, between life and death, at the margins of civilized society yet still engaged with it.

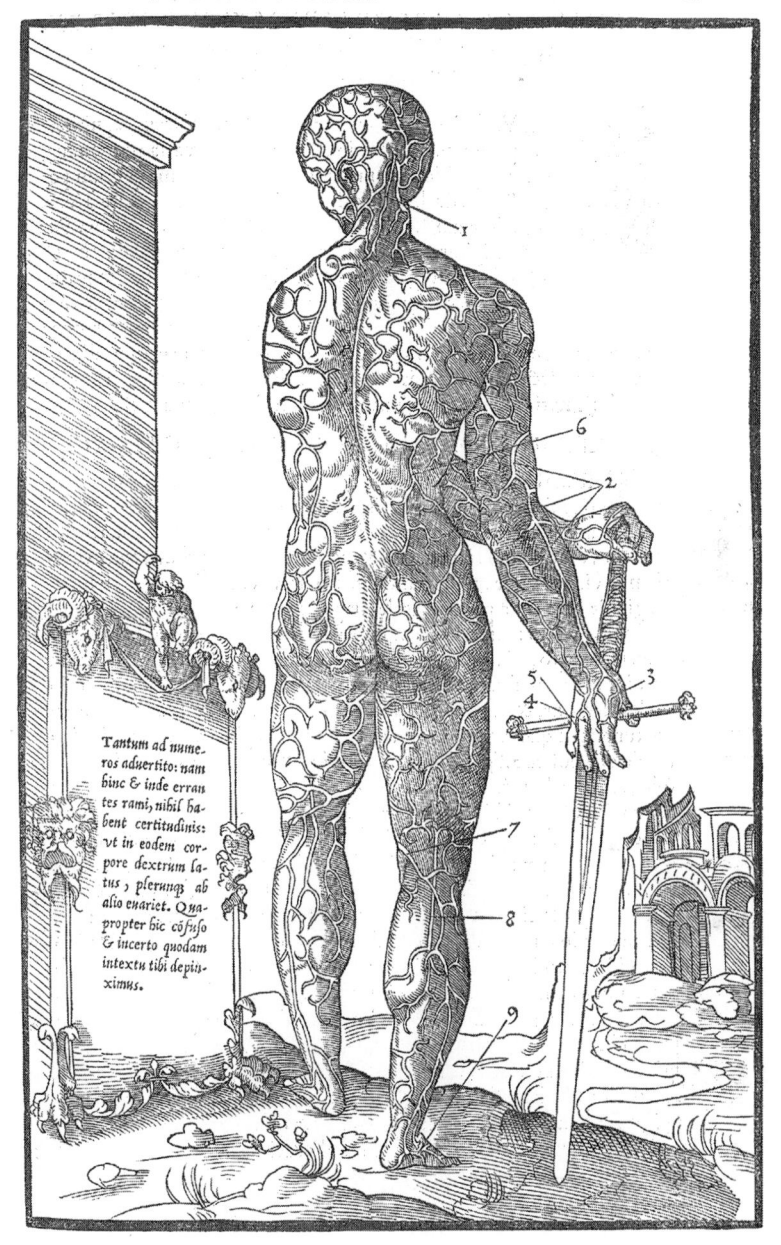

Tantum ad nume-
ros aduertito: nam
hinc & inde erran
tes rami, nihil ha-
bent certitudinis:
vt in eodem cor-
pore dextrum la-
tus, plerunq; ab
alio euariet. Qua-
propter hic cõfuso
& incerto quodam
intextu tibi depin-
ximus.

Figure 11.1 Book One showing veins and arteries. Estienne, *De dissectione*, 135

Once this body is made, it is unmade in Book Two, which shows inset views into the dissected body. Whereas today we would expect a catalog of body parts or a series of sections (or, more likely, a three-dimensional model generated from simulations or digitally controlled slices or scans), these woodcuts narrate the process of dissecting a single body. The series follows the order of anatomical dissection at the time, from lower abdomen to upper abdomen, throat and, finally, the head. In this way, Book Two serves as a companion to, or replacement for, a visceral encounter with a body in the anatomical theater (Figure 11.2). As the dissection progresses, the body becomes increasingly precarious, with the skin stitched to close previously opened areas and the body propped up by natural or architectural fragments whose state of ruin mirrors that of the body.

At a certain point, this body sheds its macerations and once again becomes graceful and nearly whole. Book Two turns its attention to the head, illustrated through eight figures in contrived yet elegant positions. The settings mirror this relative grace: fragments and ruins give way in part to more elaborate architectural settings that play on the ambiguity of interior and exterior. In three cases, windows frame a view to the sky, and bi-lobal and circular openings mimic the sectioned head, drawing an analogy between these two entities that offer communication between the inside and outside (Figure 11.3). The section cut through the head is always what we would call transverse – or, perhaps in Estienne's context, a horizontal cut separating the lower from the upper, the bodily from the celestial.

Book Three opens with ten woodcuts devoted to the female reproductive system, which gives us the treatise's only images of women. The text discusses the womb and other female anatomy, as well as techniques for handling various situations during pregnancies and births. In the woodcuts, the women display themselves in luxurious architectural settings, usually interior and above all in bedrooms with plush drapery and beds. Their legs are spread and they lounge in graceful and inviting poses, seemingly consenting to their own dissection and participating in the display of their sexual organs and interiors (Figure 11.4). In one case, a figure lifts two placentas to reveal twin fetuses in her flayed womb.[19] These sexualized images comprise the work's final new full-page woodcuts, the climactic culmination of building and dissecting the human body. Beyond this point, the book continues with detailed discussion of a few chosen parts: the eye, muscles, and spine, removed from their context of body and world and illustrated by smaller images inset in the text. Finally, the book ends with recommendations for dissection methods, tools, and the anatomy theater.

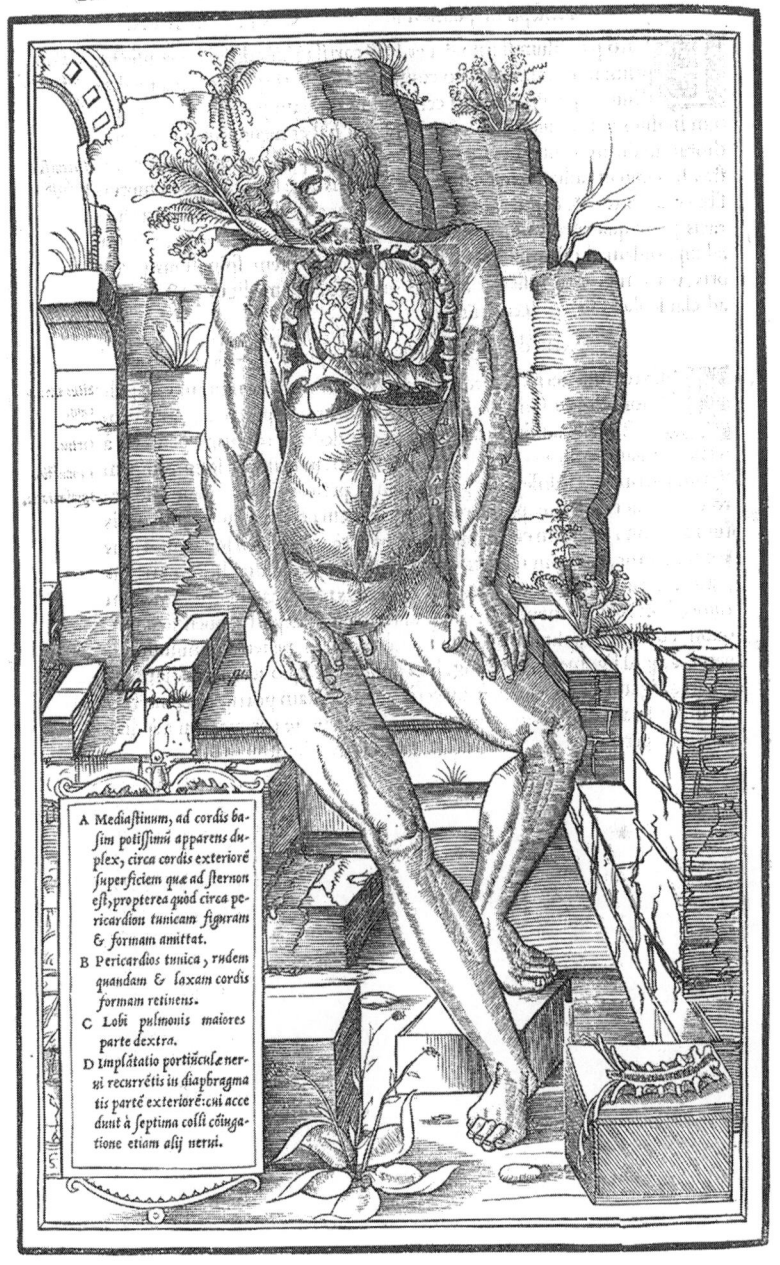

A Mediaſtinum, ad cordis ba-
ſim potiſſimū apparens du-
plex, circa cordis exteriorē
ſuperficiem quæ ad ſternon
eſt, propterea quòd circa pe-
ricardion tunicam figuram
& formam amittat.
B Pericardios tunica, rudem
quandam & laxam cordis
formam retinens.
C Lobi pulmonis maiores
parte dextra.
D Implãtatio portiũculæ nerui recurrētis in diaphragma
tis partē exteriorē:cui acce
dunt à ſeptima colli cõiuga-
tione etiam alij nerui.

Figure 11.2 Book Two showing the lungs. Estienne, *De dissectione*, 210

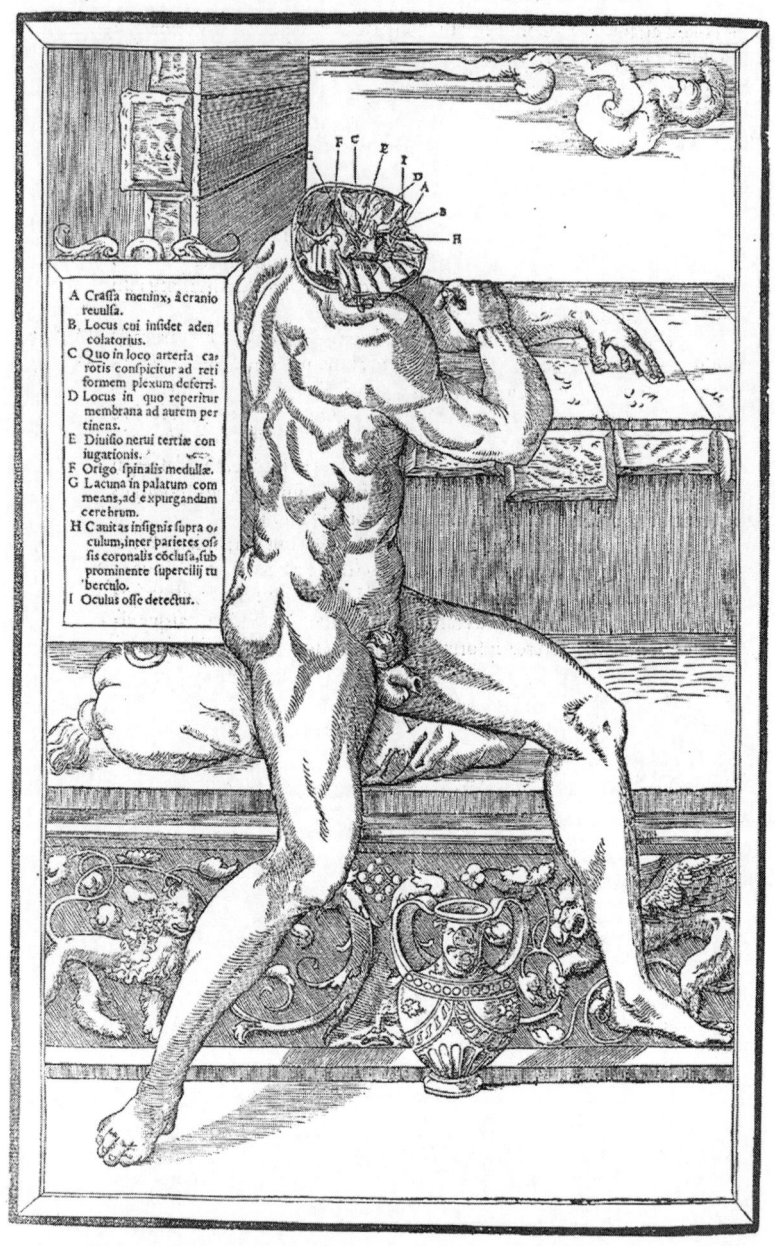

A Crassa meninx, à cranio
  reuulsa.
B. Locus cui insidet aden
  colatorius.
C Quo in loco arteria ca-
  rotis conspicitur ad reti
  formem plexum deferri.
D Locus in quo reperitur
  membrana ad aurem per
  tinens.
E Diuisio nerui tertiæ con
  iugationis.
F Origo spinalis medullæ.
G Lacuna in palatum com
  means, ad expurgandum
  cerebrum.
H Cauitas insignis supra o-
  culum, inter parietes os-
  sis coronalis côclusa, sub
  prominente supercilij tu
  berculo.
I Oculus osse detectus.

Figure 11.3 Book Two (after Caraglio's Mars) showing structures surrounding
the brain. Estienne, *De dissectione*, 250

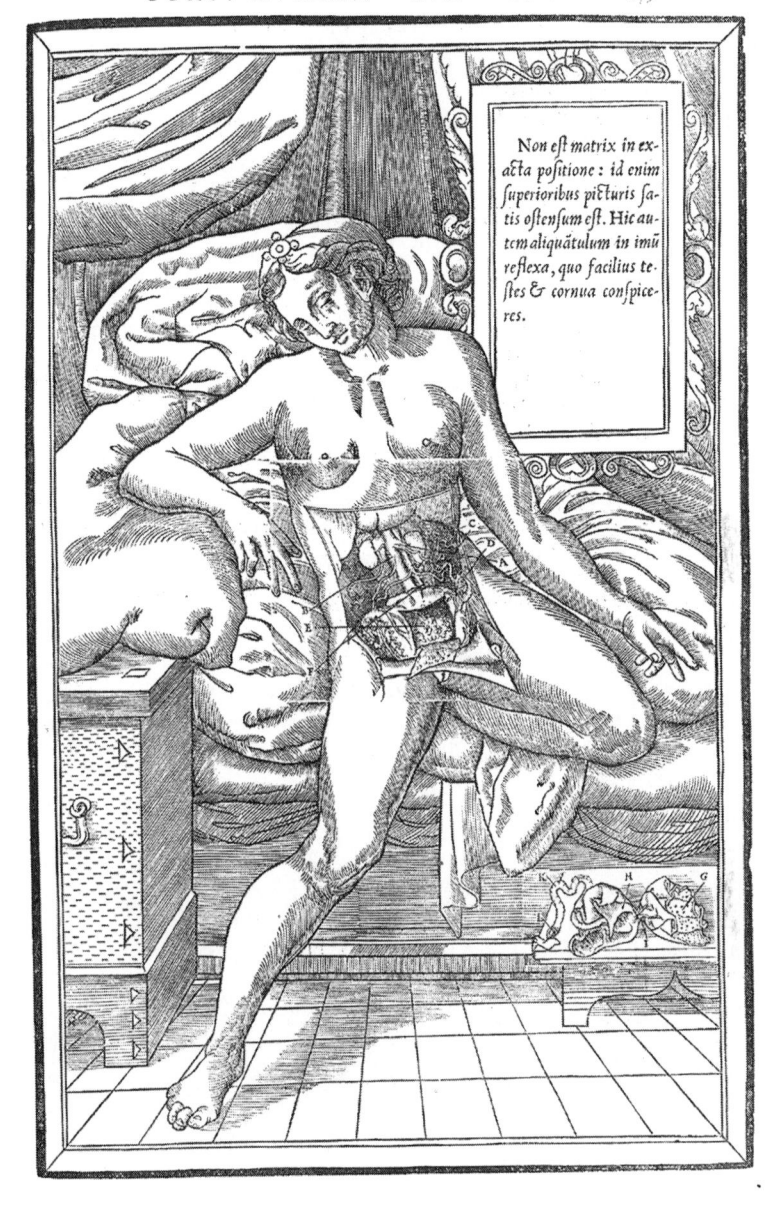

Non est matrix in ex-
acta positione: id enim
superioribus picturis sa-
tis ostensum est. Hic au-
tem aliquatulum in imu
reflexa, quo facilius te-
stes & cornua conspice-
res.

Figure 11.4 Book Three (after Caraglio's Venus) showing the womb. Estienne,
De dissectione, 210

Loves of the gods

Our eyes are drawn back to the young women at the opening of Book Three. Posed in suggestive positions, these women call attention to themselves in a manner unlike any others in the treatise. Talvacchia and medical historian Charles Kellett have traced nine of the ten female figures back to two drawings by Rosso Fiorentino and eighteen by Perino del Vaga for Caraglio's *Loves of the Gods*, a series of engravings depicting pairs of Greek gods in erotic embraces (Figure 11.5).[20] The women were not whisked directly out of Caraglio but underwent two transformations before the anatomical views were inset in their torsos. First, each goddess was redrawn without her male god, a process that required slight adjustments to her limbs. Second, the settings were changed from the mythical to the mortal realm, exchanging putties and divine allegorical symbols for more human, architectural surroundings.

Estienne's choice of these women remains enigmatic. *Loves of the Gods* was popular in France and particularly in the humanist court of François I, an avid patron of Italian erotic art. As such, it seems that the figures were meant to be recognized. Talvacchia suggests that Estienne wanted to benefit from the "cover" of a mythological setting to legitimize otherwise unabashedly erotic images[21] Kellett, in contrast, suggests that it was a question of convenience, possibly reusing figures drawn by Rosso for his own unfinished anatomy.[22] Neither explanation is satisfying. First if the mythological setting legitimized the erotic, then the exchange of mythological and divine attributes and environment for earthly and mortal ones seems implausible. On the other hand, the overall cost and elaborateness of the treatise, and the procedures necessary to adapt the figures while retaining the original reference, seem too involved to make convenience a likely choice – particularly given the sophistication of Estienne's humanist and courtly audience in reading visual quotes and subtle allegories. I propose another reading.

The love of mortals

Plato's *Symposium* contains a whimsical fable told by Aristophanes on the origins of human difference and desire. As Sawday observes, this tale became a crucial text in the Renaissance exegesis of Christian and Neoplatonic sources, and Estienne would have been familiar with it through his family's publications of Plato.[23] In this story humans were originally spherical with two heads, four arms, four legs joined at the torso, and a terrible hubris. Zeus plotted their punishment:

> "Methinks [said Zeus] I have a plan which will humble their pride and improve their manners; men shall continue to exist, but I will

Figure 11.5 Jacopo Caraglio, *Mars and Venus* (after Perino del Vaga), Istituto Nazionale per la Grafica, Rome, FC5934

cut them in two" . . . and as he cut them one after another, he bade Apollo give the face and the half of the neck a turn in order that man might contemplate the section of himself: he would thus learn a lesson of humility.[24]

The anatomical subject in the sixteenth century was a sacrificial body with many meanings: as it was often an executed criminal, the body on the dissection table embodied the fallen mortal and, therefore, the sacrificial body of Christ. Could it, for Estienne, also have evoked Plato's fallen mortals, made to consider their sins through the site of their own dissection? Aristophanes continues:

> Apollo was also bidden to heal their wounds and compose their forms. So he gave a turn to the face and pulled the skin from the sides all over that which in our language is called the belly . . . and took out most of the wrinkles . . . he left a few, however, in the region of the belly and navel, as a memorial of the primeval state . . . each of us when separated, having one side only, like a flat fish, is but the indenture of a man, and he is always looking for his other half.[25]

The belly, the container for the womb, was where the original spherical man was cut in half and where this wound was healed; Zeus' dissection ends one life and engenders another. In his narrative of the transgression of life both through death in dissection and through fertility, Estienne mimics this primeval anatomy.

The goddesses of *Loves of the Gods* were banished from their divine height to earth and severed from their godly lovers. Estienne's women, however, are shown not in the moment of their fall, but their ascent: arms and legs spread for an embrace which eluded them in life, they seek a vision of wisdom, a revelation of their primeval wholeness through the contemplation of their section. Once mortals have fallen, as Plato writes in *Phaedrus*, they forever desire to re-grow their wings through love, in order to ascend and glimpse a wisdom normally hidden from our mortal eyes.[26] Peering into the body's secrets through dissection promises such a glimpse, bringing anatomist, anatomized, and audience closer to God through a revelation of his work.

The womb has long been understood to emit a symbol of death in its menstrual blood while offering transcendence of death through its fertility. In sixteenth-century anatomy, which was understood as a process intended to ritually transcend mortal death, the womb was a particularly privileged site. The womb is what Vesalius exposes in the dissection on his frontispiece, under the masterful hand of the anatomist at the center of a swirling crowd of onlookers (Figure 11.6).[27] Like Vesalius, I would suggest, Estienne centers his anatomy on the womb as the most apt site for this allegory of fall and ascent, decay and fertility.

What happened to the male gods once separated from their lovers? Caraglio's Mars, the lover of Venus and possessor of a generative virility, appears as the penultimate male figure in the text. Twisting his body to offer

Figure 11.6 Andreas Vesalius, *De humani corporis fabrica libri septem*. (Basel: Ex officina Joannis Oporini, 1543), frontispiece

the viewer a glimpse into his sectioned brain, his head is tipped enough that were his brain filled with fluid, it would spill. On the ground between his legs is a vase, positioned so that it might receive this flow from his brain – or more directly, from his suggestively spout-like penis poised above the vessel. The suggested passage between brain, penis, and vessel recalls the theory of generation that Leonardo da Vinci illustrated in his sketch of human copulation. Leonardo, who like Estienne was brought from Italy to the court of François I, depicts the fluid of male fertility passing from the brain, through the spinal cord, and out the male member. Likewise, a close-up of the sectioned head reveals that Estienne has chosen this figure to represent (Figure 11.3 at F) the connection between the head and the neck in the beginning of the spinal cord. This section also cuts (Figure 11.3 at I) through the eye.

These two woodcuts depicting the male brain and the female womb are brought together in their unfulfilled embrace, separated by the divide between Books Two and Three. They are elaborated with more care than the books' other woodcuts. I would like to suggest that Estienne brought these two together in order to describe the male brain and female womb as generators of human fertility – a mysterious and crucial process that, like sixteenth-century anatomical dissection, transcends our mortal condition. On the other hand, what modern viewers would consider the site and deliverers of male fertility, the genital organs including the testes and vas deferens, have no significant place in the treatise.

Genius as Eros

The idea of male fertility originating in the head recalls Marsilio Ficino's emphasis on the soul and vision, the sixteenth century's newfound faith in mankind's creative capacities, and as historian D. T. Starnes describes, the Renaissance concept of genius as developed through interpretations of Plato's *Timaeus* and *Apology*.[28] Ficino, translator of Plato and the most influential Christian Neoplatonist of the fifteenth century, had insisted that the human soul was divine, with immense creative powers. Creativity, however, depended on our ability to partake of divine order through vision, through which we can receive a glimpse of the universe's original and divine order. Vision in the sixteenth century was as carnal as it was celestial; for Ficino, a lover's desirous gaze could pierce and wound his beloved. According to architectural historians Alberto Pérez-Gómez and Louise Pelletier, the Dominican philosopher Giordano Bruno, likewise, found an erotically tangible vision in the sight of the magus, who had to both seduce and fall in love with his subject in order for his magic to take effect.[29] Charles Estienne, in his *Dictionarium historicum et poeticum* of 1553, ties the notion of genius and its creative (literally, generative) capacity to this kind of vision that is at once lustful and divine:

> The ancients called Genius the god of nature, who had the power of generating all things; hence each thing was said to have its genius. . . . Some suppose Genius to be the soul or mind itself, or a god, or a spirit, which incites human beings to pleasure or lust. Therefore the ancients named those Geniales who were much concerned with external appearance and pleasure. Hence the proverb, to indulge one's Genius.[30]

As Estienne's description of the spinal cord's central canal is considered to be his most important scientific contribution to anatomy, it is fitting that he should include an allegory endowing it with a significant role as the conduit of imagination and fertility.[31] Brought together, I would suggest that the head and womb offer a potent image of fertility in the creative genius of lust and the sight of beauty.

In turn, the sixteenth-century reader's appreciation of these eroticized drawings might recall another experience of Venus' charms, implicating the reader in the visceral and carnal nature of anatomy while turning the treatise's pages. That the dissected views into the women's bodies comprise a mere two to five percent of their images' printed areas should suggest that the explicit depiction of anatomical detail, as separate from its context, was not the priority.[32] Rather, the dissected views are literally inserted into a rich, subtle, and much wider visual context. Because of their small size, even as the dissected women willingly invite the reader's gaze, there are limits to what you can see. Perhaps the experience of peering into these images serves as a proxy for being in the anatomy theater, straining to catch a glimpse of what you are told is there. The reader's experience also mimics the ultimate mystery of bodily knowledge. As Sawday observes about anatomical practices in general, "the 'thing' – the secret place, the core of bodily pleasure or knowledge of the body – always escapes representation."[33] This elusive character, I would suggest, is less pornographic than it is erotic, inviting and endlessly deferring our desirous gaze. In this sense, I would argue that these sexualized images were not in their context primarily degrading or, in Talvacchia's terms, sadistic. Instead, they offered a means through which mortal men and women could strive towards an encounter with celestial order, by becoming inspired towards creativity and fertility.

What strikes us as surprising and unsettling in *De dissectione* is that Estienne places the human body not against a background of objectivity, but rather, embeds it through allegory and rhetoric within layers of meanings and intentions. Visually representing a cut and opened body was a relatively new process in Estienne's time, and it was also not a neutral one. *De dissectione* is at once erudite, with a deep knowledge of Galenic medicine and historical references; scientific, with "numerous excellent and original observations contained in the text"; erotic, with its opened and suggestively posed women and men; and philosophical and religious, with its cosmological and ethical implications. Vesalius' much more famous work, in comparison, has been shown to be just as laden with symbolism, but his more polished visuals allow us to gloss over his carnal and theological content while admiring his prescient modernity.[34] Estienne's treatise has images that are not fully formed, contradictory, and less beautiful to our eyes – and they give us pause.

Notes

1 C. E. Kellett, "Two Anatomies," *Medical History* 8 (1964): 343.
2 Charles Estienne, *De dissectione partium corporis humani libri tres* (Paris: Apud S. Colinaeum, 1545).
3 Although modern use of the word "pornography" is a nineteenth century phenomenon, according to Lynn Hunt, the modern pornographic tradition begins in sixteenth century Italy and 17th century France and England. Lynn Hunt, "Introduction," in *The Invention of Pornography: Obscenity and the Origins of Modernity, 1500-1800*, ed. Lynn Hunt (New York: Zone Books, 1996), 10, 13–14. Sawday describes the images of women in *De dissectione* as "posed in an extravagantly sexualized manner." Jonathan Sawday, *The Body Emblazoned: Dissection and the Human Body in Renaissance Culture* (New York: Routledge, 1995), 194.
4 K.B. Roberts and J.D.W. Tomlinson, *The Fabric of the Body: European Traditions of Anatomical Illustration* (Oxford: Oxford University Press, 1992), 171–2.
5 Bette Talvacchia, *Taking Positions: On the Erotic in Renaissance Culture* (Princeton: Princeton University Press, 1999), 187.
6 Arthur Tilley, "Humanism Under Francis I," *The English Historical Review* 15, no. 59 (July 1900): 456–78.
7 As Roberts and Tomlinson describe, Estienne was awarded his medical doctorate in 1542. Roberts and Tomlinson, *Fabric of the Body*, 168.
8 Charles Estienne, *Praedium Rusticum* (Paris: Apud Carolum Stephanum, 1554); Lazare de Baïf and Charles Estienne, *De re vestiaria libellus* (Lyon: Gaspar & Melchior Trechsel, 1536); and Charles Estienne, *La guide des chemins de France, reueue & augmentee pour la troisiesme fois. Les fleuues du royaume de France, aussi augmentez* (Paris: Charles Estienne, Imprimeur du Roy, 1553).
9 Charles Estienne, *Dictionarium historicum, geographicum, poeticum* (Paris: Apud Carolum Stephanum, 1553); and Charles Estienne, *La dissection des parties du corps humain* (Paris: Apud S. Colinaeum, 1546).
10 Marcus Tullius Cicero, *Opera Omnia* (Paris: Charles Estienne, 1555).
11 For Estienne's biography, see Jules Balteau, Marius Barroux and Michel Prévost, "Estienne," in *Dictionnaire de Biographie Française* (Paris: Letouze et Ané, 1933), 95; and Fred Schrieber, *The Hanes Collection of Estienne Publications: From Book Collecting to Scholarly Resource* (Chapel Hill: University of North Carolina Press, 1984), 1–8.

12 On the expense of *De dissectione*, see Kellett, "Two Anatomies," 343. On the lawsuit, see George P. Burris, "The Illustrations in the *De Dissectione Partium Corporis Humani Libri Tres* (1545) of Charles Estienne (1504-1564)," *Proceedings of the Oklahoma Academy of Science* 46 (1966): 151.

13 Sawday, *Body Emblazoned*, 106.

14 Katharine Park discusses belief in the power of vision in the context of sixteenth-century holy anatomy. Katharine Park, *Secrets of Women: Gender, Generation, and the Origins of Human Dissection* (New York: Zone Books, 2006), 52, 255.

15 Sawday, *Body Emblazoned*, 106.

16 Sawday discusses how this symbolism helped to overcome the taboo of opening and looking inside the body. Sawday, *Body Emblazoned*, 84.

17 Hunt, "Introduction," 10.

18 Kellett untangles the ties that linked Estienne to Aretino within the French court. Kellett, "Two Anatomies," 345.

19 Charles Estienne, *De dissectione*, 276.

20 Kellett, "Two Anatomies," 344–5; and Talvacchia, *Taking Positions*, 164. See also Monique Kornell, "Rosso Fiorentino and the Anatomical Text," *The Burlington Magazine* 131, no. 1041 (December 1989), 842–7; and D. Kenneth Keele, "Leonardo da Vinci's Influence on Renaissance Anatomy," *Medical History* 8, no. 4 (October 1964): 369.

21 Talvacchia, *Taking Positions*, 166.

22 Kellett, "Two Anatomies," 344.

23 Sawday, *Body Emblazoned*, 185.

24 Plato, *Symposium* 190c–e, in *Selected Dialogues of Plato*, trans. Benjamin Jowett (New York: Modern Library, 2001.

25 Ibid., *Symposium*, 190e–191d in *Selected Dialogues of Plato*.

26 Ibid., *Phaedrus*, 250a–252c.

27 Andreas Vesalius, *De humani corporis fabrica libri septem*. (Basel: Ex officina Joannis Oporini, 1543).

28 D.T. Starnes, "The Figure Genius in the Renaissance," *Studies in the Renaissance* 11 (1964): 234.

29 Alberto Pérez-Gómez and Louise Pelletier, *Architectural Representation and the Perspective Hinge* (Cambridge: The MIT Press), 330.

30 Estienne, *Dictionarium*, 239. Translation by Dewitt T. Starnes.

31 On Estienne's description of the spinal cord, see Antoine Augustin Renouard, *Annales de l'imprimerie des Estienne; ou, Histoire de la famille des Estienne et de ses editions* (Paris: J. Renouard et cie, 1843), 356; and Gernot Rath, "Charles Estienne: Contemporary of Vesalius," *Medical History* 8, no. 4 (October 1964): 357.

32 Roberts and Tomlinson go further to estimate that the dissected areas comprise "no more than one-fiftieth of the printed area." Roberts and Tomlinson, *Fabric of the Body*, 172.

33 Sawday, *Body Emblazoned*, 12.

34 For an example of Vesalius' symbolism, see Sawday's discussion of his frontispiece. Sawday, *Body Emblazoned*, 69–70.

12

THE TACTILE LEGACY OF ALVAR AALTO AND ITS RELEVANCE TO CONTEMPORARY PRACTICE

Kenneth Frampton

Among the pioneers of the Modern Movement Alvar Aalto remains the one figure whose seminal contribution to the field seems just as valid now as it was at the end of his life. This claim may be justified on many levels, not least of which is the inherent sustainability of Aalto's architecture, sustainable above all in his preference for using brick and wood which remain the two materials with the least embodied energy in terms of production. Apart from this attribute these materials would also ensure the social accessibility of his work and it is my belief that Aalto's manner, particularly over the years from 1934 to 1968, was more accessible to the man-in-the-street than the architecture of any other pioneer whose work came to maturity over the same period. As Eduard and Claudia Neuenschwander were to demonstrate, in their study of the first decade of Aalto's post-war work, in their book *Alvar Aalto and Finnish Architecture* of 1954, Aalto's production was a symbiotic extension of Finnish environmental culture in every conceivable sense, encompassing not only his lifelong allusion to National Romanticism but also his recognition of the fact that the origin of Finnish vernacular culture was ultimately grounded in a perennial interface between wood, water and rock.

It was precisely Aalto's sensitivity towards his native culture which enabled him to render his architecture accessible to society as a whole and it is this surely that is still one of the most fundamental challenges confronting the profession today, namely, how to continue with a liberative project of the Modern Movement, while also conveying a sense of security without descending into kitsch. Aalto recognized this challenge well before many of his contemporaries and it is my contention that through his biorealist corporeal vision of modernity Finland came closer than any other modernizing state to resolving this dilemma, particularly over the last two thirds of the twentieth century. In this regard, Scandinavian functionalism was always more nuanced than the normative aspirations of the Neue Sachlichkeit as this prevailed throughout the 1930s, particularly in Germany, Holland and Switzerland. This contrast between so called funkis manner and the productive preoccupations of the Neue Sachlichkeit was already manifest in Gunnar Asplund's Stockholm Exhibition of 1930 which, as a subset of the international style, was softer in its syntax and thereby more humanly accessible than the Deutsche Werkbund Weissenhof Exhibition, staged in Stuttgart three years before. This shift exerted a decisive influence on Aalto as we may judge from his initial response to the Stockholm Exhibition:

> The deliberate social message that the Stockholm Exhibition is intended to convey is expressed in the architectural language of pure spontaneous joy. There is a festive elegance, but also a childlike lack of inhibition about it all . . . this is not a composition of glass, stone and steel as a visitor who despises functionalism might imagine, it is a composition of houses, flags, flowers, fireworks, happy people and clean table cloths.[1]

Aalto sympathized with the latent social democratic ethos as this had been conceived by the director of the Swedish Arts and Crafts Society, Gregor Paulsson. The funkis sensibility seems to have arisen out of a some kind of symbiotic exchange between Asplund and Aalto just prior to the Exhibition for with its cylindrical skylights, lacquered mushroom columns, wooden handrails, and louvered ceiling lamps, Aalto's Turun Sanomat Building, realized in Turku in 1929 evidenced a subtly nuanced sensibility within the overall severity of its cubic form. In fact Aalto's Turku building may have prompted Asplund to liberate himself from the rigid civility of Nordic Classicism not only on the occasion of the Stockholm exhibition but also in his Brandenburg department store, completed in Stockholm in 1935. This was the same year in which Aalto realized his Viipuri Library, the initial design for which had been influenced by Asplund's Stockholm public library of 1926. With its cylindrical anti-glare skylights, ergonomic handrails, Artek timber furniture and its serpentine acoustic ceiling, the Viipuri Library achieved a new kind of tactile functionalism that went beyond the populism of the Stockholm Exhibition (Figures 12.1 and 12.2).

Among the facts brought to light by Göran Schildt's biography of Aalto of 1984 is the strong bond that obtained between Aalto and Paulsson.

Figure 12.1 Alvar Aalto, Viipuri Library, interior photo; image courtesy of Alvar Aalto Foundation

Figure 12.2 Alvar Aalto, Viipuri Library, interior photo; image courtesy of Alvar Aalto Foundation

According to Schildt, Aalto was deeply affected by the cultural socialism of Paulsson's book of 1916, entitled *The New Architecture*. Aside from sympathizing with Paulson's progressive view, the foundation of Artek in 1935 enabled Aalto to realize Paulsson's ideal of industrially produced, low cost quality furniture to be made available to society as a whole. In fact, Aalto's Artek furniture in bent and laminated wood would prove to be one of the keys to the accessibility of his architecture; a quality which without compromising the liberative drive of the modern project transcended the reductive functionalism of the European avant-garde which Aalto had encountered at the end of the 1920s when he acquired for his own use Marcel Breuer's Wassily chair in tubular steel. In his seminal address "Rationalism and Man," given to the Swedish Society of Industrial Design, in 1935 Aalto argued that however rational and efficient it may be from a productive standpoint, the high thermal conductivity of steel was unsympathetic to human touch. In his address Aalto extended this critique to formalist light fittings, such as the Bauhaus white opalescent spherical lights much favored by the Neue Sachlichkeit particularly when suspended in the center of the room. In his anti-glare counter-argument in favor of indirect and/or diffused light, Aalto would come close to anticipating Richard Neutra's concept of biorealism as this was advanced in his book *Survival through Design* of 1954.

Aalto's tactile approach to both form and material first emerges in his own house constructed in the Helsinki suburb of Munkkiniemi between 1934 and 1936 (Figure 12.3). Comprised of whitewashed load-bearing brickwork and vertical timber siding, this is for the first time when we will encounter this particular juxtaposition in his work, the juxtaposition of milled timber, the opposition that is between milled timber cladding and rough timber balustrading from which only the bark has been stripped; the two being brought together in conjunction with plate glass and a rubble stone walling. This modern reinterpretation of the Finnish vernacular will come more fully into its own with his Finnish Pavilion designed for the World Exhibition staged in Paris in 1937 (Figure 12.4). This last was built almost exclusively of wood consisted of single story open-sided gallery, which culminated in a top-lit exhibition hall clad, on all four sides, with ribbed timber siding. The exhibition, staged at the height of the Spanish Civil War, was followed in 1939 by the New York World's Fair and by the outbreak of the Second World War. In Finland these events were accompanied by a three and a half month bitter struggle against the Soviet Union, the so-called Winter War, a conflict, which will be resumed in the so-called Continuation War of 1941 to 1945.

Alvar and Aino Aalto first visited the United States in 1938 and Alvar Aalto would return there in the following year to supervise the construction of the Finnish National Pavilion at the New York World's Fair. Aalto's

Figure 12.3 Alvar Aalto, Aalto's Munkiniemi House, 1934 photo, image courtesy of Alvar Aalto Foundation

pavilion in New York was another tour de force in timber construction, which as an interior was virtually an inversion of the Paris pavilion (Figure 12.5). At the same time, the thematic was virtually identical, namely, the representation of Finland as a rising industrial nation, based on a forest economy and committed to a social-democratic program of modernization. In physical terms this pavilion was a fifty-two foot high cavernous space dominated by an undulating inclined wall made up of a reiteration of vertical timber patterns and divided horizontally into a geometrically progressive sequence of four successive tiers, respectively representing the country, the people, the workaday world, and, at the lowest level, the products of the national timber industry, which varied from the rolls of newsprint to skis, propellers and Aalto's bent and laminated Artek furniture. Above this tactile display of industrial products on the ground floor, the various facets of Finnish life were represented by large blown up photographs of varying size and shape. There was something about the rhythmic dynamism of this montage that recalled El Lissitzky's agit prop setting for the Soviet contribution at the International Hygiene Exhibition staged in Dresden in 1930. What was unique here, however, was Aalto's particular approach to the plasticity of the

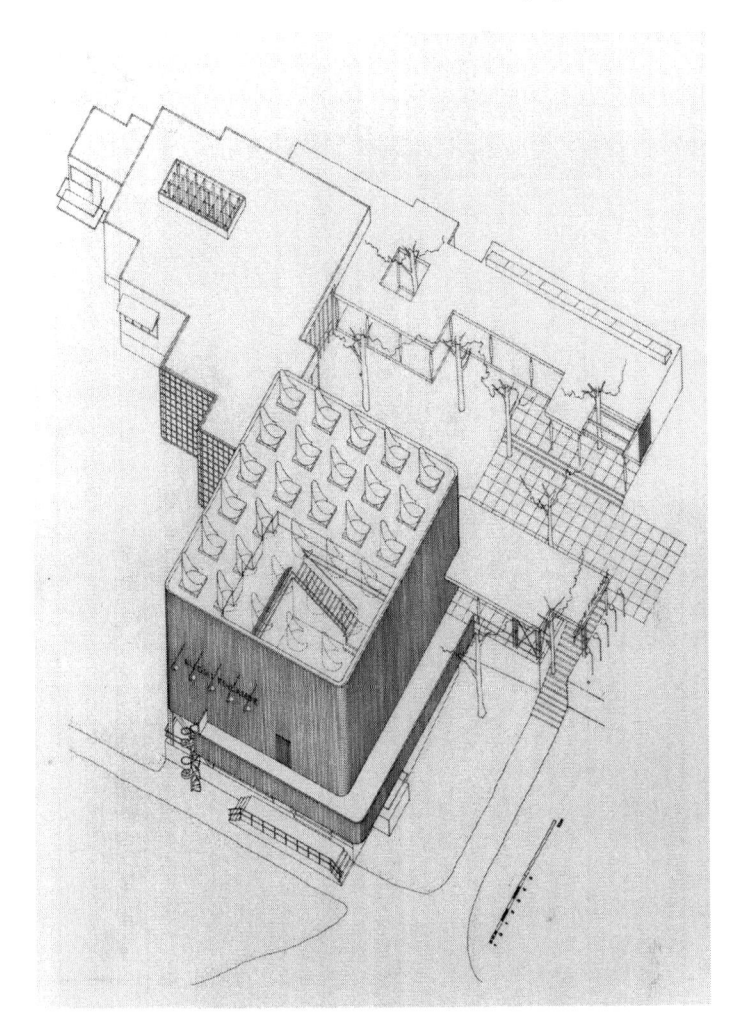

Figure 12.4 Alvar Aalto, Finnish Pavilion, Paris, 1937 axonometric view; image courtesy of Museum of Finnish Architecture

space which, as with his famous Savoy vase of 1936, derived from his feeling for the organicism of the Finnish landscape inundated with lakes.

Apart from this vision of a mutually beneficial interplay between nature and culture, Aalto, like Gregor Paulsson, was convinced that a truly liberative modernity could not be achieved without the integration of architecture and design with radical social reform and it is this conviction no doubt that

Figure 12.5 Alvar Aalto, Finnish Pavilion, New York, 1939 perspective; image courtesy of Alvar Aalto Foundation

lay behind his traumatic disillusionment when the Soviet Union gratuitously invaded Finland in 1939. Around this time Aalto, together with Paulson and his wife, Aino Aalto, would become preoccupied with cultivating a Third Way between the totalitarianism of the USSR and the freewheeling rapacity of American capitalism. Their particular brand of welfare state humanism was to have been proselytized through publication of an international magazine entitled *The Human Side*, a project which, despite having selected topics and authors for the first issue, was totally eclipsed by the outbreak of the Second World War.

Aalto's successive exhibition pavilions for the Finnish state exemplified this progressive ideology while, at the same time, affording him occasions on which to demonstrate the organic heterotopia of his emerging maturity, first, in 1937, in a quasi-constructivist reinterpretation of the Karelian vernacular, and second, in 1939, when he produced a mesa-like metaphor for the edge of a forest in the form of an undulating cliff-like face which will be later transposed into the brick escarpment of the Baker House dormitory block, completed to his designs in Cambridge, Massachusetts, in 1949 (Figures 12.6.a and 12.6.b).

Figure 12.6.a Alvar Aalto, Baker House, plan; image courtesy of Alvar Aalto Foundation

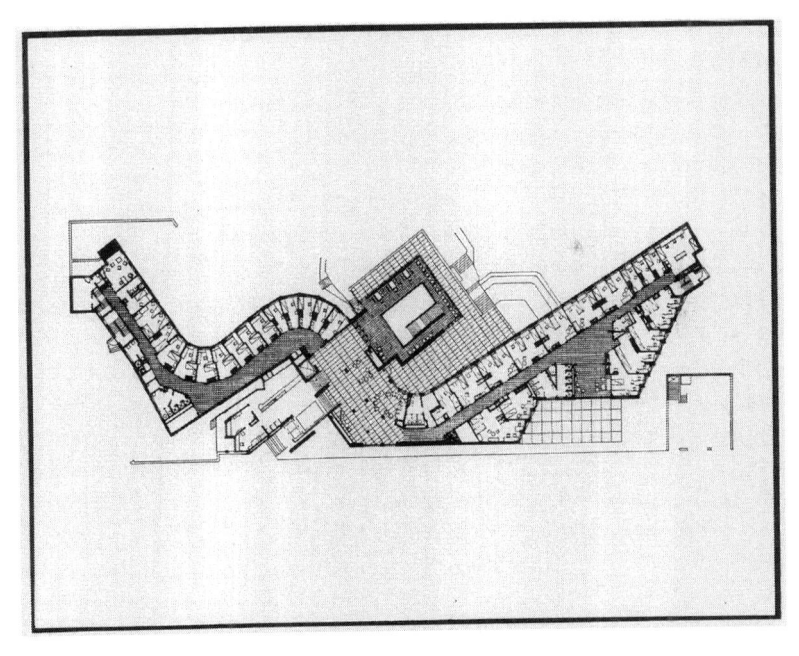

Figure 12.6.b Alvar Aalto, Baker House, perspective; image courtesy of Alvar Aalto Foundation

The Villa Mairea, designed for Mairea Ahlstrom and her husband Harry Gullichsen and completed in Noormarku, ten years before in 1939, was the apotheosis of Aalto's reinterpreted Karelian vernacular which, despite the evident Japaneserie of its black lacquered columns bound in cane, prompted the hypersensitive critic Gustaf Strengell to see it as the new Niemela farm, by which Strengell was referring to the Helsinki open air museum of vernacular buildings, founded at Seurasaami in 1909.

Aalto's move into brick as the primary material came with the brick-faced pulp mill that he designed for Ahlstrom; a vast industrial plant built on a backwoods site in Sunila in 1938. However, this shift did not entail any kind of aversion to wood as we may judge from Aalto's Otaniemi sports hall and the Karhula Glassworks Warehouse, both dating from the early 1950s and both demonstrating quite brilliant tectonic exercises in the use of timber structure. Much the same may be found in the numerous industrial structures that he built over this same period as in the timber clad, steel-framed Varkaus saw mill of 1946.

Aalto's most comprehensive projection at this time in relation to Finland's rapidly expanding timber industry was his regional plan for Imatra worked out over the years 1947–53 (Figure 12.7). In this and other regional plans of the period, Aalto developed his somewhat mythical concept of the "forest town," as opposed to the Anglo-American Garden City as first fully exemplified in Unwin and Parker's Hampstead Garden Suburb of 1905. In total contrast, Aalto's Imatra plan posited a relatively dense cellular residential aggregation which would be integrated as interstitial form into an organic patchwork of arable land, densely wooded areas and industrial enclaves, the whole being fed by a continuous linear road and rail infrastructure, thereby establishing a continuous nature/culture mosaic in which anything as altruistically controlling and conformist as a public park would have been totally out of place.

It was a sign of postwar austerity that Aalto's next canonical building was not a luxury villa but a small municipal building, namely, the brick-clad Saynatsalo Town Hall which was the winning design of a competition held in 1949, the building being realized two years later. Comprising a spiraling mass-form which culminated in the mono-pitched roof of its council chamber, Saynatsalo, comprising both the town hall and the local library, was laid out around the square arena of an elevated atrium situated one floor above the general level of the street (Figures 12.8.a, 12.8.b and 12.8.c). This podium would be accessed by two different kinds of stairways, the one monumental in dark granite, and the other a roughly stepped approach covered with grass, where the rudimentary risers were made of split tree trunks held in place by stakes. Where the former, dressed in stone so as to signify civic deportment, brought one to the level of the public library and

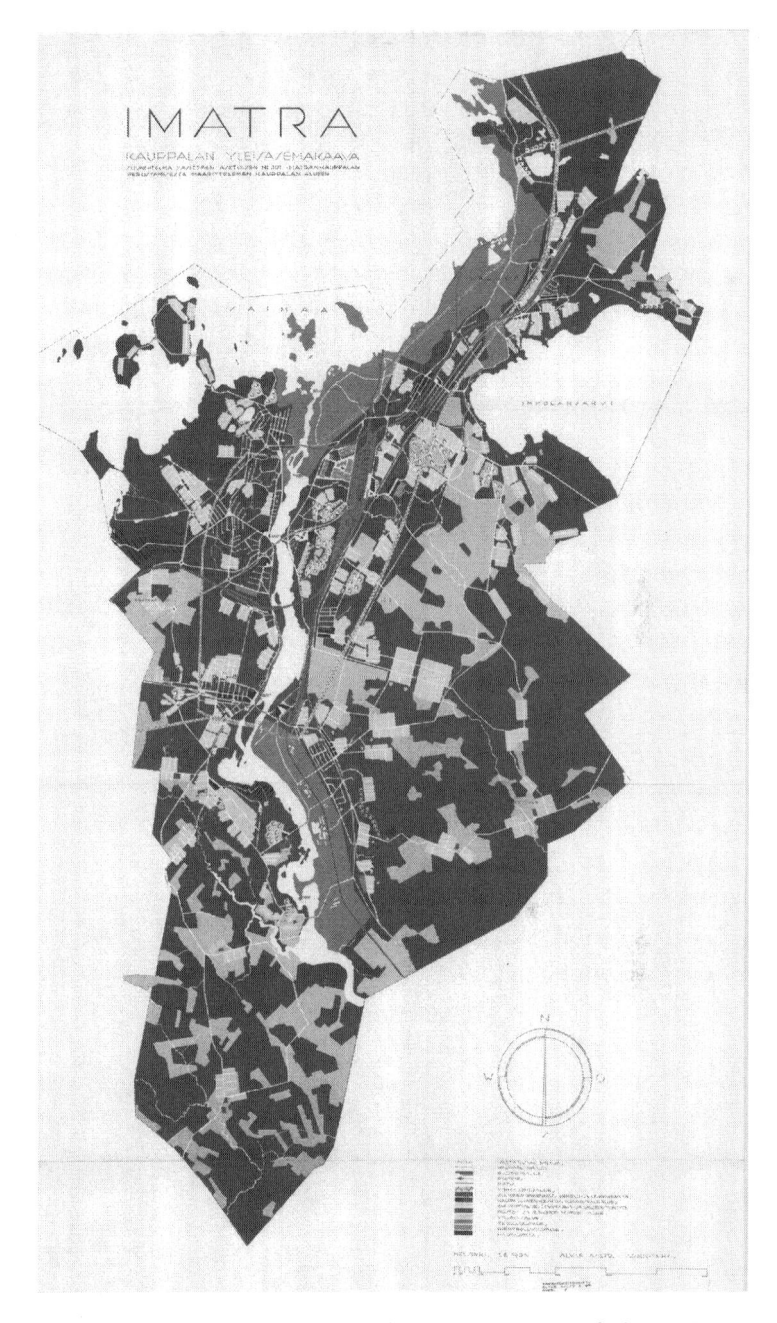

Figure 12.7 Alvar Aalto, Imatra town plan; image courtesy of Alvar Aalto
Foundation

the municipal offices, the latter alluded to the vernacular roots, which were always lying just beneath the surface in Aalto's architecture. That Aalto valued brickwork very highly is evident from all the industrial work that he built during this period and from the praise that he accorded to the masons who built Saynatsalo. Something of the Baltic vernacular was surely hinted at in the false crenulations of its brick walls and in the atypical twin timber trusses fanning out above the council chamber to support the purlins of the mono-pitch roof.

Equally crucial in Saynatsalo is the phenomenological experience of the spatial promenade which, paved in brick throughout, leads up from the entry foyer via a right angled stair, to deposit the subject on the timber floor of the council chamber itself, thereby passing the solid presence of the brick stair underfoot to the altogether less stable feel of the polished floor boards of the council chamber flexing slightly under one's weight. At the same time one notes that wood is just as much an honorific material as the granite steps leading up to the podium from the street.

This brings me to that which is still one of most fertile aspects of Aalto's on-going legacy, namely, his proclivity from Saynatsalo onwards to treat almost every building as if it were a micro-landscape in itself and, further,

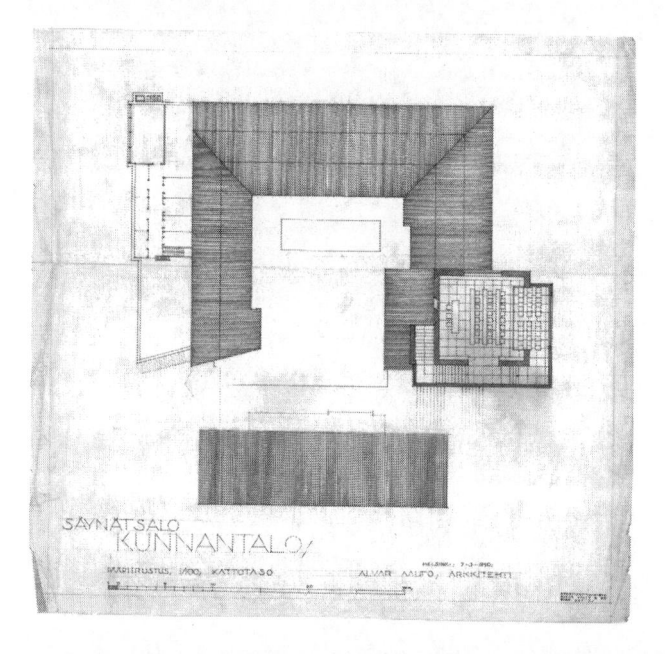

Figure 12.8a Alvar Aalto, Saynatsalo, plan; image courtesy of Alvar Aalto Foundation

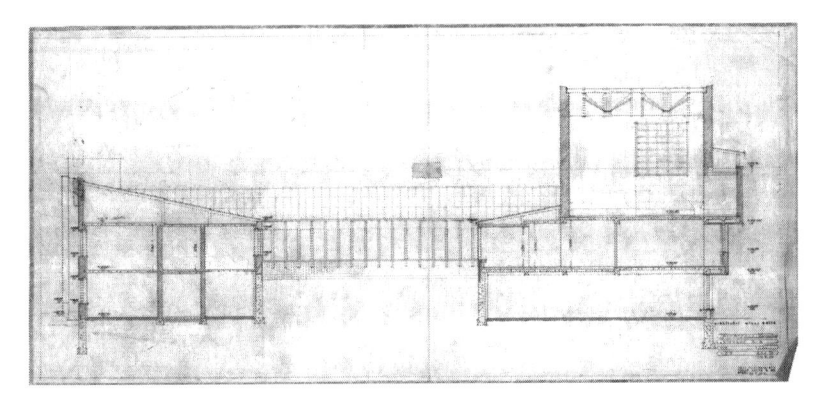

Figure 12.8b Alvar Aalto, Saynatsalo, section A; image courtesy of Alvar Aalto
Foundation

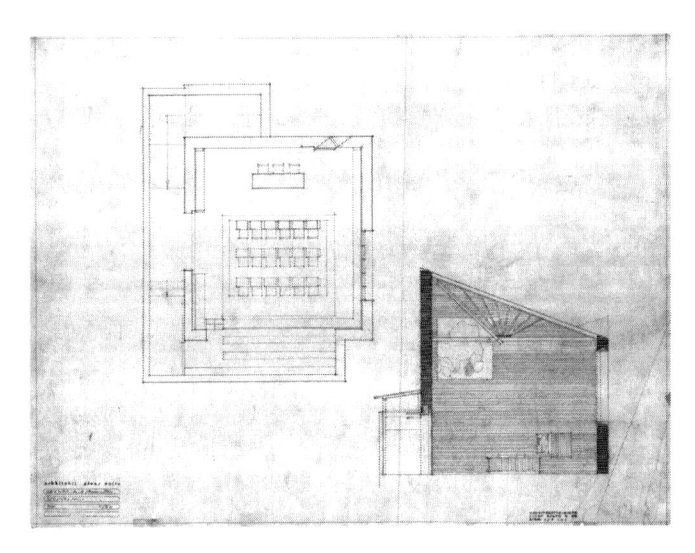

Figure 12.8c Alvar Aalto, Saynatsalo, section B; image courtesy of Alvar Aalto
Foundation

by virtue of this intrinsic topographic inflection, to open the building not
only to an organic grounding of the work in a specific site but also to the
rhythmic reciprocal articulation, not to say animation of the site in terms of
what is, in effect, nothing more than singular intervention. But beyond this,
depending on the circumstances and the scale, Aalto would also conceive a
potential civic intervention as a megaform capable of being read as an artificial land-form in itself.

Perhaps we first encounter, this last, in an unequivocal way, in Aalto's Vogelweidplatz Sports and Concert Center projected for Vienna in 1953. Herein a 25,000 seat hall to serve both purposes is covered by a suspended catenary roof in such a way as to assume the profile of a truncated artificial mountain around which a whole spread-eagled cluster of orthogonal sports facilities, ball-courts etc. are arrayed in such a way as to constitute the "foothills" of the mountains, covered by the same roof, with an Olympic sized swimming pool set to one side, constituting the enclosing flank thereby creating a civic plaza which in its turn opens directly into the stadium. This design anticipates the heroic topographic manner in which Aalto will attempt to come to terms with the mass ownership of the automobile with his remarkable *paysagiste* proposal of 1962 for integrating the automobile into the center of Helsinki. Here the strategy was to encroach on the existing nineteenth-century railhead entry into the city with a high-speed multi-lane autoroute which in its turn would feed into tri-level covered parking for 4000 cars, with each level being the occasion for a landscaped terrace.

What is one of most surprising and refreshing aspects of this proposal, at least as we may perceive it in model form, is that the autoroute entry and the existing railhead are treated as part and parcel of the same plastic composition, as are the one-off cultural buildings to be built as a sequence on the other side of the Toölö Lake. Even more compelling perhaps is that the historic content of the city would have been incorporated into this large scale intervention had it been executed. Existing institutions such as the Parliament, the National Museum and the Olympic Stadium would have been harmoniously incorporated into the panoramic vision. In this scalar and strategic range, passing from the Imatra Plan to the Vogelweidplatz stadium and his automobile topographic proposal for the center of Helsinki, we have ample evidence of Aalto's continuing relevance for the specific challenges facing the practice of architecture and urbanism today.

I have in mind Paul Ricoeur's recognition of the continual uprooting of the late modern world where the challenge increasingly becomes, as he put it, how to become or remain modern and yet, at the same time, return to sources. Similarly, we have to recognize that the megalopolis is a universal condition that we have no choice but to come to terms with as a universal phenomenon. In this regard, it is increasingly clear that some form of landscape urbanism offers the most plausible generic strategy with which to overcome the loss of the historic city. Thus, Aalto's informal linear city mosaic of Imatra may well serve as a valid strategic model, wherein urbanism is posited more as a critical ecological pattern than as any kind of coherent whole. And it is under a similar rubric that the one-off building, either as a megaform or as a more modestly scaled civic intervention, may yet be brought to yield unforeseeable catalytic ramifications for the future of urban form.

This, then, is the range of Alvar Aalto's continuing legacy extending from the phenomenological subjective experience of relatively intimate continuing environments to the strategic potential for appropriate large scale interventions in which the ultimate aim is not some identifiable whole or norm but rather the confirmation of a fragmentary yet nonetheless relatively harmonious large scale organic process and prospect.

Notes

1 Alvar Aalto, "The Stockholm Exhibition 1930," in Göran Schildt, Ed., *Alvar Aalto in His Own Words* (New York: Rizzoli, 1998): 72.

Interlude C

Sigmund Freud or the dark ~~forest~~ room revisited

Natalija Subotincic

Favorable conditions[1]

Do you recall?

During that time you were having such difficulties writing about the dreams.

You said, "What I don't like about them is the style. I was quite unable to find any simple or distinguished expression and degenerated into jocular circumlocutions with a straining after pictorial imagery."[2]

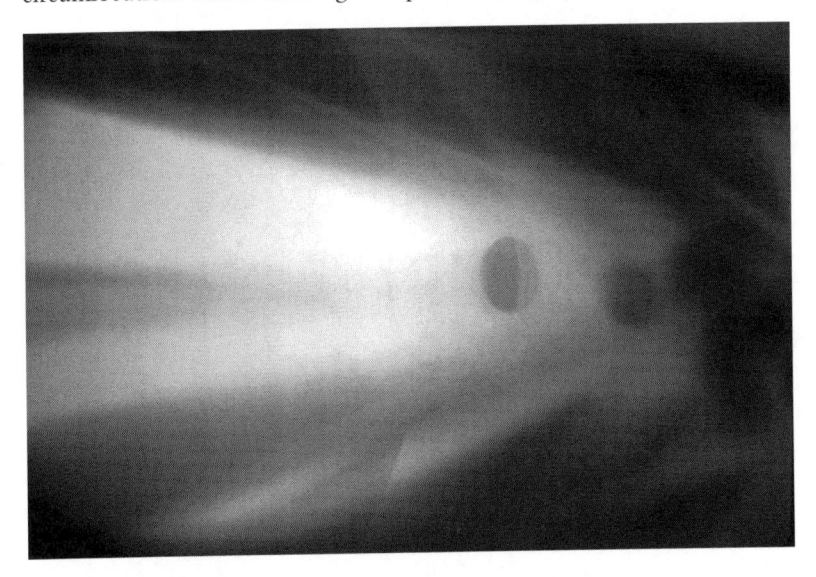

Figure C.1 POLYPHILO 1, Natalija Subotincic

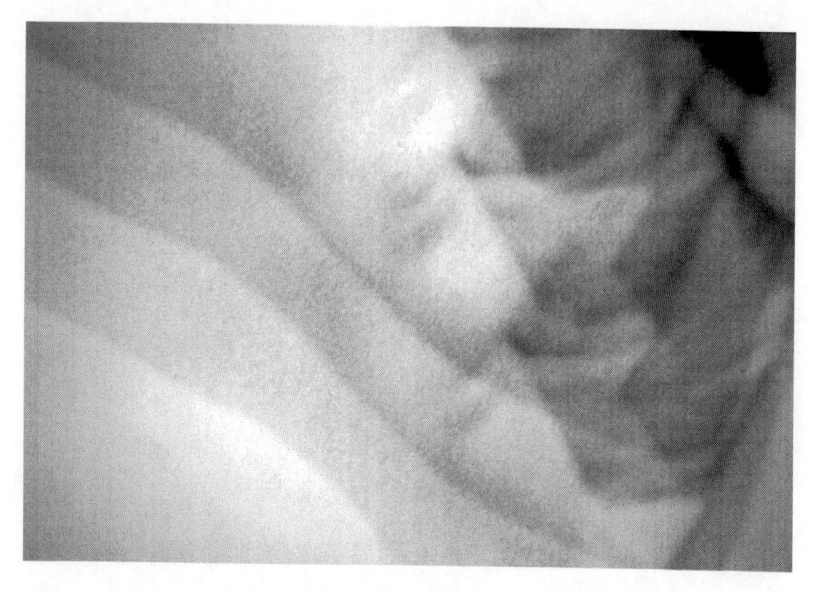

Figure C.2 POLYPHILO 2, Natalija Subotincic

Perhaps, at that point you were prepared, "to accept the ambiguity of meaning, one recognized as inhabiting the surface of the image yet [remains] resistant to clarification in language."[3] Your struggle came to a head when you were grappling with how to structure the overall collection of dreams and other inclusions, in your soon to be published interpretation of dreams – *POLYPHILO or The Dark* ~~Forest~~ *Revisited*. Finally with much relief, you revealed in a letter the construction of an image that appeased your great concerns.

> The whole thing is now arranged on the analogy with a stroll in the forest. At the outset, the dark wood of authors (who do not see the trees), without any outlook and full of blind alleys. Then, a concealed path along which I conduct the reader – my collection of dreams, with their peculiarities, details, indiscretions, and bad jokes – And then, suddenly, the heights, the prospect, and the inquiry, 'Where should you like to go from here?'[4]

Come doctor, let's leave the dark forest and venture into the dark room . . .

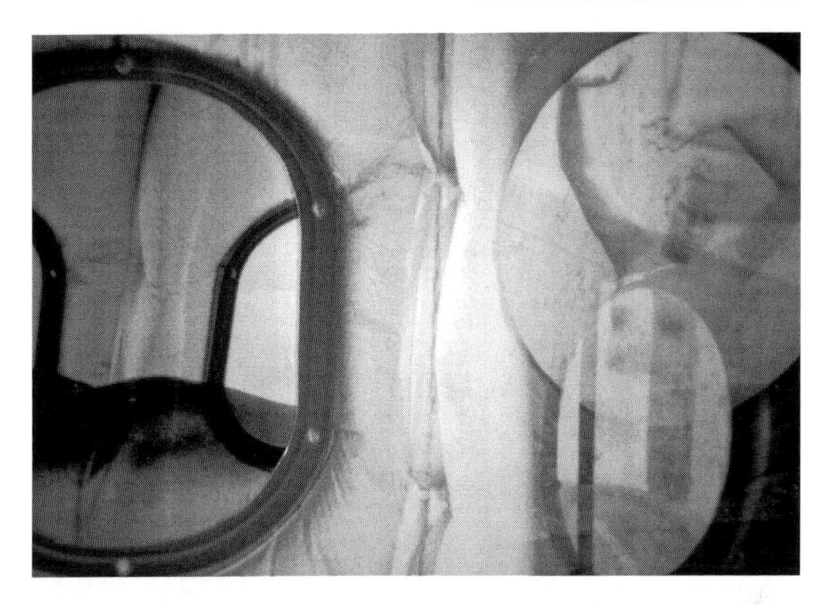

Figure C.3 POLYPHILO 3, Natalija Subotincic

The outer world[5]

I am a part of all that I have met;
Yet all experience is an arch where through
Gleams that untraveled world, whose margin fades
For ever and for ever when I move.
How dull it is to pause, to make an end,
To rust unburnished, not to shine in use!
As though to breathe were life. . . ."[6]

You constructed a distinctly spatial articulation, *an architecture of the psyche*, that included three realms: the "external world" existing outside our body but perceived and sensed by it; the "inner world" or *unconscious* existing within the deepest recesses of our body; and caught between these two, the "outer world," or space of *consciousness*. To name this in-between the outer world, is to situate the external world within us, recognizing we are never distinct from it, and that the space of consciousness is a place where inner and external worlds convene. This is also where you situate dreams, implying that similar reverberations occur between consciousness and our dreams.

Your notion of *space* relates, "to the topographical nature of the mind, particularly of the unconscious," whereas "time is absent in the

Figure C.4 ROE_Single Eros_detail, Natalija Subotincic

unconscious . . . confined to the more conscious layers."[7] And, that "concrete concepts" exist in the unconscious and it is only when impressions arrive at a level of consciousness that we become able to verbally articulate them.[8] So, what you are proposing, is that the unconscious is *silent* and *strictly spatial* and that we can utter only from within the *space and time* of consciousness. . . .

A piece of real experience

" . . . Gradiva, 'the girl splendid in walking'."[9]

" . . . her eye, which gazed calmly ahead, bespoke absolutely unimpaired powers of vision and thoughts quietly withdrawn. . . ."[10]

This resonant penumbral expanse from the unconscious to consciousness silently traced its path across your room. This is not a place where subtlety is explained or made obvious, no Oedipus, you are too clever for that. Rather, this place is where the obvious, buried deep within the subtle, seeps slowly into consciousness. As I wander, my experience resides within that silent space of a breath caught between imagining and articulating. This room speaks as I speak in my dreams, through fragments mysteriously tethered to the external world.

Figure C.5 ROE_Gradiva_detail, Natalija Subotincic

Figure C.6 ROE_Freud thinking_detail, Natalija Subotincic

"Yet he felt that what was passing through his mind stood in too strong contrast to the happy naïveté of the couple" who "were not meditating profoundly over the essential nature of a girl who had died two thousand years ago, but, without any weariness, were taking pleasure in an enigmatical problem of their life of the present."[11]

Moving through this place, from artifact to artifact, I find myself slightly askew, in a dream world where things do not always appear as themselves or as we have come to *know* them.

Figure C.7 ROE_Gradiva_Eros array_detail, Natalija Subotincic

" . . . he had a dark feeling that their bright, merry eyes might look through his forehead into his thoughts and thereby assume an expression as if they did not consider him quite in his right mind."[12]

Transmutation and transposition run rampant between artifacts and their referents in the external world. Carefully choreographed arrangements foreshadow those to come, or obscure those already past.

"Please stay quite still – my colleague is right; the method is really good and she has used it with the greatest success."[13]

Internal adjustments begin to occur as I allow events to unfold. Experience is where consciousness is continually interrupted by the incessant arrival of new communications from our deeper recesses, and where these disturbances are intricately interwoven with perceptions arriving from the external world that we are always desperately trying to make sense of.

> . . . a couple of times . . . the feeling had seized him that she looked as if she were seeking for access to his inmost thoughts and were looking

Figure C.8 ROE_ Eros array in motion_detail, Natalija Subotincic

Figure C.9 ROE_ Eros pair_detail, Natalija Subotincic

Figure C.10 ROE_ Eros triad and hand_detail, Natalija Subotincic

about them as if with a bright steel probe. He was obliged, therefore, to take great care that she might come upon nothing foolish in his mental processes.[14]

But our dream worlds do not always make sense, and the external world is not always objectively revealed to our consciousness the way many would

Figure C.11 ROE_ Full painting, Natalija Subotincic

have us believe. We reside through our experiences within this penumbral expanse that is often full of conflict. The outer world constructed within this place is where our collective consciousness and dreams do not part ways but form our unpredictable foundations.

"Thus he saw her putting one foot across the interstice while the other was about to follow, and as he contemplated the girl, her immediate and more remote environment rose before his imagination like an actuality."[15]

The unhurried, haunting atmosphere of this place encourages us to confront what we think we know. It makes present to our consciousness this penumbral zone of sensibility, that has always, and will always exist within our experience of the external world but is all too often repressed by our inner desires to fully comprehend. This becomes apparent the moment we finally step back outside and can't help but utter, "Where am I?"

So tell me doctor, "Where should you like to go from here?" . . .

Acknowledgement

Natalija Subotincic would like to acknowledge: The Sigmund Freud Museum in Vienna, Austria; The Sigmund Freud Museum in London, England; The University of Manitoba and the Faculty of Architecture in Winnipeg, Manitoba, Canada for their generous support of this research.

Notes

1 The three initial photographs in this offering were created by the author in 1989 and became part of the illustrations for POLYPHILO or The Dark Forest Revisited (Cambridge, MA: MIT Press, 1992).

2 Sigmund Freud in a letter to Wilhelm Fleiss, September 11th, 1899, in Ernest Jones, The Life and Work of Sigmund Freud: The Formative Years and the Great Discoveries, 1856 – 1900, vol. 1 (New York: Basic Books Inc., 1953), 360.

3 Alberto Pérez-Gómez and Louise Pelletier, Architectural Representation and the Perspective Hinge (Cambridge, MA: MIT Press, 1997), xxi.

4 Sigmund Freud in a letter to Wilhelm Fleiss, August 6, 1899, in Jones, The Life and Work of Sigmund Freud, vol. 1, 359.

5 The remaining images are selections from the author's recently completed painting entitled "Reflecting on Eros from Vienna to London" that examines the evanescent presence of Eros panning across the *space* and *time* of Freud's consulting rooms. This painting forms the most recent part of the author's ongoing body of research on the architecture integral to Freud's cabinet.

6 Excerpt from Alfred Lord Tennyson's poem "Ulysses" written in 1833 and published in 1842 in his third publication entitled *Poems*. See the Poetry Foundation, accessed May 10, 2012, www.poetryfoundation.org/poem/174659.

7 In 1914 Sigmund Freud wrote a letter to a friend where he briefly alluded to having finally solved to his great satisfaction "the psychological problem of space and time!" Although he unfortunately didn't reveal any further details, his biographer Ernest Jones surmised that Freud's ideas about *space* and *time* (which are presented here) were based on Freud's essay "The Unconscious," which was being written at that time but was not published until a year after the letter. See Ernest Jones, The Life and Work of Sigmund Freud: Years of Maturity, 1901 – 1919, vol. 2 (New York: Basic Books Inc., 1955), 175. See also Sigmund Freud, "The Unconscious (1915)," in The International Psycho-Analytical Library, vol. 4, no. 10, Collected Papers, ed. Ernest Jones and trans. Joan Riviere (New York: Basic Books Inc., 1959), 98.

8 Sigmund Freud's thoughts summarized in Jones, The Life and Work of Sigmund Freud, vol. 2, 326.

9 Wilhelm Jensen, Gradiva, A Pompeian Fancy, trans. Helen Downey (New York: Moffat, Yard and Co., 2010, [1918]), 5.

10 Ibid., 4.

11 Ibid., 81.

12 Ibid.

13 Ibid., 82.

14 Ibid., 85.

15 Ibid., 6.

PART IV
Fusion of horizons

13

VOICES OF TRANQUILITY

Silence in art and architecture

Juhani Pallasmaa

> Only in complete silence one starts to hear; only when language resigns, one starts to see.[1]
>
> *Carthusian Monks, Grand Chartreuse*

Loss of silence and time

"Nothing has changed the nature of Man so much as the loss of silence," the Swiss philosopher Max Picard argues in his remarkable book *The World of Silence* (written in 1948).[2] The nearly seven decades that have passed since the publication of the book have only made the philosopher's concern more urgent. The oppressive thought that we may be losing the innate silence of our souls is becoming increasingly evident. Today we can even catch ourselves escaping silence into excessive noise in our panicked search for privacy and intimacy. This pathological reversal of behavior makes me think of Erich Fromm's thought provokingly paradoxical theme of "escape from freedom" in his seminal book with this very title.[3] We seek freedom obsessively, but as Fyodor Dostoyevsky has already suggested, when we, pitiful human beings, finally have it, we do not know what to do with it, and we end up voluntarily closing up the very door to freedom.

The loss of silence and freedom is accompanied with the continued escalation of speed. In the fifteenth century the clocks of Nuremberg began to strike every quarter hour, and, as Marcel Proust recalls, the measure of minutes arose to human consciousness with the introduction of railway traffic. Now our digital watches measure time in seconds. Isn't it absurd to remember in the morning the precise clock reading when you happened to wake up for a moment at night? Through its exaggerated numerical precision, the reading of time has lost its analogic correspondence with the course of the sun as well as its human meanings. Experiential time has withered into a mere numerical fact. At the same time, we have unnoticeably turned our body position in relation to the progression of time. The Greeks understood that the future came from behind their backs while the past receded away in front of their eyes. We have turned our face towards the future and the past is disappearing behind our backs.[4]

"The world's magnificence has been enriched by a new beauty; the beauty of speed," Filippo Marinetti declared in the Futurist Manifesto in the 1920s.[5] Paul Virilio, the architect–philosopher, has recently remarked that the most important product of the contemporary culture is speed. Yet, Milan Kundera makes the alarming observation about the relationship of speed and memory, "The degree of slowness is directly proportional to the intensity of memory; the degree of speed is directly proportional to the intensity of forgetting."[6] Aren't we on our way to total amnesia through the constant acceleration of the speed of life?

Our effort to avoid boredom strengthens the desire for newness. But as the Norwegian philosopher Lars Svendsen suggests, the obsession with newness is bound to result in repetition and, eventually, in boredom. "As the new is searched only because of its newness, everything becomes identical, because it has no other properties but its newness," Svendsen laments.[7]

Fragments of silence

"Silence no longer exists as a *world*, but only in fragments, as the remains of a world. And as man is always frightened by remains, so he is frightened by the remains of silence," Picard reasons.[8] We are, indeed, frightened by fragments of silence, as they reveal to us our sad loss of domicile and home. These fragments also make us conscious of our fundamental loneliness, an experience that we nowadays tend to escape into a collective identity through cultural noise, mass communication, entertainment, and fashion. The primal stillness of the world – I would like to say the ontological silence of the universe – is increasingly contaminated and eradicated by cultural noise and clatter, in the same way that the primal darkness is polluted by man-made light. This loss of silence and benevolent darkness reflects the disastrous secularization and materialization of life. Our sphere of life becomes filled with racket, "visual noise" and an excessive abundance of disturbing and distracting stimuli. The world is losing its mystery and poetry as well as its sensuous appeal. In my view, the grand task of art is to re-create and maintain the mythical, poetic and sensuous reality of the world.

Silence of nature

As the opposite of our noisy lifestyle today, tranquility is a contemplative, mystical and solemn state. The silence of nature evokes a pantheistic experience, which connects us with cosmic dimensions. This silence also evokes the unity and singularity of the world and a sense of healing participation; I am part of the singularity of the world, not cast into an irreversible solitude and isolation.

Sounds of nature are not noise, as they reinforce nature's primal causalities and quietude. The rippling of water, birds' twitter, rustling of grass in the wind, or even the roar of thunder, strengthens the experience of the innate tranquility of nature. The sound of wind or a stream calms us as it makes us aware of the processes of nature and their underlying silence. More importantly, I am connected with my own self, and guided to experience a moment of wholeness. These sounds of nature are an essential ingredient of nature's primal silence. As a consequence, even the most powerful voices of nature are comforting, as they enfold us in nature's majestic logic and causality.

Sound arises from silence, not silence from sound. Silence slows down time and permits us to experience phenomena beyond our normal awareness. Just think of the slow time and quietude in Anton Chekhov's first novel, *Steppe*, where the reader's mind is slowed down and sensitized to hear and follow the flight of a single fly.

The notion and experience of silence is evidently connected with emptiness, the concept that is central in eastern thinking. Emptiness is the spatial and visual equivalent of the primarily aural experience of silence. However, the senses constantly interact, and both experiences can be sensed through vision and hearing. In fact both silence and emptiness invite subtle multi-sensory experiences, as if they were voids that invoke imaginary sensations.

Silence is not merely an auditory experience of the absence of sound; it is a multi-sensory and existential experience of being, rather than of listening. It is this existential "thickness" and richness of silence that gives it its poetic authority. Silence reveals the essence of things, as if it were perceived by the human senses for the first time. Silence is an atmospheric and qualitative perception that fuses the percept and the perceiver. It is always an affective experience, as silence is not outside me, it is my very soul that has been silenced.

Silence in the arts

The significance of silence for music, poetry and other arts is clear enough. "Poetry comes out of silence and yearns for silence," Picard writes.[9] Also great paintings and architecture arise from and create tranquility. "It must be immense, this silence, in which sounds and movements have room," Rainer Maria Rilke advices the aspiring poet Kappus in his touching book *Letters to a Young Poet*.[10] For Rilke, silence is always accompanied by solitude: "Works of art are of an infinite solitude," and "what is necessary, after all, is only this, vast inner solitude."[11] He maintains that solitude and silence are essential for a poet, and, I would suggest, it is also essential for an architect or any artist, for that matter. But are we able to tolerate solitude and silence in our current lifestyle?

The paintings of Piero della Francesca, Johannes Vermeer and J.M.W. Turner silence all sound. The events of these paintings take place as if carved into a beautiful marble of silence. Regardless of today's tendency towards increasing noise also in art, the greatest of modern and contemporary paintings are impressive spaces of tranquility. The subject matter of Giorgio Morandi's still life paintings is eternal immobility and tranquility. His timid objects seek support and safety from each other, evoking the most haunting question of all: why do things exist, rather than not? The paintings of Claude Monet project vague sounds, like the ripple of water, or the sound of peaceful breathing. The artistic tranquility is the silence of existence. As Constantin Brancusi advices us, "Art must give immediately, all at once, the shock of life, a sensation of breathing."[12]

The stillness in the images of the metaphysical painters seems to draw the spectator into the vacuum of their muteness; this is a threatening voicelessness, the suffocation of sound. The smoke of a train that frequently appears in De Chirico's paintings emphasizes the total soundlessness of the space. If the moist air in Monet's paintings is meant to be felt by the skin, these paintings are heard as much as seen.

I would like to argue that all great painters paint silence. Just look at the soft silence of the light in Mark Rothko's paintings! Masterful architecture, likewise, evokes silence. This stillness of the arts is not a mere absence of sound, but an original sensory and mental state, an observing, listening and knowing quietude. It brings us back to a beginning. It is a mental state, which evokes a feeling of melancholy, as it reminds us of our own transitory nature and irretrievably lost innocence. At the same time, it integrates our sense of self and existence with our very being in the world.

Silence in architectural experience

A powerful architectural experience eliminates noise and turns our consciousness to ourselves, to our own existential experience. Just think of the materialized silence of Romanesque monasteries and convents, which fuse light and silence into a singular haptic experience. Also the contemporary church interiors of Alvar Aalto and Juha Leiviskä in Finland are cast similarly in a benevolent and therapeutic silence. In any impressive architectural or artistic space, we hear only our own heartbeat. The innate silence of this experience results, it seems to me, from the fact that the work focuses our attention on our own inner experience; the work re-orientates my very sense of being. I find myself listening to my own existence. The mental task of art is to concretize our being in the world and to make us conscious of our selves. The painter wants "to make visible how the world touches us," Maurice Merleau-Ponty describes our experience of Paul Cézanne's paintings.[13] Also all meaningful architecture mediates and structures our experience and understanding of the world, or perhaps, understanding our being in the world. Moreover, architecture makes visible how the world touches us. The art of architecture should create, safeguard and maintain silence. As architects, we need to follow Søren Kierkegaard's advice: "Create silence! Bring men to silence!"[14]

The language of architecture is the drama of tranquility. Great buildings are silence turned into matter, and in its very essence architecture is petrified stillness. As the racket and clatter of construction work fades away, as the shouting of workers ceases, the building turns into a timeless monument of quietude. And what a silent faithfulness and patience can be felt in old buildings! They safeguard their silences in the folds of their material structures, and embrace us with this extraordinary treasure. Experiencing architecture is not only a matter of appreciating spaces, forms and surfaces, it is also a way of listening to the building's characteristic silence. Every great building has its unique voice of tranquility, and there are indications that early human constructions in history were actually conceived for hearing rather than vision.

Through specific architectural silences, we can experience the lifestyles and temporal rhythms of past cultures, and also the experience of the depth of time resides in these magnificent silences. As we enter a Gothic cathedral, we can feel its ancient, embracing silence as a haptic sensation that evokes images of past rituals and forms of life, and invites us to imagine echoes of Gregorian chants bouncing off the ribbed vaults. This is a tactile silence with a deep memory. This is a haptic silence, experienced by the skin rather than the ears. This experience of haptic silence with a distinct gravity is not limited to pre-modern structures: as we enter Crown Hall in Chicago by Ludwig Mies van der Rohe, the Kimbell Art Museum of Louis Kahn in Fort Worth, or the Thermal Baths at Vals by Peter Zumthor, we are struck by the majestic calm and stillness of these spaces. Our ears appreciate each in consonance with the eyes and the body. Great artistic experiences always strengthen and unify our sense of self.

Light and silence

Light belongs to silence, whereas the stillness of night is mere lack of sound; night is a sleeping sound. Silence and light create the innermost essence, the mental core, of architecture. "Sun never knows how great it is until it hits the side of a building, or shines inside a room," Louis Kahn remarks.[15] Paradoxically, every silence has its sound; the great Mexican architect, Luis Barragan spoke of the "placid murmur of silence," and you can hear it in his spaces as the colored light touches your skin like a warm liquid.[16] Great architecture is a true art of alchemy: light turns into a liquid and a tactile sensation; gravity turns into a thought; silence into sound; and matter into emotion. The greatest silences that I have experienced are the Pharaonic silence of the Karnak temple, the Roman silence of the Pantheon, and the whispering silences of the Japanese Zen gardens, such as Ryōan-ji in Kyoto.

Picard writes perceptively and poetically of the significance of silence for architecture. "The colonnades of the Greek temples are like boundary lines along the silence. They become ever straighter and ever whiter as they lean against the silence . . . Wandering amongst the Greek pillars is a wandering in a radiant silence," he writes. "Just as ivy grows round a wall for centuries, so the cathedrals have grown around the silence. They are built around the silence."[17] Picard speaks of cathedrals as "museums of silence," and of Greek statues as "vessels," or "white islands of silence."[18] For this philosopher of silence, even "the forest is a great reservoir of silence out of which the silence trickles in a thin, slow stream and fills the air with its brightness."[19]

The calming, protecting and healing silence of the forest has a special mental meaning for us Nordic people. For us the forest is the parents' comforting embrace and the mother's protective womb, whereas the Central Europeans usually fear the darkness and silence of the forest. We escape danger into the forest, whereas central Europeans run away from the forest.

Two architectures

It is useful to distinguish between two architectures in our time: the architecture of form, on the one hand, and the architecture of essence, on the other. The architecture of form attempts to charm us with its excessive and loud manipulation of forms and suggestions. This architecture wants us to be concerned with itself, it wants to entertain us and entice our attention and senses. While the architecture of form aims at fashionable curiosities, the architecture of essence aspires for the timeless poetic content of life and architecture itself. It poeticizes the commonplace and casts an aura of uniqueness on the everyday. The architecture of essence focuses our attention on life, and it emancipates our senses and awakens an attending receptiveness and quietude.

In my view, architecture is a background phenomenon that creates settings for human events and acts of life. Yet, in all areas of communication and artistic expression, our consumerist culture tends to favor quick, forceful, noisy and emotionally overwhelming experiences. A commercially oriented image effect, a sort of an image shock, has gained popularity in the competition for the attention of the over-stimulated consumers. As a consequence, the architecture of today's "society of spectacle," is increasingly a product of sensationalism.[20] Trying to compete with other media, architecture becomes an eye-catching image or a form of entertainment, creating an obsession with uniqueness and unforeseen novelty. But this is a misunderstanding of the role of architecture and its fundamental task as a framing device for perception and understanding as well as for the various events of life. The power of architecture is in its silent but perpetual presence and prestige in our daily lives. This persistent presence creates an unnoticeable frame of pre-understanding for our entire existential experience. We perceive, understand and remember through our architectural structures, and these settings are extensions and externalizations of our nervous system and consciousness.

Profound architecture does not dictate or force distinct behaviors, reactions and emotions. It is moderate, tactful and generous. Jean-Paul Sartre, the philosopher–writer, points out this necessary element of generosity in the art of literature:

> The writer should not seek to *overwhelm*; otherwise he is in contradiction with himself; if he wishes to *make demands* he must propose only the task to be fulfilled. Hence the character of pure presentation which appears essential to the work of art. The reader must be able to make a certain aesthetic withdrawal. . . . Jean Genet justly calls it the author's politeness towards the reader.[21]

Architecture definitely needs the same aesthetic withdrawal, politeness and silence.

Silence and anonymity

In today's consumerist culture we are mislead to believe that the qualities of art and architecture arise from expression of the artist's or architect's *persona*.

However, as the philosopher Maurice Merleau-Ponty writes, "We come to see not the work of art, but the world according to the work."[22] Balthus (Balthazar Klossowsky de Rola), one of the greatest figurative painters of the last century, makes a thought provoking comment on artistic expression:

> Modernity, which began in the true sense with the Renaissance, determined the tragedy of art. The artist emerged as an individual and the traditional way of painting disappeared. From then on the artist sought to express his inner world, which is a limited universe: He tried to place his personality in power and used paintings as a means of self-expression. But great painting has to have universal meaning. This is sadly no longer so today and this is why I want to give painting back its lost universality and anonymity, because the more anonymous painting is, the more real it is.[23]

In his work and teaching, the dignified Finnish designer, Kaj Franck, also sought anonymity; in his view, the designer's persona should not dominate the experience of the object. In my view, the same criterion applies fully to architecture; profound architecture arises from facts, causalities, and experiences of life, not from personal artistic inventions. As Alvaro Siza, one of the greatest architects of our time argues, "Architects do not invent anything, they just transform conditions."[24] In a television interview in 1972 Alvar Aalto made an unexpected confession: "I don't think there's so much difference between reason and intuition. Intuition can sometimes be extremely rational. . . . It is the practical objectives of constructions that give me my intuitive point of departure, and realism is my guiding star. . . . Realism usually provides the strongest stimulus to my imagination."[25]

In my own work I have always wanted to pull myself away from the work before it is finished. The work needs to express the beauty of the world and human existence, not any idiosyncratic ideas of mine. Yet, this call for anonymity does not imply lack of emotion and feeling. Meaningful design re-mythicizes, re-animates and re-eroticizes our relationship with the world. I wish my designs to be sensuous and emotive, but not to express any emotions of mine. I aim at a distinct visual silence, a receptive, courteous and sensitized state of awareness.

Life in silence

Maybe, the idea of turning life back to the unpretentious appropriateness and silent prestige that we admire in the peasant's sphere of life, or in the most refined creations of Modernity, proves to be a groundless nostalgia, but man has never mourned for a homecoming more than today. In the middle of today's virtual and digital utopia we desire to re-encounter the fundamental causalities of life. And man has never yearned for silence as the focus of his being more than we do in our era of surreal and hysterical consumption and noise.

The Finnish poet Bo Carpelan evokes the nobility of restrained life and meditative tranquility in one of his poems in the collection entitled *Homecoming*:

> There are still houses with low ceilings,
> window-splays where children climb up
> and squatting, chin against knees,
> watch the wet snow falling
> peacefully over dark, narrow courtyards.
> There are still rooms that speak of lives,
> of cupboards of clean, hereditary linen.
> There are quiet kitchens where someone sits
> reading with the book propped against the loaf of bread.
> The light falls there with the voice of a white blind.
> If you shut your eyes you can see
> that a morning, however fleeting, awaits
> and that its warmth mingles with the warmth in here
> and that each flake's fall
> is a sign of homecoming.[26]

(The first version of this essay was given as a lecture at the Embassy of Finland in Washington DC on 28 September 2011. The essay was further developed for a lecture at the American Academy in Rome on 11 November 2013.)

Notes

1 Carthusian Monks, Grand Chartreuse, quoted from a letter by Nic Baker III to the author, October, 2013.
2 Max Picard, *The World of Silence* (Washington, DC: Gateway Editions, 1988), 145.
3 Erich Fromm, *Pako vapaudesta* (Helsinki: Kirjayhtymä, 1976).
4 Robert M. Pirzig, "An Author and Father looks Ahead at the Past," *The New York Times Book Review* 89, March 4, 1984, 7–8.
5 As quoted in Thom Mayne, "Statement," in *Peter Pran*, ed. Liyang Qiu (China: Dut Press, 2006), 4.
6 Milan Kundera, *Slowness* (New York: Harper Collins Publishers, 1966), 39.
7 Lars Fr. H. Svendsen, *Ikävystymisen filosofiaa* (Helsinki: Tammi Publishers, 2005), 75.
8 Picard, *The World of Silence*, 212.
9 Ibid., 145.

10 Rainer Maria Rilke, *Letters to a Young Poet* (New York: Random House, 1986), 106.

11 Ibid., 23, 54.

12 Eric Shanes, *Constantin Brancusi* (New York: Abbeville Press, 1989), 67.

13 Maurice Merleau-Ponty, "Cezanne's Doubt," in *Sense and Non-Sense* (Evanston, IL: Northwestern University Press, 1964), 19.

14 Picard, *The World of Silence*, 231.

15 Louis Kahn, paraphrasing Wallace Stevens in "Harmony between Man and Architecture," in *Louis I Kahn Writings, Lectures, Interviews*, ed. Alessandra Latour (New York: Rizzoli International Publications, 1991), 343.

16 Luis Barragan, "1980 Pritzker Architecture Prize Address," in *Barragan: Complete Works*, ed. Paul Rispa (London: Thames and Hudson, 1995), 205.

17 Picard, *The World of Silence*, 161, 168.

18 Ibid., 162–169.

19 Ibid., 19.

20 Guy Debord, *The Society of the Spectacle* (New York: Zone Books, 1994), 12.

21 Jean-Paul Sartre, *Basic Writings*, ed. Stephen Priest (London and New York: Routledge, 2001), 268.

22 Maurice Merleau-Ponty, as quoted in Iain McGilchrist, *The Master and His Emissary: The Divided Brain and the Making of the Western World* (New Haven, CT: Yale University Press, 2009), 409.

23 Cristina Carrillo de Albornoz, *Balthus in His Own Words* (New York: Assouline, 2001), 6.

24 Alvaro Siza, as quoted in Kenneth Frampton, "Introduction," in *Labour, Work and Architecture* (London: Phaidon Press, 2002), 18.

25 Interview for Finnish Television, July 1972, in Göran Schildt ed., *Alvar Aalto in His Own Words*. (Otava Publishing Company, Helsinki: 1997), 273–274.

26 Bo Carpelan, *Homecoming*, trans. David McDuff (Manchester: Carcanet, 1993), 111.

14

AN ARCHITECTURAL CREATION MYTH BORROWED FROM THE PHENOMENOLOGY OF MUSIC

Stephen Parcell

Sound versus musical sound

One of the many books in the music library that illuminate architecture obliquely is Thomas Clifton, *Music as Heard: A Study in Applied Phenomenology.*[1] In the late 1970s Clifton and another philosopher of music, F. Joseph Smith, carried out separate phenomenological studies, methodically bracketing out peripheral circumstances to discern essential premises of music. To make a long story very short, both concluded that the human experience of sound is the starting point of music. Smith distinguishes between sound and musical sound:

> Musical sound is more than just raw sound. The roar of the ocean is not yet music, though it is primordial sound. Raw sound becomes musical sound only after it has been processed through . . . definite categories.[2]

Clifton adds,

> Music is an ordered arrangement of sounds and silences whose meaning is presentative rather than denotative. . . . This distinguishes music . . . from sounds as purely physical objects. . . . The same sound, under different circumstances, can be interpreted as either music or nonmusic.[3]

We understand most of the sounds around us in a denotative way, relying on them – in conjunction with visual sights and other clues – to denote particular features in our surroundings, especially nearby things that are moving. Meanwhile, we may understand other sounds around us as musical because they are organized deliberately and are meaningful in a different way. Music is presented *in* the sounds (and silences). Normally we do not regard musical sounds denotatively: to denote, for example, that there is an oboe buzzing around the room. Both Clifton and Smith indicate that the basic distinction here is between sounds and musical sounds. They emphasize that sound is essential: "The sound source . . . must be there if we are to experience music at all."[4]

Pythagorean theory

This scenario may seem self-evident, but Western music theory is based on different premises. Followers of Pythagoras in the fifth century BCE noticed that pairs of tones that sound consonant are generated by a taut string that is subdivided into different lengths with simple ratios: 2:1 produces an octave; 3:2 produces a fifth; 4:3 produces a fourth, etc. This seemed to provide a rare empirical proof that the universe is based on simple numbers. Consequently, music theory based on mathematics was regarded as a form of universal knowledge and later became instituted as one of the four liberal arts of the quadrivium. Although the experience of sound provided the initial evidence, writers on music theory, especially Boëthius in the sixth century CE, emphasized the numbers and declared that sound is only a secondary, non-essential attribute. He stated, "Pythagoras . . . put no credence in human ears, which are subject to change."[5] Discussing the cosmic music of the spheres, Boëthius also suggested that the extremely fast motions of heavenly bodies produce sounds but they are inaudible to humans.[6]

One consequence of this belief in musical mathematics is that Western music has relied primarily on pitch intervals: not absolute pitches that are high or low, but proportional relations between pitches.[7] In theory, a C-major triad in a low register is identical to a C-major triad in a high register. This proportional relationship was the basis of harmony in Western music.[8] Due to Pythagorean mathematics and the Neoplatonic and Christian connotations it had acquired, listening to medieval chants could be understood as witnessing perfect numerical proportions; the sound then would be incidental. Similarly, observing medieval religious buildings could be understood as witnessing perfect numerical proportions; the substance then would be incidental. Western architecture theory has been based primarily on form, starting from the ratio between the lengths of adjacent sides of a rectangle. This proportional relationship was the basis of harmony in Western architecture. In both disciplines the numerical proportions were believed to provide a glimpse of the divine order of the universe.

Meanwhile, music was understood not just as numbers. Alongside this universal music theory was a tradition of musical performances for human enjoyment; however, the two traditions were kept separate to avoid contaminating the religious concepts. Church officials warned against complex melodies and rhythms that would distract worshippers and "stir lascivious sensations in the loins."[9] Similarly, architecture was understood not only as numbers. Alongside this universal architecture theory was a medieval tradition of building in which materials were used skillfully to make things that compensate for intrinsic human weakness.[10] This tradition also was grounded in religion but did not share the mathematical premises of church architecture.

Timbre and materiality

When analyzing even a single sound, focusing on its primary pitch implicitly downplays its other characteristics: intensity and especially timbre. As Clifton notes,

> In our culture, a great deal of importance is given to the role of pitch and interval . . . while texture, timbre, gesture, dynamics, and duration are frequently thought of as secondary, something that pitches and intervals *have*. If a French horn prolongs an open E, and then quickly mutes it, is it the same E? Logically, yes; but in terms of musical behavior, I think not.[11]

In nineteenth-century music theory, timbre was conceived as a tertiary characteristic of sound: an incidental quality that can be defined only indirectly, as the leftover attribute that differentiates two sounds with the same pitch and intensity.[12] To compose music in this way, one would start with different pitches and perhaps different intensities, then add timbre for flavor. Both pitch and intensity can be quantified and notated easily (e.g., middle A at double forte; or 440 cycles per second at 55 decibels) but timbre cannot. To analyze timbre objectively, several components would have to be considered: the attack and decay with which the sound begins and ends, the many constituent pitches within the timbre, and the different intensities of those pitches.[13] To build up the complex properties of a particular timbre from scratch would be a difficult task.

Timbre is difficult to conceive but easy to perceive. All creatures recognize timbre intuitively from experience and memory. Sitting still with our eyes closed, we rely largely on different timbres to recognize things in our surroundings: the turning of a page, the boiling of a kettle, or a knock at the door. From a timbral standpoint, pitch is merely one simplified component of timbre, not a primary attribute in its own right. Most of the sounds around us do not have only a single primary pitch. To compose music that emphasizes timbre, one would work directly with sound and not be overly concerned with primary pitches or their graphic notation.

When analyzing even a single substance, focusing on its primary form implicitly downplays its other characteristics: size and especially materiality. Western architecture theory regards materiality as a tertiary characteristic of substance: an incidental quality that can be defined only indirectly, as the leftover attribute that differentiates two substances with the same form and size. To compose architecture in this way, one would start with different forms and perhaps different sizes, then add materiality for flavor. Both form and size can be quantified and represented easily (e.g., a cube, 2' x 2' x 2') but materiality cannot. To analyze materiality objectively, several components would have to be considered: its texture and resilience, its tones and colors, and its many constituent forms at different scales.[14] To build up the complex properties of a particular material from scratch would be a difficult task.

Materiality is difficult to conceive but easy to perceive. All creatures recognize materiality implicitly from experience and memory. Moving around with our eyes and ears closed, we rely largely on materiality to recognize things in our surroundings: the delicacy of paper, the steam from a kettle, or the solidity of a door. From a material standpoint, form is merely one simplified component of materiality, not a primary attribute in its own right. Most of the substances around us do not have only a single primary form. To design architecture that emphasizes materiality, one would work directly with substance and not be overly concerned with primary forms or their graphic notation.

Music versus non-music

Underlying the distinction between Pythagorean theory and everyday performance, as well as the distinction between pitch interval and timbre, is a more basic issue: the grounds on which one defines what is and what is not music. Pythagorean theory relies on numerical relations that are essentially silent and autonomous. Clifton's phenomenological analysis points instead to actual sounds that are perceived by humans.[15] He acknowledges that sounds exist objectively, like trees and mountains, but says that music requires a receptive listener to distinguish the denotative sounds of one's surroundings from the presentative sounds of musical order. Certain sounds that one hears in the forest might be recognized as musical. The situation here includes only the sound and the human listener, not yet the intentions of a composer. To focus on this basic musical event, Clifton brackets out peripheral elements, including a composer, an act of composition, instruments, performers, and a score. He notes that one person may recognize certain sounds in the forest as musical whereas another may not; however, we tend to agree on such things. Musical sounds in the forest need not emphasize pitch intervals. We tend to focus on pitch but can recognize musical order also in rhythms and in sequences of timbres. Music we don't like may be dismissed as "noise," but we still recognize it as music.

In distinguishing music from non-music, Clifton points out that music is perceived not as a set of individual sounds but as a larger figure with rhythm, form, motion, direction, and degrees of stability and instability.[16] The primary phenomenon is gesture.[17] Musical events create their own time; they do not happen *in* time. Describing music as fast, smooth, high, low, ascending, descending, bright, or colorful indicates that we experience music not only temporally and aurally but also in a quasi-spatial way that recognizes forces.[18] It tends to rely on tonality, which provides the narrative structure for most Western music: harmony exerts a pull on dissonant sounds to bring them back to a state of rest.[19] These descriptions suggest that we rely on previous bodily experience to interpret what the music is doing.[20] Here, Clifton's approach follows that of philosopher Maurice Merleau-Ponty, who stressed that we understand our surroundings reciprocally through the body, in a continuous intertwining that provides the essential ground for any subsequent abstractions.[21] No one has written a phenomenological analysis of architecture that is comparable to what Clifton wrote for music, so approaching architecture circuitously via the phenomenology of music is a second option.

Architecture versus building

Like "music," "architecture" is an abstract noun. It is inherently singular and does not designate particular things such as songs and buildings. Paul Valéry suggested that music and architecture share a special relationship because they exist in our surroundings and, unlike other arts, do not rely on representational images or words as intermediaries.[22] However, recognizing architecture has become much more difficult. As Friedrich Nietzsche noted, "In general, we no longer understand architecture – at least, not nearly as well as we understand music."[23] A recognition of music relies on an intuitive perception of order, whereas a recognition of architecture relies on attributes that are esoteric, sophisticated, and often contradictory.[24] Architectural theorists have drawn many different lines between what is and what is not architecture. They have proposed various criteria to distinguish an architectural attribute from a non-architectural attribute: proportionate versus non-proportionate, ornate versus plain, grand versus humble, complex versus simple, unique versus typical, rich versus poor, sacred versus secular, etc. All of these criteria are illustrated by Nikolaus Pevsner's statement, "A bicycle shed is a building; Lincoln Cathedral is a piece of architecture."[25] Pevsner's two examples sit at opposite ends of an ascending scale: Lincoln Cathedral has all seven architectural attributes, whereas the bicycle shed has all seven non-architectural attributes. By avoiding the middle zone, where a building might be ornate but simple, proportionate but secular, or sacred but plain, Pevsner avoided drawing a more decisive line between architecture and building. However, even if he had done so, the line would be arbitrary and debatable because architecture and building are situated on a continuous sliding scale. There is no categorical distinction between them – only a graduated distinction that requires a well-educated critic to employ the overlapping criteria. The graduated scale has no intrinsic division, so there is plenty of opportunity for debate over whether a given building qualifies as architecture. The ascending scale from building to architecture is unidirectional: buildings aspire to be architecture but architecture does not aspire to be building. Pevsner's prime architectural example of Lincoln Cathedral is recognized also as a building, so the lower designation is encompassed by the upper one. Due to the many overlapping criteria it has acquired, the word "architecture" has become sufficiently ambiguous to be adopted for novel domains such as "molecular architecture" and "computer architecture" that are not associated with buildings.[26]

Architectural education and practice have reinforced these sophisticated definitions of architecture. Since the mid-nineteenth century, the discipline of architecture has been studied increasingly at a university level.[27] It is now regarded as a composite subject that is defined in an indirect way, based on the multiple facets it shares with other subjects: art, engineering, sociology, psychology, history, etc. Because architecture has no presence in primary or secondary education, it is assumed to be an esoteric subject with no roots of its own in childhood experience. Aptitude for architecture often is assumed from a student's previous abilities in cognate subjects such as drawing and mathematics, or from equal strengths in arts and sciences. Due to the many responsibilities that architectural education has acquired, design tends to emphasize productive lessons with direct applications.[28] As a practice, architecture is defined by government legislation and regulated by professional bodies that set the criteria and standards to determine who is and who is not an architect. By law, only registered architects can make architecture. Meanwhile, anyone can make music. This is not to suggest that everyone should be permitted to make buildings, but simply to point out that the word "architecture" is reserved for advanced professional activities and that we have no equivalent concept or word for more basic experiences and activities involving substance (and space) in our surroundings.[29]

Tecture versus non-tecture

In distinguishing music from non-music, Clifton elaborates on the basic human condition described by Merleau-Ponty: A human is immersed in worldly surroundings and uses bodily experience to develop a reciprocal understanding of the world and oneself. The world is recognized as a continuation of the flesh of the body. If the world has three dimensions, depth must be the first, as it presumes human involvement from the beginning.[30] Merleau-Ponty strongly opposes any subject–object dichotomy and he struggles to describe this continuity in words, due to the resistance in Western languages that presume discontinuity and dichotomy. Even the word "surroundings" suggests an opposition of center and circumference. Merleau-Ponty regards the human experience of worldly immersion as the precondition for developing any subsequent abstractions.

In a similar way, Clifton's distinction between music and non-music focuses on the sounds (and silences) in our surroundings and relies on a human observer to detect the subtle presence of musical sounds amidst other, denotative sounds. This is a creation myth for music: a momentous first occasion that remains an essential benchmark for all subsequent developments and abstractions. In the creation myth this could happen out in the forest, where denotative sounds would denote the features of one's surroundings and any presentative musical sounds would be recognized immediately as belonging to a separate epistemological category (Figure 14.1).[31]

Some of our surroundings are sounds (and silences); some of our surroundings are substances (and spaces). In a parallel creation myth, alongside the one for music, most of the substances in the forest would denote one's surroundings, but something is recognized as a subtle but deliberate organization that cannot be attributed to nature; it presents something different. The word "architecture" cannot be used here because it carries sophisticated connotations and employs an ascending scale that uses "building" rather than "substance" as its foil, so let's introduce an irritating placeholder word – "tecture" – that avoids those connotations.[32] In this forest setting the basic distinction is between substances and tectural substances – equivalent to the denotative–presentative distinction between sounds and musical sounds.

Figure 14.1 Forest (photo by author)

Similar to what Clifton noted for music, substance must be present if we are to experience tecture at all. "Non-tecture" denotes the ambient features of one's surroundings, whereas tecture presents a deliberate order of some kind. A paraphrase of Adolf Loos offers an illustration: "When we come across a mound in the wood, six feet long and three feet wide, raised to a pyramidal form by means of a spade, we become serious and something in us says: somebody lies buried here. *This is [tecture].*"[33]

Another illustration is offered by the Scottish sculptor Andy Goldsworthy, who works outdoors and reorganizes natural elements in a subtle way to savor what might be described as the threshold between tecture and non-tecture. Goldsworthy is following in the footsteps of earlier land-art sculptors such as Robert Smithson.[34] This sculptural tradition modifies existing surroundings in the world rather than fabricating new objects for a gallery setting. Their work is more like montage than drawing.

In standing out from its denotative, non-tectural surroundings, tecture would be recognized not merely as a set of individual substances but as a larger figure with implicit rhythm, form, motion, direction, and degrees of stability and instability. As in music, the primary phenomenon would be gesture. Tectural events would create their own space; they would not happen *in* space. They might be experienced not just spatially and visually but also in a quasi-temporal way that recognizes forces. As in musical tonality, tecture might rely on a narrative structure that exerts a pull on incompatible substances to bring them back to a state of rest. These various descriptions would suggest that we rely on previous bodily experience to recognize what the tecture is doing (Figure 14.2).

Tectural practice

This description of tecture portrays a first moment of a discipline that is more basic than architecture.[35] As a creation myth, it is not part of recorded history but of separate, prehistoric origin. It could be stored away in a corner of architectural theory, filed under prehistory, phenomenology, or music–architecture parallels, alongside other architectural creation myths. Alternately, it could be germinated and cultivated to imagine the discipline into which it might grow. Initially, this would require a bracketed setting where subtleties of tecture can be distinguished from a background of non-tecture. It would also require a receptive, fictional frame of mind in which these fabricated words are less irritating. As in Clifton's creation myth for music, such a setting would start not from a blank slate but amidst surroundings of substances

Figure 14.2 Beach (photo by author)

(and spaces) – perhaps a forest or a generic building interior. This setting would include not only objects but also humans with senses, experiences, and memories.[36] It would invoke early childhood experience and perhaps even animal awareness.

The discipline of tecture might develop very slowly, starting with observation and recognition. To practice tecture beyond this initial stage, some parallels might be drawn from the discipline of music.[37] A musician proceeds gradually through a series of increasing challenges: listening, performing, improvising, and composing. A "tecturian" might proceed gradually through an equivalent series of activities, rather than leaping immediately to composing or designing. There is no rush to be productive or useful; as in music, the tectural engagement with substance (and space) starts as an enjoyable form of play that is done for its own sake, as a simple human challenge rather than as an external problem to be solved. As in musical sounds (and silences), tectural substances (and spaces) are engaged directly, not through representational notation. Paper and graphic instruments might be used for rubbings but not for drawings or writing. A tecturian might learn to play tecture on various instruments that modulate substances (and spaces). As the different timbral qualities produced by a musical instrument suggest different ways to play it, the different material qualities produced by a tectural instrument might do the same. Tectural performances might even "stir lascivious sensations in the loins." Solo practice and performance would develop skill but collaborative improvisation might be even more enjoyable. Tectural composition, the most advanced activity, might begin with temporary bodily gestures in air or sand, rather than with permanent representational drawings that are abstracted from one's surroundings. At this stage, every bodily gesture is full-scale. Every worldly site is half-finished. Just as Merleau-Ponty had to steer a linguistic course through existing terms and categories, the fictional discipline of tecture might have to do the same when it branches out into the larger world. Along with selected examples from Loos and Goldsworthy, it might invoke certain recognizable figures, actions, and projects in craft, sculpture, and building. To recognize allies, tecturians would rely mainly on their own bodily experience of substance (and space), rather than abstract principles obtained vicariously from others. With its roots in phenomenology, alongside Clifton's intuitive recognition of music, tecture would be cautious and selective when adopting practices and examples from the history of architecture.[38] This would draw a line between tecture and architecture. In turn, this might leave architecture free to focus on larger, more complex organizational projects. The current practice of architecture – from teapots and furniture to buildings, cities, and regions – has become too vast for one discipline anyway. On the other hand, architects who believe in the tectural creation myth might formulate an alternate definition of architecture that is based on the human experience of substance (and space). Retroactively, this would enable them to have been architects since birth.

Notes

1 Thomas Clifton, *Music as Heard: A Study in Applied Phenomenology* (New Haven: Yale University Press, 1983), 232.

2 F. Joseph Smith, *The Experiencing of Musical Sound: Prelude to a Phenomenology of Music* (New York: Gordon and Breach, 1979), 169.

3 Clifton, *Music as Heard*, 1.

4 Ibid., 2.

5 [Anicius Manlius Severinus] Boëthius, *De institutione musica* 1.10, trans. Calvin M. Bower, in *Fundamentals of Music*, ed. Claude V. Palisca (New Haven: Yale University Press, 1989), 17.

6 Boëthius, *De institutione musica* 1.2, in *Fundamentals of Music*, ed. Palisca, 9.

7 The use of a vertical spatial metaphor to map pitches is common throughout history and around the world but its directionality is culturally specific. Our current Western distinction between high and low pitches may seem self-evident but the ancient Greeks reversed these directions: bass voices were "high" while soprano voices were "low." They relied on different analogies: "high" pitches were associated with long strings, tall pipes, and dominant males. See Edward Arthur Lippman, "Music and Space: A Study in the Philosophy of Music" (PhD diss., Columbia University, 1952), 136–51.

8 These Western premises are culturally specific. Other advanced forms of music were developed from different premises. African drumming, for example, relied on absolute pitches, not pitch intervals. See John Miller Chernoff, *African Rhythm and African Sensibility: Aesthetics and Social Action in African Musical Idioms* (Chicago: University of Chicago Press, 1979), 75–9.

9 John of Salisbury (twelfth-century bishop of Chartres), quoted in Lydia Goehr, *The Imaginary Museum of Musical Works: An Essay in the Philosophy of Music* (Oxford: Clarendon Press, 1992), 132.

10 This was theorized in the medieval concept of architecture as a mechanical art. See Hugh of St Victor, *The Didascalicon of Hugh of St Victor: A Medieval Guide to the Arts*, trans. Jerome Taylor (New York: Columbia University Press, 1961), 76. See also Stephen Parcell, "Hugh of St Victor and the Mechanical Arts," in *Four Historical Definitions of Architecture* (Montreal: McGill-Queen's University Press, 2012), 59–104.

11 Clifton, *Music as Heard*, 6.

12 Hermann von Helmholtz formulated this theory in 1862 and it has remained the standard since then. He refers to the three properties as force [intensity], pitch, and quality [timbre]. See Hermann von Helmholtz, *On the Sensations of Tone as a Physiological Basis for the Theory of Music*, trans. Alexander J. Ellis (New York: Dover, 1954), 10, 19, 65–9. For a broader discussion of timbre, see Erik Christensen, *The Musical Timespace: A Theory of Musical Listening* (Aalborg, Denmark: Aalborg University Press, 1996), 12, 16–19, 68–75; and Jean-Claude Risset and David L. Wessel, "Exploration of Timbre by Analysis and Synthesis," in *The Psychology of Music*, ed. Diana Deutsch (New York: Academic Press, 1982), 24–58.

13 See Gerald J. Balzano, "What are Musical Pitch and Timbre?" *Music Perception* 3, no. 3 (1986): 297–314.

14 The short film *Powers of Ten*, by Charles and Ray Eames (1977), shows that substance has recognizable forms at different scales, from macro to micro.

15 See Clifton, *Music as Heard*, 1–18.

16 Ibid., 11.

17 Ibid., 21.

18 Ibid., 14. See also Lippman, "Music and Space."

19 See Susan McClary, "Music, the Pythagoreans, and the Body," in *Choreographing History*, ed. Susan Leigh Foster (Bloomington: Indiana University Press, 1995), 82–104; and Susan McClary, "What was Tonality?" in *Conventional Wisdom: The Content of Musical Form* (Berkeley: University of California Press, 2000), 63–108. Christopher Small, *Musicking: The Meanings of Performing and Listening* (Hanover, NH: Wesleyan University Press, 1998), 187, refers to tonality as a grand, comforting metanarrative: "a bedtime story told to adults."

20 Clifton, *Music as Heard*, 45.

21 Maurice Merleau-Ponty, *Phenomenology of Perception*, trans. Colin Smith (London: Routledge and Kegan Paul, 1962), 140; and Maurice Merleau-Ponty, *The Visible and the Invisible; Followed by Working Notes*, trans. Alphonso Lingis (Evanston, IL: Northwestern University Press, 1968), 152.

22 Paul Valéry, "Eupalinos, or The Architect," in *Dialogues*, trans. William McCausland Stewart, vol. 4 of *The Collected Works of Paul Valéry*, ed. Jackson Mathews (New York: Pantheon Books, 1956), 93–6.

23 Friedrich Nietzsche, *Human, All Too Human*, trans. R. J. Hollingdale (Cambridge: Cambridge University Press, 1996), 101.

24 Music and architecture are not timeless disciplines with an intrinsic relationship. They are related only within certain historical limits and on limited grounds, such as Pythagorean theory, nineteenth-century synaesthesia, and the fine arts classification since the eighteenth century.

25 Nikolaus Pevsner, *An Outline of European Architecture*, 6th ed. (Harmondsworth, UK: Penguin, 1960), 7. Pevsner does not elaborate on this brief philosophical statement but elsewhere his description of Lincoln Cathedral (including its minor deficiencies) cites all of these architectural attributes. See Nikolaus Pevsner, John Harris, and Nicholas Antram, *Lincolnshire*, 2nd ed.; *The Buildings of England* (London: Penguin, 1989), 444–71.

26 *Oxford English Dictionary*, 2nd ed., s.v. "architecture."

27 Arthur Clason Weatherhead, "The History of Collegiate Education in Architecture in the United States" (PhD diss., Columbia University, 1941), 24.

28 "When music teachers teach their students, they don't teach them composition by having them compose. Instead, they have them listen to music. In architecture schools very few people listen to the music, as it were. They're thrown right in and asked to design. The real problem with architecture is that students who know very little about design are asked immediately to design buildings. They form habits about what design should be without even knowing what the possibilities are." Peter Eisenman, quoted in Kathryn Anthony, *Design Juries on Trial: The Renaissance of the Design Studio* (New York: Van Nostrand Reinhold, 1991), 182.

29 The word "architecture" is only two thousand years old and has ambiguous roots. See Parcell, "Architecture as a *Technē*," in *Four Historical Definitions of Architecture*, 21–39.

30 Maurice Merleau-Ponty, "Eye and Mind," trans. Carleton Dallery, in *The Primacy of Perception*, ed. James M. Edie (Evanston, IL: Northwestern University Press, 1964), 180. The same argument is made in Merleau-Ponty, *Phenomenology of Perception*, 254–7, 267.

31 R. Murray Schafer has composed and performed music for natural settings, described in his book *Patria and the Theatre of Confluence* (Indian River, Ontario: Arcana Editions, 1991).

32 "Tecture" is an obscure word for "canopy" or "roof," from Latin *tectura* "a covering," used only in the seventeenth century. *Oxford English Dictionary*, 2d ed., s.v. "tecture." Of the 1.1 million hits for "tecture" on Google, most seem to be merely the last part of the hyphenated word "archi-tecture," but others are novel hybrids such as "eco-tecture" and "nano-tecture."

33 Adolf Loos, "Architecture," trans. Wilfried Wang, in *The Architecture of Adolf Loos*, ed. Yehuda Safran and Wilfried Wang (London: Arts Council of Great Britain, 1985), 108.

34 Terry Friedman and Andy Goldsworthy, eds., *Hand to Earth: Andy Goldsworthy: Sculpture 1976-1990* (New York: Harry N. Abrams, 2004), 13, 140.

35 It precedes Laugier's account of the primitive hut. See Marc-Antoine Laugier, *An Essay on Architecture*, trans. Wolfgang Herrmann and Anni Herrmann (Los Angeles: Hennessey and Ingalls, 1977), 11–12.

36 This exercise is less constrained than what the sensory statue encounters in Etienne Bonnot de Condillac, *A Treatise on the Sensations*, trans. Franklin Philip, in *Philosophical Writings of Etienne Bonnot, Abbé de Condillac* (Hillsdale, NJ: Lawrence Erlbaum Associates, 1982), 144–339.

37 Although the discipline of music offers certain lessons, it cannot be regarded as an ideal for the fictional discipline of tecture to emulate. Since the early nineteenth century, music has departed considerably from the direct worldly engagement that Merleau-Ponty described, due to the advent of the "work" concept that separated, redefined, and reorganized composers, notations, performers, performances, and listeners. See Goehr, *Imaginary Museum of Musical Works*, 176–242.

38 Attempts to translate musical form into architectural form usually trivialize both disciplines by framing the exercise in a highly reductive way and by relying on graphic representations rather than sound and substance. For examples, see Elizabeth Martin, ed., *Architecture as a Translation of Music* (New York: Princeton Architectural Press, 1994). Still, a lesson might be learned from the fact that students who land in architecture school recognize a void in the discipline and hope to fill it by invoking musical experience.

15

MODUS OPERANDI OF AN ARCHITECTUS DOLI

Architectural cunning in the comic plays of Plautus

Lisa Landrum

In a well-known passage at the end of *De architectura*, Vitruvius asserts that civic liberty has been more often won by the "cunning" (*sollertia*) of architects than by the power of war machines (10.16.12). Leon Battista Alberti begins his treatise on the art of building with a comparable claim: that the enemy has been more often defeated by the "ingenuity" (*ingenium*) of architects than by the sword of generals.[1] Beyond the context of battles won by wit, these authors deemed cunning ingenuity as equally imperative in peaceful situations, since it was this inventive capacity that enabled architects to perform essential tasks of their discipline: such as discovering hidden opportunities and relationships in given situations; foreseeing, with good judgment, perfect designs; adjusting these designs in relation to peculiarities of sites; and tempering ornament according to cultural contexts. This manifold capacity, which Vitruvius mainly called *sollertia* and Alberti *ingenium*, has roots and tendrils spanning a long tradition: from pre-philosophical notions of "cunning intelligence" (*mētis*) expressed in Greek myth;[2] to nuanced definitions of "practical wisdom" (*phronēsis*) described by Aristotle;[3] to humanist theories of "invention" (*inventio*) developed in the Italian Renaissance;[4] to elucidations of embodied knowledge, situated understanding, and ethopoetic imagination articulated by recent practitioners of philosophical hermeneutics.[5] But when Vitruvius and Alberti valorized cunning ingenuity as a modus operandi specifically appropriate to architects, they were also tapping into a commonplace fundamental to comic drama: a *topos* as old as comedy itself, whereby an unlikely protagonist would overcome difficulties and ultimately restore social order via admirably inventive yet paradoxically dubious means. This comic *topos* first became associated directly with architects in two Athenian dramas of the late fifth century BCE (Aristophanes' *Peace*, and Euripides' *Cyclops*), and was later reinforced and expanded in the Latin plays of Plautus staged in Rome between 201 and 184 BCE.

At least five of Plautus' twenty extant comedies involve what classicists call an *architectus doli*, an "architect of trickery." In *Miles Gloriosus*, a slave named Palaestrio is repeatedly called *architectus* by his scheming collaborators, as, under his guidance, they collectively trick a braggart warrior into releasing an abducted woman and reuniting her with her proper lover (901–2, 915, 919, 1139). In *Poenulus*, the slave Milphio calls himself *architectus* while scheming to liberate two sisters from a pimp (1110). In *Mostellaria*, another slave, Tranio, alludes to a hypothetical *architectus* while scheming to save a recklessly indulgent youth from his father's fury (760). In the prologue of *Amphitryon*, Mercury (in the guise of a slave) introduces Jupiter as "*architectus* of all,*"* while explaining that this supreme divinity will soon cause trouble, then reconciliation, by engaging in a deceptive love affair with a war hero's wife (45). Lastly, in the opening lines of *Truculentus*, the prologuist rhetorically brushes "architects" aside as he prepares to set forth the dramatic work of the comedic playwright himself (3).

Plautus' elaboration of the cunning slave character has long been considered one of his most original contributions to Latin drama; but the "architect" terms associated with these slaves (and with Jupiter) were likely transposed from the now largely lost Greek comedies that Plautus adapted and translated into Latin. These five imported "architects" were generally ignored in early studies of Plautine inventiveness.[6] They eventually gained attention, however, in an important 1952 study on *The Nature of Roman Comedy*.[7] Since then, Plautus' *architectus* figure has been interpreted in a variety of ways within classical scholarship: as a euphemism for the play's lowly agent of intrigue;[8] as a proxy for the scheming playwright;[9] and as a media-reflexive figure associated with other craft imagery used throughout Plautus' plays to qualify and vivify not only acts of scheming and plot construction, but also moral edification.[10] Yet, there are further interpretations to be made and important questions to be asked from the perspective of the architectural discipline. What links might the *architectus doli* have to the cunning ingenuity of actual architects? How can the ethically ambiguous deeds and dilemmas of the "architects" in these plays shed light on the comparable acts and conundrums of architects in society – both then and now? And, given that Plautus' plays were performed around 200 BCE (two centuries before Vitruvius' *De architectura*, and two centuries after architects arose as figures of cultural significance in Greece), how might the appearance of cunning "architects" in the speculative arena of Roman theatre be understood as participating in a re-emergent theorization of the architect's role?

This essay cannot answer these questions in full, but it will initiate an interpretation of Plautus' *architectus doli* with such questions in mind. By lifting this Roman dramatist up out of the footnotes of architectural scholarship (where he is sometimes merely credited with providing the earliest extant use of the Latin term *architectus*), the following study prepares the grounds for discovering how the cunning agents and agencies of Plautus' comedies meaningfully illuminate the modus operandi of architects.

Modes of transformation

It is appropriate to begin this discussion with the opening words of the prologuist in *Truculentus*, for it is in this play that the transformative work of the dramatist is both compared to and contrasted with the work of architects. First, however, we must set the stage by recalling that Plautus' plays were performed not in permanent stone theaters, but on temporary wooden platforms constructed for special events in the open forums and circuses of Rome. These public areas of the city were not designated for plays throughout the year, rather they were transformed into theatrical settings on certain occasions, including recurring festivals, temple dedications, military triumphs, and funerals.[11] With such civic transformation in mind, the opening words of *Truculentus* are all the more suggestive. Speaking directly to the assembled audience, the actor delivering the prologue says:

> It's Plautus' plea that you provide a plot (*locus*),
> within your pretty city, please – a spot,
> where he can rear his Athens proud and high,
> all by himself: no architects need apply.[12]

Although "architects" are involved here only to be dismissed, the manner of their dismissal suggests that dramatists and architects share – in some contentious yet complementary sense – in the related activities of place-making and plot-making. Being staged in Rome but set in Athens, this play's inaugural speech act transforms the city, or rather the spectator's perception of it, through the dramatist's architect-like powers of persuasive conjuration. Like the prologuist at the start of another comedy, *Menaechmi*, who announces "I bring you Plautus by tongue, not by hand" (3), the actor inaugurating *Truculentus* has no need for architects because (in the public place provided) Plautus will build his enduring work with dramatic language and human interaction, not stones.

We may discern in these two prologues an underlying contest between words and monuments – a polemic echoing Pindar, who once promised to erect a monument of song more lasting than stone.[13] Yet, we should also hear in these opening lines a productive complicity between dramatic and architectural modes of transformation. Plautus' inaugural words reveal a creative tension between place-making and plot-making in which these arts are not simply bound by analogy, but intertwined by their cooperatively transformative agency. In other words, by expressly dismissing "architects" the poet cunningly appropriates their craft, asserting that the dramatist's medium likewise builds on situational and social conditions already available in the urban milieu. As Vitruvius' contemporary, Ovid, would write, "the place (*locus*) itself provides the subject matter for the poet."[14] Thus, what "architects" contribute to Plautus' *Truculentus* is not a simple image of dramatic poetry as monumental work, but a more complex demonstration of dramatic action as a potent mode of civic transformation.

This dramatic sense of civic transformation is reinforced at the beginning of another play. At the start of *Poenulus*, the prologuist initially establishes the scene conventionally: providing the play's title; acknowledging its Greek model; reminding the audience of theatrical etiquette; and soliciting the indulgence of authorities (1–45). He then announces, more dramatically, that he "shall now determine the regions, limits and confines" of the "plot" (*argumentum*) – a task for which he has been designated not the play's *architectus*, but its *finitor*, or "surveyor," one who delineates boundaries (48–9). At the time of this play's performance (circa 189 BCE), a land surveyor would have been an extremely busy and controversial figure, since the Roman Republic, surging with confidence after defeating Carthage and Macedon in the second Punic War (in 201 BCE), was ramping up its policy of territorial expansion by founding numerous colonies.[15] In this colonial context, the authority of Plautus' *finitor* is called upon, comically, not to delineate a new piece of the Republic abroad, but to inscribe a commensurable area of foreign land (in this case Calydon) within Rome. This nested and comparative layering of sites reinterprets the limits, mutability, and potential reversibility of the Roman situation. Many other instances of allusively layered places and plots occur in Plautus' plays. Most overtly, midway through *Curculio*, a character refers directly to the markets, courts, colonnades, and shrines of the Roman Forum, thereby linking the actual performative situation in Rome to the play's imagined Greek setting (in Epidaurus).[16] By appropriating features of the surrounding milieu into the fictional plot, Plautus' architect-like characters invite audiences to compare real and represented places, and to consider the drama underway as an illuminating mimesis of their mutually transformative potential.

A further point must be emphasized concerning *Truculentus*. Though the opening lines of this play serve to compare the topographies of Rome and

Athens, the rhetorical dismissal of "architects" also foregrounds the power of speech to dramatically alter human circumstances. This power is demonstrated in *Truculentus* by the speech of a courtesan named Phronesium. As a cynical, yet seductive, embodiment of *phronēsis* (practical wisdom), this Athenian courtesan – who claims to have been taught by her own *ingenio* (453) – personifies both the ambiguous efficacy of language and the need for interpretation in relation to changing circumstances. This courtesan's ploys, like those of the *architectus*, are successful because she understands (and knowingly manipulates) circumstantial conditions: not least of which is the gullibility of her solicitors – those men who desire Phronesium but, ironically, possess no *phronēsis*.

Modes of deception and deliberation

By dismissing "architects," the prologuist in *Truculentus* paradoxically reveals both the dramatic agency of place-making and, reciprocally, the civic transformation implicit in drama. In the remaining plays to be introduced, cunning slaves called "architects" reveal a related modus operandi: deception, and its efficacious role in renewing social order. Plautus' leading slaves are exemplars of such deception. By orchestrating elaborate ruses with the help of various collaborators, these quick-witted, deep-thinking and shrewdly opportunistic slaves always succeed in outwitting adversaries (typically arrogant soldiers and oppressive pimps) for the benefit of their own less savvy masters who have themselves become caught up in an unfortunate predicament through some combination of bad luck, a lack of money, and a superabundance of libido. Before describing select deceptions of the *architectus doli*, it is helpful to consider the *doli* of their epithet.

Dolus and *dolosus*, meaning "trick" and "tricky," are terms used throughout the comedies of Plautus to qualify deceptive schemers, scheming, and schemes. In *Miles Gloriosus*, the *architectus*-slave practices "learned tricks" (147), concocts a "perfect trick" (248), and enlists collaborators who are themselves full of "trickery" – knowing "every phony phrase, the phony ways, [and] phony plays" (191–92).[17] Further, this *architectus* shares the "rationale" (*ratio*) behind his "tricks" (773), and teaches his collaborators to perform their *dolus* with *subdolus*, or "subtlety" (355–7). Like *architectus*, *dolus* and *dolosus* stem from Greek terms: *dólos* (δόλος) and *dólios* (δόλιος). In Greek myth, Odysseus, who embodies *mētis*, also exemplifies *dóliotēs* (trickery): as when he overcomes the Cyclops by "guile" (*dólō*), not might.[18] Elsewhere in the *Odyssey*, *dólos* names tricks involving cunning artifacts: the Trojan Horse is a *dólos* (8.494); so, too, is the bed of invisible bonds crafted by Hephaestus to ensnare his wife (Aphrodite) and her lover (Ares) in their adulterous affair (8.276). Like a fisherman's lure offered as bait for a potential catch, such artifacts (when knowingly deployed) have treacherous appeal. But Plautus' *architectus doli* does not devise treacherous artifacts. Rather, cunning schemes of action are his trick. Although these schemes involve the knowing manipulation of physical artifacts (including urban and theatrical settings), their success depends on more subtle skills akin to those that Vitruvius and Alberti would later valorize: persuasive leadership, timely judgment, practical forethought, and a keen interpretation of the limits and potential of circumstances – all thoughtfully exercised in the midst of highly problematic (even preposterous) situations.

Paradoxically, the success of tricky schemes in Plautus often depends on true deliberation. In *Miles Gloriosus*, the *architectus* earnestly deliberates before and throughout the scheme. Initially, he calls his inner wits to counsel as though convening a veritable "assembly" (197). Later, he likens a conference with fellow conspirators to a "well-attended senate meeting" (594). Such mock senatorial sessions led by a dubious architect–slave may have parodied the false counsel reputedly practiced by contemporaneous Roman senators and generals, whose strategizing was, at times, deemed as dishonorably cunning as Rome's archenemy Hannibal.[19] But, parody aside, these same scenes also show true deliberation to be imperative for concocting schemes capable not only of deceiving empowered oppressors but of liberating others from unwelcome predicaments. When such deception is enacted for the sake of accomplishing a genuine good on behalf of others, it is called a "just deception." As the tragedian Aeschylus once wrote, Zeus does not object to "just deception."[20] The scheme in *Miles Gloriosus* provides a good example, since it culminates with reunited lovers escaping oppressive misfortune on a ship, leaving in their wake a brutally punished warrior. Several other plays of Plautus end similarly, with amorous and familial reunions. The *architectus*, then, brings about justly deceptive schemes while keeping a deliberative eye on a larger plot.

Modes of representation

Together with transformation, deception and deliberation, the *architectus* in Plautus also practices modes of representation. First, Plautus and his "architects" deploy a variety of architectural metaphors, using terms drawn from related trades, including masonry, carpentry, ship-building, weaving and pottery. With such artisanal metaphors, Plautus gives representation to largely invisible processes of scheming.[21] For instance, the plan of Plautus' *architectus* is sometimes called a "piece of craft" (after the Greek *technē*), and a "fabricated thing." A fellow schemer is an "artist" and "builder," and the general work of scheming is "building." The elements of a scheme might be "glued together," as bricks are joined with mortar in a well-bonded wall.

A highly-refined plan may be "polished" like marble or silver; whereas a preliminary trick may be "hewn" and "rough-hewn" like heavy timber, or "hammered-out" after the manner of a smith working metal in a forge. Some slaves carefully "weave" an intricate plot; others quickly "stitch" an improvisatory trick. A scheme may be "moulded" in the manner of a potter working malleable clay: as Palaestrio boasts in *Miles Gloriosus*, "this affair is shaping up well under my hands" (873, 1143).[22] Palaestrio's collaborators also offer an extended analogy between devising a scheme and building a ship. As the schemers prepare to launch their trick, one remarks on how their *architectus* has firmly established the keel, setting it well "in line," now it's up to them, the "experienced builders," to complete the work on time (915–21). Beyond the relatively obvious compositional and tectonic parallels between well-crafted schemes and well-made artifacts, this imagery also makes vivid the collaborative, iterative and immersive aspects of scheming.

Plautus further uses architectural imagery to draw ethical arguments. For instance, in *Mostellaria*, the youth who misbehaves in his father's absence incants an extended monologue in which he likens himself to a house and his parents to builders (85–156). Although his parents initially raised him up with strong foundations and proper finishes (a good liberal education), he realizes that he has poorly maintained their work. Now, having suffered a storm of love, he is "being eaten away by metaphorical rain and hail," and his timbers are rotting.[23] Central to this youth's song is the problem of finding a proper model, or *exemplum*: he finds a well-built house to be an *exemplum* of man, and a self-disciplined man to be an *exemplum* for others. The slave's later introduction of "some architect" who deems a particular house exemplary (760), participates in this edifying imagery, suggesting that architects (and architecture) have some role to play in restoring ethical capacity.

Finally, the "architects" of Plautus implicate features of the setting (the *scaena*) into their scheme, giving representation to architecture's ominous, appealing and revelatory agencies. For example, in *Mostellaria*, Tranio convinces a father that his house is haunted so that he will not enter it and discover how his son misbehaved in his absence. Through situational allusions and deceit, Tranio changes not the house, but the father's perception of it. Tranio subsequently persuades the father to regard the neighbor's house as exemplary by alluding to "some architect" who praised it (760–1), and by describing appealing features of its otherwise invisible interiors. In *Miles Gloriosus*, adjacent houses also aid and abet the scheme. With a secret tunnel and well-placed windows, Palaestrio, the *architectus*, makes one woman appear as two to those less skilled in the interpretation of appearances. These portals perform epistemologically, giving selective access to the truth of events. The *architectus* in this play persuasively controls what is seen and unseen, and how what is seen and unseen are understood.[24] Having initially involved the *scaena* to make the warrior's slave not see what he has seen, Palaestrio later involves his collaborators to make the warrior see what he has not. Preoccupied with his own image, this warrior, who brags of his own ability to blind enemies with radiant weaponry, is shown, ironically, to be himself blind to the subtle devices mobilized against him. Seeing only what he desires, the braggart succumbs to flattery, perceiving the architect's trick only after it is too late.

Negotiating ambiguity

In the prologue of *Amphitryon*, Mercury introduces Jupiter as "architect of all" – of all "good deeds" performed for the people (45). This seemingly straightforward qualification of Jupiter's benevolent omnipotence takes on subtler layers of meaning when considered in dramatic context, since Jupiter himself performs in this comedy as a deceptive schemer in pursuit of mortal love. Impersonating a returning war general, Amphitryon, Jupiter enjoys the affections of this general's wife, Alcmena. Meanwhile, Mercury, impersonating Amphitryon's slave Sosia, ensures that Jupiter's philandering goes unnoticed. The play unfolds as a series of episodes involving double, mistaken, and lost identities, and culminates with a near tragedy when Amphitryon discovers what he believes to be his wife's infidelity. This crisis turns to comic resolution, however, when Jupiter reveals himself as the source of trouble and reconciles the situation by adjusting time such that Alcmena gives birth to twin sons: one mortal, one divine. Thus, when Mercury introduces Jupiter as "architect of all," this "all" implies the play's every action (large and small), every complication (good and devious), plus the tragicomic resolution. This comprehensive plot-making realigns the *architectus* figure with the dramatist Plautus, who may well have played the role of Jupiter himself.[25]

Beyond reinforcing performative similarities between architects and dramatists, *Amphitryon* reveals the complex status shared by these comparable agents: a shifty, ambiguous, and contradictory status somewhere between a lowly actor (on par with a wily slave) and a supreme god (acting as a mortal general). Mercury delights in these ambiguities, urging the audience to pay attention while Jupiter stoops to take up the "histrionic art" (86–90, 152). As a comedic playwright, Plautus, likewise, delights in ambiguities of status. All his plot-driving agents of *doli* and *ingenium* were officially powerless: slaves, women, prostitutes, old men, and foreigners. Like actors and dramatists, builders and architects in the Roman Republic were generally foreigners, freedmen, or slaves.[26] Yet, in spite of their subordinate position, they were tasked with authority and obliged to act with expertise and comprehensive knowledge. Like slaves in Roman society, architects were mercurial mediators: moving between echelons of society, between public and private domains, and between noble intentions and underhanded means. Given twenty-first century anxieties over the authority, respectability, and relevance of architects, the architect–slaves of Plautus provide a timely model for theorizing persistent ambiguities of status inherent to the architect's role.

Conclusion

This essay has largely emphasized the good intentions of an *architectus doli*, and the ethical benefits of their transformative, deceptive, deliberative and representative deeds. But the actions and intentions of cunning architects are not always good. Indeed, the word "architect" has been used as a pejorative epithet for villainous schemers since at least the fourth century BCE.[27] When Vitruvius and Alberti composed their respective treatises, they were each eager to distance the architect's modus operandi from malfeasance. For instance, although Vitruvius valued *sollertia* as a kind of cunning proper to architects, he also sought to distinguish true architects from those who "term themselves architects falsely" (6.pref.7). Similarly, although Alberti valued *ingenium* and wit, he also deemed "deceit and guile" of the masses and "unscrupulous cunning" of the powerful to be serious threats to civic order.[28] Plautus' *architectus doli*, then, should be seen as treading a thin line between propriety and impropriety, helping us to recognize and navigate the ethical ambiguities architects face while striving for happy endings.

Notes

1 Joseph Rykwert, Neil Leach and Robert Tavernor, *Leon Battista Alberti: On the Art of Building in Ten Books* (Cambridge, MA: MIT Press, 1988), 4.

2 Marcel Detienne and Jean-Pierre Vernant, *Cunning Intelligence in Greek Culture and Society*, trans. Janet Lloyd (Sussex: Harvester Press, 1978).

3 *Nicomachean Ethics* 1140a24–1145a11.

4 Ernesto Grassi, *Rhetoric as Philosophy: The Humanist Tradition* (University Park: Pennsylvania State University Press, 1980).

5 Richard Kearney, *The Wake of Imagination: Toward a Postmodern Culture* (Minneapolis: University of Minnesota Press, 1988); and Mario J. Valdés, *A Ricoeur Reader: Reflection and Imagination* (Toronto: University of Toronto Press, 1991). In architectural discourse, see Marco Frascari, "Sollertia," *Off Ramp* 1, no. 5 (2001): 51–3; David Leatherbarrow, "Adjusting Architectural Premises: The Conscience of Design," *Practices* 5–6 (1997): 175–84; and Alberto Pérez-Gómez, "The Architect's Métier," in *Carleton Folio* (Ottawa: Carleton University, 1985).

6 Eduard Fraenkel, *Plautine Elements in Plautus*, trans. Tomas Drevikovsky and Frances Muecke (Oxford: Oxford University Press, 2007), first published as *Plautinisches im Plautus*, 1922.

7 George E. Duckworth, *The Nature of Roman Comedy* (Princeton: Princeton University Press, 1952).

8 George Fredric Franko, "The Characterization of Hanno in Plautus' *Poenulus*," *American Journal of Philology* 117, no. 3 (Autumn 1996): 425–52; and C. Stace, "The Slaves of Plautus," *Greece & Rome* 15, no. 1 (April 1968): 64–77.

9 Stavros A. Frangoulidis, "Palaestrio as Playwright: Plautus, *Miles Gloriosus* 209–212," *Studies in Latin Literature and Roman History* 7, no. 227 (1994): 72–86; Timothy J. Moore, *The Theater of Plautus: Playing to the Audience* (Austin: University of Texas Press, 1998), 75–6; Alison Sharrock, *Reading Roman Comedy: Poetics and Playfulness in Plautus and Terence* (Cambridge: Cambridge University Press, 2009); Niall W. Slater, *Plautus in Performance: The Theatre of the Mind* (Princeton: Princeton University Press, 1985); and Eva Stehle, "Pseudolus as Socrates, Poet and Trickster" in *Classical Texts and their Traditions: Studies in Honor of C.R. Trahman*, ed. David F. Bright and Edwin S. Ramage (Chico, CA: Scholars Press, 1984), 239–51.

10 W. Forehand, "The Use of Imagery in Plautus' *Miles Gloriosus*," *Rivista di Studi Classici* 21 (1973): 5–16; Mason Hammond, Arthur M. Mack and Walter Moskalew, *T. Macci Plauti: Miles Gloriosus* (Cambridge MA: Harvard University Press, 1963, reprinted 1997), esp. 48; and Eleanor Windsor Leach, "*De exemplo meo ipse aedificato*: An Organizing Idea in the *Mostellaria*," *Hermes* 97, no. 3 (1969): 318–32.

11 Gesine Manuwald, *Roman Republican Theatre* (Cambridge: Cambridge University Press, 2011), 41–68.

12 James Tatum, trans., *Plautus: The Darker Comedies, Bacchides, Casina, and Truculentus* (Baltimore and London: Johns Hopkins University Press, 1983), 153. Unless otherwise noted, all other translations of Plautus in this essay are from Wolfgang de Melo, ed., *Plautus*, Loeb Classical Library, 5 vols (Cambridge, MA: Harvard University Press, 2011).

13 *Olympian Ode* 6.1–4.

14 *Fasti* 4.807.

15 Erich S. Gruen, "Plautus and the Public Stage," in *Culture and National Identity in Republican Rome* (Ithaca: Cornell University Press, 1992), 124–57.

16 For an interpretation of this scene, see Timothy Moore, "*Palliata Togata*: Plautus, *Curculio* 462-86," *American Journal of Philology* 112, no. 3 (Autumn 1991): 342–62.

17 Plautus. *Three Comedies: The Braggart Soldier, The Brothers Menaechmus, The Haunted House*, trans. Erich Segal (New York: Harper & Row, 1969).

18 *Odyssey* 9.406–8.

19 On Plautus' parodying of military strategizing, ambitions and triumphs, see Fraenkel, *Plautine Elements in Plautus*, 163–6.

20 Aeschylus Frag. 301.

21 For an introduction to this *topos*, see M. L. West, "Poetry as Construction," in *Indo European Poetry and Myth* (Oxford: Oxford University Press, 2007), 35–6.

22 See note 10 above for references to craft imagery.

23 I use Kristina Milnor's words here to capture the gist, see "Playing House: Stage, Space, and Domesticity in Plautus's *Mostellaria*," *Helios* 29.1 (2002): 10.

24 On "vision and confusion" in Plautus, see Sharrock, *Reading Roman Comedy*, 100–15.

25 David Christenson, ed., *Plautus, Amphitruo* (Cambridge: Cambridge University Press, 2000), 2.

26 James C. Anderson, *Roman Architecture and Society* (Baltimore: Johns Hopkins University Press, 1997), 37; and Manuwald, *Roman Republican Theatre*, 90–1.

27 Demosthenes, *Speeches* 40.42; 56.11.

28 *De re aedificatoria*, 5.1; and Caspar Pearson, *Humanism and the Urban World: Leon Battista Alberti and the Renaissance City* (University Park, PA: The Pennsylvania State University Press, 2011), 119–20.

16

TOWARDS AN ECOLOGY OF THE PALLADIAN VILLA

Graham Livesey

> . . . our house would emerge as permeated from every direction by streams of energy. . . . Its image of immobility would then be replaced by an image of a complex of mobilities. . . .[1]
>
> *Henri Lefebvre*

The villas by Andrea Palladio (1508–1580) in the sixteenth century for the terra firma, or mainland, region of the Veneto were designed primarily for the nobility of Vicenza and Venice. They were typically the centerpieces of working farms, and supplemented the incomes of the owners; they also provided a place for culture, recreation, leisure, and entertainment. The Palladian villa remains a distinct and comprehensively studied sub-type within the historical typology of the villa, and yet much of the scholarship surrounding the Palladian villa concentrates on the formal qualities of the buildings; relatively little has been written about how the Palladian villa was occupied. Here the functional organization of the villa and the use of furniture will be briefly studied in order to address the notion that all buildings and environments constitute ecologies.

An ecology is defined as the vital interaction between organisms and the environments they occupy, and is a concept that was devised in the mid-nineteenth century.[2] Ecologies are measured in terms of how they function as habitats, which necessitates examining flows of populations, energy, water, waste, nutrients, and the like. Ecologies can be productive or not, and they are subject to a wide range of events. Ecologies constructed by humans also include technologies, economies, and socio-political systems, as humans modify and adapt to environments through the creation of clothing, objects, shelter, settlements and organizations. The overall behavior of an environment evaluates the productivity of that environment in terms of the energy employed, the distribution of nutrients and waste, the health of populations and also the economic, social and political dynamics of the system. Over time well-functioning ecologies support a complex range of species and tend towards dynamic balance, despite being continuously subject to changing arrays of forces.

The landscape ecologist Richard T.T. Forman has developed a method for examining the behavior of ecologies based on the "patch," "corridor," and "matrix."[3] This method examines the structure and performance of landscapes against various flows and population systems. Patches are defined territories or spaces that have a discernible composition, shape, size, edge characteristics, and adjacencies.[4] A patch or territory, for example a room in a building or a small park in a city, has a latent functionality that is activated by populations that inhabit it and by the characteristics of the patch. In the case of architecture this has to do with how internal spaces are arranged, and how these relate to a larger context. Landscape ecologists employ the notion of "patch dynamics" to describe how a group of spaces might behave over time according to changing arrangements.

The behavior of a group of patches is influenced by the boundaries that both separate and unite adjoining territories or spaces. Boundaries, such as walls, and how they are composed, is also an essential factor in looking at the performance of an architectural ecology.[5] Buildings are arrangements of spaces that are either functionally predetermined or open. The productivity of a building's arrangement depends on the dynamics that occur within the internal spaces, and between the building and its context. Much of this depends on the size, shape, and location of a space, and the porosity of the boundaries that define that space. For example, walls in buildings function like membranes in that they filter a wide range of flows from heat, light, sound, and water, to animals, humans, and vegetation. Doors and windows are used in architecture as devices for crossing boundaries, and for regulating flows. The arrangement of spaces in a building and the interconnections between the spaces establish an ecological and functional potential. This is completed by how humans interact with the spaces, and how they modulate the environment through the use of furnishings and possessions.

Agostino Gallo, writing in 1566, describes in detail the pleasure of villa life including the benefits of fresh air and good food, the freedom and ease of living in the country, the enjoyment of watching peasants working, and the various activities the inhabitants enjoyed (hunting, conversing, reading, playing games, dining, and listening to music). His protagonist portrays a typical day in the villa:

> First of all, I usually get up at dawn, and these days I join my companions at that hour to go out hawking. . . . Then we come home and often eat together. . . . Over the meal we talk about what we have discovered and caught . . . until it is time to rest or to attend to some necessary business. After that we often find ourselves getting together again to read, play cards or board games or chess, sing or play musical instruments. . . . After we have amused ourselves in this way, we walk in a group to visit this friend or that. . . .[6]

In particular this passage describes the social and recreational activities of noblemen enjoying the benefits of life in a late Renaissance villa. The women who also occupied the villa would have had a much more restricted existence, following very different patterns of living.[7] This wide range of activities would have been supported by a host of servants whose labor was essential to operating the house and the farm.[8]

In his famous treatise *The Four Books on Architecture* (*I quattro libri dell'architettura*), originally published in 1570, Palladio, in his precise manner, elaborates on a villa in which the owner can pass his time "improving his property and increasing his wealth through his skill in farming," and enjoy the benefits of life in a rural setting.[9] The siting of the villa as part of a working farm was a crucial decision, and despite the lack of site drawings in Palladio's oeuvre, contemporary studies demonstrate how carefully he located the villas.[10] In siting the villa and outbuildings, and arranging internal spaces, Palladio was very conscious of factors such as access, wind, orientation to the sun, views, and less commodious factors such as dampness.[11] A range of outbuildings, including the barchessa, either attached to the villa, or not, would have accommodated servants, animals, implements, and storage. In the flat landscape of the Veneto the villas were typically located facing a river or canal; this landscape had been engineered for some time in order to provide drainage, irrigation, and transportation systems.[12] Ultimately, the siting of the building and the arrangement of the internal spaces contribute to the ecological effectiveness of a design.

The internal organization of the villa that Palladio developed responded precisely to the needs of his clients, judging from the popularity of his designs. Palladio's villas followed a repeating pattern that organized rooms according to public (*entrate, sale*), semi-private (*stanze, camere, camerini*), and servant's areas. The servants' working spaces were typically arranged on the lower level with kitchens, cellars, and the like, while the main rooms were formally grouped on the *piano nobile*, which was elevated above ground level, around the main *sala*; the upper mezzanine levels were typically used as granaries and servant's quarters.[13] The *piano nobile* was sandwiched between the working, or less noble, areas of the house, internal stairs were discretely hidden within the fabric of the villa to accommodate the functioning of the villa, and external stairs typically provided dramatic access to the loggia from the estate.

The loggia was a vital element in the house working in tandem with the *sala* (Figures 16.1 and 16.2), or main hall, as it provided a transitional space between interior and exterior and was used for leisure, dining, and viewing the surrounding countryside.[14] The *sala* (and entrances), as the most public space in the house, would have been used mainly for entertaining, conducting business, and for parties, banquets, performances, and weddings, and was typically a large formal room. The other, more private, rooms (*stanze, camere*) were equally distributed on either side of the public spaces and were multi-functional.[15] The Palladian villa plan is characterized by its careful and symmetrical arrangement of spaces within a controlled form, akin to that of the human body. To some extent the organization of the villas reflected the arrangement of the palaces Palladio's clients occupied in Vicenza and Venice, the Venetian palace being formally organized on the *piano nobile* level around the *portego*.[16] Palladio writes of convenience, that it "will be provided when

Figure 16.1 Andrea Palladio, Villa Godi (1537), view from *loggia* (image courtesy of Johannes Niemeijer)

Figure 16.2 Andrea Palladio, Villa Pisani (1543–45), view of *sala* or main hall (image courtesy of Johannes Niemeijer)

each member is given its appropriate position, well situated, no less than dignity requires nor more than utility demands; each member will be correctly positioned when the loggias, halls, rooms, cellars, and granaries are located in their appropriate places."[17] The rigorous "systematization"[18] of the villa plan was a new aspect of Palladio's designs, as was the controlled balancing of the facades and placement of openings (Figure 16.3).

Palladio, through the establishment and refinement of the villa plan was creating a series of spaces, or an ecology, that responded to both internal and external forces. The differing sizes of rooms (small, medium, and large) were suitably arranged, proportioned, and connected in order that they can be "mutually useful."[19] In his treatise, Palladio writes:

> The small ones [rooms] should be divided up to create even smaller rooms where studies and libraries could be located, as well as riding equipment and other tackle which we need everyday and which would be awkward to put in the rooms where one sleeps, eats, or receives guests. It would also contribute comfort if the summer rooms were large and spacious and oriented to the north, and those for the winter to the south and west and were small rather than otherwise, because in the summer we seek the shade and breezes, and in the

Figure 16.3 Andrea Palladio, Villa Pisani (1543–45), view of facade facing courtyard (image courtesy of Johannes Niemeijer)

winter, the sun, and smaller rooms get warmer more readily than large ones. But those we would want to use in the spring and autumn will be oriented to the east to look out over gardens and greenery. Studies and libraries should be in the same part of the house because they are used in the morning more than at any other time.[20]

From this quote it is evident that Palladio very carefully oriented each of the rooms; it can also be deduced that the occupation of spaces shifted according to the seasons and times of the day. The size, shape, and proportion of rooms were vital to the functioning of the house and the harmony of the architecture, as was the relationship between rooms and the outdoors, as precisely determined by the placement and size of doors and windows.[21]

Beyond the design and arrangement of the rooms in the villa, are the vital connections between spaces and the site itself. In the treatise Palladio also devotes some text to describing the size, location, and ornamentation of doors, windows, and stairs. For example, writing about windows, he states:

One should, therefore, take great care over the size of the rooms which will receive light from them [windows], because it is obvious that a larger room needs more light to make it luminous and bright than a small one; and if the windows are made smaller and less numerous than necessary, they will be made gloomy; and if they are made too large the rooms are practically uninhabitable because, since cold and hot air can get in, they will be extremely hot or cold depending on the seasons of the year, at least if the region of the sky to which they are oriented does not afford some relief.[22]

The size and number of windows were determined by size of a room, by climatic factors, and by the facade. Equally important was the placement of doors, size of doorways, and the direction of the door swings. Further, many of the Palladian villas featured finely frescoed interior walls depicting themes conducive to villa life, and executed by established Venetian artists; this is evident in the frescoes by Giovanni Antonio Fasolo dating from the 1560s in the *salone* of the Villa Caldogno (attributed to Palladio).

The attention to creating a harmonious whole, through the arrangement of spaces and the careful design of openings in walls, remains a hallmark of the Palladian villa. Despite the seeming neutrality and formality of the spaces, the various rooms that comprised the living rooms of the villa were carefully sequenced and each had distinctive qualities based on size, shape, and location.[23] The villas were normally occupied during the warmer seasons, particularly during the planting and harvesting months. Activities on the *piano nobile* level of the villa included sleeping, dressing, eating, socializing, recreation, study, entertaining, and working; each of these uses required spaces, furniture, and other objects.[24] The use of the rooms would vary, depending on who occupied the house, with any of the larger *stanze/camere* able to be a bedroom.[25] When not occupied, the villas would have been relatively bare except for beds, and a few remaining items; the smaller rooms that were used as libraries or studies likely retained possessions throughout the year.[26] Therefore, vital to the functioning of the villa was the employment of furniture, which allowed for the continuous rearrangement of the internal spaces; a defined group of spaces to be given a functional flexibility that allowed the entire group of spaces, or the dynamic of a group of patches, to be reorganized, or adjusted to changing ecological factors.

As Jean Baudrillard points out in his book *The System of Objects*, objects employed in traditional everyday life involved forms of embodied energy, energy that came from human labor and animals.[27] Baudrillard writes, that in traditional, or pre-industrial settings:

> Man's profound gestural relationship to objects . . . epitomizes his integration into the world, into social structures. . . . We cannot help but admire scythes, baskets, pitchers or ploughs, amalgams of gestures

and forces, of symbols and functions, decorated and stylized by human energy and shaped by the forms of the human body, by the exertions they imply and by the matter they transform. . . .[28]

These objects, including furniture, necessarily engage in the exertions and gestures of the human body and its involvement in space. It can be inferred that furniture mediates between ourselves and the spaces we inhabit, engages in a variety of energy flows, and allows for the creation and maintenance of ecologies. Baudrillard notes that objects in traditional systems were based on human efforts that were "embedded in human relations." Similarly, the occupants of the Palladian villa, through their own actions and those of servants, participated in an ongoing negotiation with their environment through architecture and its furnishings. J. Macgregor Wise has described the creation of home, or habitat, as the continuous "organization of markers (objects) and the formation of space. . . . Home can be a collection of objects, furniture, and so on that one carries with one from move to move."[29] He suggests the arranging of objects, the organizing of space, and the presence of family and friends, is part of the identity making associated with home. As Wise states, the creation of home is a continuous activity that occurs everywhere we go, through "the arrangement of objects, practices, feelings and affects."[30] The flows of energy in a house create both harmonious and conflicted conditions, aided by the arranging of furniture, or the continuous creation of "home."[31] Domestic actions participate in a wide range of flow patterns and continuous exchanges of energy.[32]

The owners of Palladian villas would have brought their furniture (*móbili*) and smaller personal items with them on each visit by cart or barge, packing these up when returning to town (Figure 16.4).[33] This supported the adaptability of the internal spaces. Discussing the *camere*, or secondary rooms, found in Venetian palaces, Patricia Fortini Brown notes that they were spaces primarily used for sleeping, being occupied by beds and fireplaces. However, they had further functions:

> The *camere* were also used for dining, for small formal dinners and for large banquets when guests spilled over from the *portego*, as well as for everyday meals during cold weather. . . . Tables on trestles, which could easily be set up in different rooms, were the norm in this period. Wall hangings, table linens and other objects were moved around as needed.[34]

One must assume that the secondary rooms in the Palladian villas were used in a similar manner. Beds would have occupied the spaces, and would not

Figure 16.4 A Renaissance bed, chair, stool, urinal and incense burner in Bartolomeo Scappi, *Opera dell'arte del cucinare*, Venice, 1570

have been moved back and forth between villa and palace like the smaller furnishings (tables, chairs, stools, benches, chests, etc.). Beds were often the center of the house during the Renaissance, and were often shared, being "important sites for sociability."[35] Brown notes that after the bed, the chest was the most important piece of furniture in the Venetian *camere* of the period, and like the room itself, was multi-functional in that it provided storage (for clothing, linen, books, and small items), acted as a seat, could be used as a table, and provided a display surface for a runner or carpet.[36] Chairs, tables, and a variety of fabrics would have completed the furnishings.[37] Beyond the sleeping and dining functions, these spaces would also have been used as work and social places for women. Servants would have also been engaged in setting up rooms upon arrival, rearranging them as needed, and packing up for the return to Venice or Vicenza.

Life in the villa, despite the emphasis on rural tranquility, would have been busy, supported by the daily activities of served and servants. Much of the functioning of the villa would have depended on the interaction of spaces and flows of organisms, energy, air, water, nutrients, waste, and the like. The organization of building would have both enhanced and negated flow patterns. In particular, flows of energy are active in all aspects of villa from the embodied energy found in the material aspects of the house, to the active and passive energy systems, and the energy of the daily routines of living. As suggested above furniture plays a vital role in continuously modulating the various interior and exterior environments. This involves managing flow patterns, creating new ones, and dealing with the inevitable forces of inefficiency in the system.

The basic design of the Palladian villa appears to have been successful in meeting the needs of the Venetian and Vicentine clients, and has been a source of inspiration for subsequent generations of architects. Despite the symmetry of the villa plan, each room has particular qualities based on its size, shape, location and adjacent relationships (internal and external); when combined, this established a complex set of potentials. Palladio was sensitive to the specific needs of his clients, and to the concept of the rooms being multi-functional. Furniture was truly mobile and was used to continuously adjust the spaces of the house to changing users and to the seasons. In other words a productive relationship between furniture (*móbili*) and building (*immóbili*) was established. This resulted in a creative use of space, negotiated through changing furniture and spatial arrangements, rarely found in modern architecture.

As a repeating group of spaces, the patch dynamics of the Palladian villa was supported by the siting of the villa, and the ability on the part of the users to move functions around in the various spaces of the building. The Palladian villa balanced urban and rural life, and responded to the landscapes and climate of the Veneto. The villas were simple and relatively inexpensive to build, and they reflected Palladio's late Renaissance classicism and inherent analogies to the human body. The Palladian villa was a formal and repeating arrangement of rooms and elements guided by both urban and agricultural factors, that was then adjusted continuously in response to client needs and site forces. The villas brought together material elements (building, furniture), flows (air, water, energy), bodies (clients, servants, visitors), languages (speech, codes of behavior), and territorialities (rooms, landscapes) into a dynamic construct.

Acknowledgements

I would like to thank the editors for their input in developing the essay, Dr. David Monteyne for providing insightful comments on a late draft, and Johannes Niemeijer for graciously giving permission to reproduce images originally published in *Palladio, the Villa and the Landscape* (Basel: Birkäuser, 2011), co-authored with Gerrit Smienk.

Notes

1 Henri Lefebvre, *The Production of Space*, trans. D. Nicolson-Smith (Oxford: Basil Blackwell Ltd., 1991), 93.
2 The term "ecology" was devised in 1866 by the German scientist Ernst Haeckel.
3 See Richard T.T. Forman, *Land Mosaics: The Ecology of Landscapes and Regions* (Cambridge, UK: Cambridge University Press, 1995).
4 Ibid., 43–142.
5 Ibid., 145–176.
6 Agostino Gallo, "The Advantages of Villa Life," in James S. Ackerman, *The Villa: Form and Ideology of Country Houses* (Princeton: Princeton University Press, 1990), 131.
7 See Joanne M. Ferraro, *Venice: History of the Floating City* (Cambridge, UK: Cambridge University Press, 2012), 79.
8 See Guido Guerzoni, "Servicing the *Casa*," in *At Home in Renaissance Italy*, ed. Marta Ajmar-Wollheim and Flora Dennis (London: V & A Publications, 2006), 146–151.
9 Andrea Palladio, *The Four Books on Architecture*, trans. Robert Tavernor and Richard Schofield (Cambridge, MA: MIT Press, 1997), 121.
10 See Gerrit Smienk and Johannes Niemeijer, *Palladio, the Villa and the Landscape* (Basel: Birkäuser, 2011).
11 Palladio, *The Four Books*, 121–122.
12 See Denis Cosgrove, "Platonism and Practicality: Hydrology, Engineering and Landscape in Sixteenth-Century Venice," in *Water, Engineering and Landscape*, ed. Denis Cosgrove and Geoff Petts (London: Belhaven Press, 1990), 35–53.
13 See Paul Holberton, *Palladio's Villas: Life in the Renaissance Countryside* (London: John Murray, 1990), 206–209, 229.
14 See Paolo Portoghesi, *The Hand of Palladio* (Turin: Umberto Allemandi & Co., 2008), 89–96. See also Palladio, *The Four Books*, 56–57.
15 Palladio, *The Four Books*, 57.

16 See Patricia Fortini Brown, *Private Lives in Renaissance Venice: Art, Architecture, and the Family* (New Haven and London: Yale University Press, 2004).

17 Palladio, *The Four Books*, 7.

18 Rudolf Wittkower, *Architectural Principles in the Age of Humanism* (New York: W.W. Norton & Co., 1971), 70.

19 Palladio, *The Four Books*, 78.

20 Ibid.

21 Ibid., 60–61.

22 Ibid., 60.

23 Holberton, *Palladio's Villas*, 208–209.

24 See Robert Woods Kennedy, *The House, and The Art of Its Design* (New York: Reinhold Pub. Corp., 1953), 132–133.

25 Holberton, *Palladio's Villas*, 225.

26 Ibid., 226.

27 Jean Baudrillard, *The System of Objects*, trans. J. Benedict (London: Verso, 1996), 48.

28 Ibid.

29 J. Macgregor Wise, "Home: Territory and Identity," *Cultural Studies* 14, no. 2 (2000): 299.

30 J. MacGregor Wise, "Assemblage," in *Deleuze: Key Concepts*, ed. Charles Stivale (Montreal: McGill-Queen's Press, 2005), 79.

31 Mihaly Csikszentmihalyi and Eugene Rochberg-Halton, *The Meaning of Things: Domestic Symbols and the Self* (Cambridge, UK: Cambridge University Press, 1981), 86.

32 Ibid., 195.

33 Holberton, *Palladio's Villas*, 225. See also Sir Harold Acton, "Introduction," in Peter Lauritzen, *Villas of the Veneto* (London: Pavilion Books, 1988).

34 Patricia Fortini Brown, "The Venetian Casa," in *At Home in Renaissance Italy*, 58–59.

35 Elizabeth S. Cohen and Thomas V. Cohen, *Daily Life in Renaissance Italy* (Westport, CT: Greenwood Press, 2001), 221–222.

36 Brown, "The Venetian Casa," 61.

37 See Cohen and Cohen, *Daily Life in Renaissance Italy*, 221–224.

Interlude D

Transformative power of Architecture

Steven Holl

> I believe in the social contract, therefore I teach. I believe the university is one of the last places that protects and preserves freedom; therefore teaching is also a sociopolitical act, among other things.[1]
>
> *John Hejduk*

Trying to make sense out of what we are doing as architects today requires a reexamination of values. It requires asking, what are our core values? Questions of ethics might be considered.

This world's social inequity, where roughly one-third of all people on the planet live on less than two dollars per day, and unprecedented environmental degradation set architecture in a particular twenty-first-century framework. Unlike the modern architects of the early twentieth century, we should have a new global view. Today, we have unparalleled and comprehensive information about our fragile planet. As architects, we face our limitations with concrete geometric desires – yet we want our aspirations to have meaning. We try to imagine ideals and make idealistic proposals for particular situations. However, ambiguous circumstances prevail.

The ambiguities of cultural and economic change are compounded by record environmental and climatic change. Are there also fundamental epistemological changes? Let's assume we can still reflect on ethics in a similar spirit as Kropotkin did in his *Ethics: Origin and Development*.[2] Kropotkin removed ethics from religious and metaphysical spheres and placed ethical teaching back in the natural environment and the everyday world. He asked questions significant in the life and thought of all beings. For Kropotkin, a basis of human ethics was the "physics of human conduct." He saw ethics not as an "abstract science of human conduct but a concrete scientific discipline whose object is to inspire humans in their practical activities."[3] As one of the responsible and practical arts, architecture is challenged with inventing new possibilities. Architecture's potential to unburden life lies in its invention.

Today fundamental questions concerning prominent architecture are rarely asked. Instead we are inundated with information, much of it useless. Today architecture is viewed in a rapid fire of narrow screen images. Flashes of new buildings irrespective of site or local culture are, as Pérez-Gómez notes, "equivalent to a mindless search for consumable novelties."[4]

An alternative is to reinvent specific architecture case by case. Each work of architecture is organized as if to build its site. Rather than an object occupying a site, specific architecture is inspired by its site. This can be an ethical aspect of focusing architecture on social dimensions. As I have described in previous text,

> Architecture is bound to situation. Unlike music, painting, or literature, a construction is intertwined with the experience of a place. The site of a building is more than a mere ingredient in its conception. It is its physical and metaphysical foundation.[5]

Alberto Pérez-Gómez, Juhani Pallasmaa and I carried these thoughts much further in our collection of essays in the *Questions of Perception* with Professor

Figure D.1 For Alberto, Steven Holl

Pérez-Gómez continuing the cause, when he clearly states that, "The cultural specificity of practices in our global village is absolutely crucial."[6]

There is a transformative power to architecture. Architecture has much more to offer than pragmatic solutions to problems of the environment or technical solutions to programmatic needs. As Pérez-Gómez argues, architecture "incites us to real meditation, to personal thought, and imagination, opening up the space of desire . . . unveiling a glimpse of the sense of existence."[7] He argues for the urgency of the poetic imagination of the architect, wherein lies the potential of the real transformative power of architecture in the twenty-first century. In Pérez-Gómez's words, "works of architecture, art, and poetry are indeed capable of moving us; they transform our life and ground our very being."[8]

Notes

1 Herbert Muschamp, "John Hejduk, an Architect And Educator, Dies at 71," *New York Times*, July 6, 2000.
2 Prince Kropotkin, *Ethics: Origin and Development*, trans. Louis S. Friedland and Joseph R. Piroshnikoff (New York: The Dial Press, 1924).
3 Ibid., xiii.
4 Alberto *Pérez-Gómez*, "Relevance of Beauty in Architecture," in *Cultural Role of Architecture*, ed. Paul Emmons, John Hendrix and Jane Humolt (New York: Routledge, 2001), 164.
5 Steven Holl, *Anchoring: Selected Projects, 1975-1988* (New York: Princeton Architectural Press, 1989), 9.
6 Alberto *Pérez-Gómez*, "Relevance of Beauty in Architecture," in *Cultural Role of Architecture*, ed. Paul Emmons, John Hendrix and Jane Humolt (New York: Routledge, 2001), 165.
7 Alberto *Pérez-Gómez*, "Architecture and the Body," in *Art and the Senses*, ed. Francesca Bacci and David Melcher (New York: Oxford University Press, 2011), 576.
8 Alberto *Pérez-Gómez*, "70 Architect(e)s . . . longing for beauty and the common good," in *70 Architect(e)s: On Ethics and Poetics*, ed. Marc J. Neveu and Negin Djavaherian (Montreal: McGill University, 2007).

PART V
After the crisis

17

JUAN O'GORMAN AND THE GENESIS AND OVERCOMING OF FUNCTIONALISM IN MEXICAN MODERN ARCHITECTURE

Juan Manuel Heredia

Under the title *La Génesis y Superación del Funcionalismo en la Arquitectura*, the first published version of Alberto Pérez-Gómez's seminal book *Architecture and the Crisis of Modern Science* appeared in Mexico in 1980.[1] Devoid of Husserlian allusions, Pérez-Gómez's Spanish title gave no hint of his phenomenological emphasis but was more suited to the Mexican audience. The term functionalism had been at the center of debate in Mexico ever since a group of "radical functionalist" architects initiated that country's modern movement in the late 1920s. Denying any relevance to art, aesthetics, or "spiritual necessities," these architects gained their reputation thanks to their uncompromising attitude and the strikingly austere and utilitarian character of their buildings. Conceiving architecture as "engineering of buildings," their work was also inextricably linked to the creation of the *Escuela Superior de Ingeniería y Arquitectura* (ESIA) of the *Instituto Politécnico Nacional* (IPN), Pérez-Gómez's alma mater and the sponsor of his book. Founded in 1936 inspired by the example of the *École Polytechnique* in Paris, the IPN embodied the positivistic legacy targeted by Pérez-Gómez and embraced in Mexico at many levels of culture since the end of the nineteenth century. Founded four years earlier but immediately incorporated into the IPN, the ESIA advocated the teaching and dissemination of a "technical architecture" in service of post-Revolutionary Mexico. In retrospect, Pérez-Gómez's book constituted an indirect criticism of his school, of Mexican functionalism, and of Mexican modern architecture in general.

Four decades before the book's publication, however, an architect also affiliated to the ESIA attempted in Mexico an earlier criticism of functionalism. Indeed, shortly after the school's opening, its founder and the most radical of Mexican "radicals," Juan O'Gorman, retreated from his views that regarded functionalism as a vehicle for social emancipation and began considering it an instrument of capitalistic accumulation. O'Gorman's repentance would not only lead into his formal retirement from the profession but, fifteen years later, to his dual architectural swan song: the mosaic-clad library of the University of Mexico and his surrealistic cave/house on the outskirts of Mexico City. His criticism of functionalism and the implicit and explicit appeals to corporeality and meaning contained in it show many parallels to Pérez-Gómez's academic work. The deterministic character of his thinking that added to his conflicted personality, however, led him into theoretical conundrums that greatly differed from the latter's more rigorous and fertile theorizing. Nevertheless O'Gorman's career as an architect developed with certain autonomy from his theories, showing throughout the years a level of maturation that went unsuspected to the architect himself (Figure 17.1). This essay traces O'Gorman's architecture and his embrace and criticism of functionalism, acknowledging his importance in the history of modern architecture and in doing so helping to situate the legacy of his unsuspected successor.

Born in Mexico City in 1905, Juan O'Gorman was a central figure of Mexico's post-revolutionary culture.[2] A descendent of British diplomats and Mexican Independence fighters he grew up in a sophisticated environment cultivating a strong nationalistic spirit and a cosmopolitan taste for the humanities, the natural sciences and the arts. Encouraged to pursue his artistic sensibilities through painting, O'Gorman eventually joined the ranks

Figure 17.1 Juan O'Gorman, CTM Union building project, Mexico City, 1936

of the socialist artists surrounding Frida Kahlo and Diego Rivera. Instead of painting, however, he decided to study architecture and enrolled in 1922 in the school of architecture of the National University, then the only school of architecture in the country. O'Gorman studied during a transitional period when most of the school's faculty adhered to an eclectic pedagogy legacy of more than a century of academic instruction in Mexico, but when the combined spirit of renewal of the Mexican Revolution (1910–1920) and the *Neues Bauen* was strongly felt.[3] As a student O'Gorman was in fact pivotal in renovating the school of architecture, mobilizing his classmates to request the support and inclusion of faculty of a more modern persuasion. From these teachers he inherited a structural-rationalist view of building, a proficient knowledge of concrete construction, and a preference for stripping down surfaces from inessentials.[4] His most influential teacher, Guillermo Zárraga, transmitted to him a patriotic spirit and an idea of architecture as service for the provision of shelter for the people, yet also encouraging him to consult international periodicals for learning and inspiration. An alleged "anti-Vignolist," Zárraga was also probably who first introduced him to the work of Le Corbusier.

Indeed, O'Gorman discovered Le Corbusier during his last years at the university. Reportedly the young student became so enthralled with his books that he became known in the corridors of the school as the "kid with Le Corbusier under his arm." Not surprisingly, as he began practicing architecture, the imprint of Le Corbusier's work became pervasive on his own. O'Gorman's often too literal interpretations betrayed the enthusiasm of a young and rebellious architect introducing in Mexico the preeminent symbol of architectural renovation in the world. These interpretations, however, were highly selective, mainly concentrated on the formal and theoretical aspects that he needed for his own polemical uses. Working in a country just emerging from a revolutionary war but with great prospects of reconstruction ahead of it, O'Gorman borrowed from Le Corbusier a technocratic and socially minded mentality, leaving aside the more poetic and transcendental aspects of his work. Moreover, if for Le Corbusier architecture was a substitute for revolution, for Gorman as for indeed most of Mexican modern architects, it was its product and guarantee. O'Gorman's buildings for their part rehearsed the most distinctive motifs of Le Corbusier's architecture. This was more evident in his houses, which were often direct emulations of his projects.

In a series of domestic commissions dating from 1929 to 1935 (and that famously included the twin houses for his friends Kahlo and Rivera), O'Gorman demonstrated a precocious assimilation of Le Corbusier's formal vocabulary (Figure 17.2). More interested in external details and the

Figure 17.2 Juan O'Gorman, Frida Kahlo and Diego Rivera house-studios, Mexico City, 1931

exposure of electrical, mechanical, and tectonic features (wiring, plumbing, concrete frames and surfaces etc.), however, his projects resulted in largely iconographic exercises bent on expressing a possible modernity for Mexico. Notoriously absent were the formal strategies that could have generated the spatial complexity and sequences that characterized Le Corbusier's architecture. In aligning the partitions to the structural frame, O'Gorman in fact created highly compartmentalized interiors closer to the idea of *existenz-minimum* than to a Corbusian "promenade." Moreover, their proportions were not the result of a careful study of human uses but of a building module (the three-meter spacing of concrete reinforcement for load bearing walls) subdivided or multiplied in consideration of a "function" abstractly and univocally conceived. Along with these modernist features the houses also incorporated a series of "vernacular" motifs: vibrant colors, clay bricks, dry-stone terraces, and cactus fences, etc. Presumably introduced for economic reasons, these elements actually reinforced the houses' expressive and pictorial character. At any rate, O'Gorman never rationalized his houses in regional terms but instead referred to them as the first "functionalist" houses in Mexico.

By functionalism O'Gorman meant when architecture's form "completely derived from its utilitarian function."[5] Elsewhere he defined functional architecture as that "only useful for the mechanical aspects of life," and that "exclusively satisfied the need for shelter."[6] These definitions were in turn based on the "theoretical principle" of "minimum expenditure for maximum efficiency," and were thus justified in view of the need to act with the outmost economy, objectivity and expediency in Mexico. Circularity of argumentation apart, O'Gorman's definitions represented the most deterministic notions of function in those years.[7] On the one hand, they exhibited a dualistic conception of life that sharply separated corporeal ("mechanical") from intellectual or spiritual existence. On the other hand, they were oblivious of the codetermining relation between built form and human action.[8] More importantly, O'Gorman's idea of function disregarded the metaphorical meaning that the term had historically possessed since its adoption by architects in the nineteenth century.[9] As it has been recently argued, this meaning was still present in twentieth century functionalism, and was present in O'Gorman's work.[10]

Indeed, despite his claims O'Gorman's buildings were conceived as metaphorical, not literal, embodiments of function. Both their modernistic and "traditional" elements were more a matter of display than of actual operation. Admittedly these elements *performed*, to different degrees of success, in the ways prescribed by the architect. Yet they did it also, but stronger, in the theatrical sense of the term. A collection of pictorial and didactic motifs, the houses lacked the internal and external articulations that could elevate them to a "higher" narrative or poetic level.[11] Moreover, O'Gorman's modular design was exacerbated by his strong interest on spatial economy. This produced very rigid arrangements that made the owners alter them, paradoxically questioning the architect's claims. This was perhaps more evident in the house for his friend Kahlo: a beautiful object but a rather oppressive setting that obliged its disabled owner to flee into the more spacious adobe of her youth.

Rivera's patronage of O'Gorman, however, unexpectedly led in 1932 to the architect's appointment as head of the Department of School Construction of Mexico's Ministry of Education. Far from gratuitous his appointment obeyed the government's interest in his theories, and its dissatisfaction with the way public schools had been built until that time, not keeping pace with an increasing demand or with the project for establishing a socialist education in Mexico.[12] O'Gorman's first initiative was the construction and renovation of over fifty elementary schools with an overall budget of one million pesos, the sum normally destined for the construction of a single school designed in the standard eclectic fashion. Although built with the same construction technique, modular logic, and exposed elements as his houses, O'Gorman's "functionalist" schools were less formally indulgent and designed in real view of economy and potential growth (Figure 17.3). Yet they transpired a similar didactic spirit, which given their programmatic character, was perhaps more appropriate. Linearly and symmetrically arranged, they had a regimented character only alleviated by the strategic detachment of columns in vestibules. O'Gorman also painted the buildings in different colors to make them more agreeable to the people who would inhabit them. More graphically he painted, or rather wrote, the phrase *Escuela Primaria* ("elementary school") on selected walls on the outside to make them more recognizable. Giving continuity to the work initiated a decade earlier by Rivera, O'Gorman also invited a group of muralists to decorate the vestibules with frescoes displaying political and pedagogical themes. Despite their realistic style and the seeming lack of correspondence with the buildings' abstract language, these frescoes could be seen from a variety of perspectives, repeating but extending the didactic character of his houses. Compared to them, however, they were more articulate projects, with a more assertive presence and a greater sense of appropriateness.

O'Gorman's growing reputation led him, almost immediately, to become part of the committee in charge of establishing the guidelines of technical

Figure 17.3 Juan O'Gorman, Elementary School in Portales, Mexico City, 1932–33

education in the country. As the only architect on the committee, he was also put in charge of establishing a new model of architectural education. Thus, in 1932 O'Gorman transformed a preexisting construction trade school into the *Escuela Superior de Construcción* (ESC).[13] The immediate predecessor of the ESIA, the ESC offered the degree of "building engineer," and in this sense materialized O'Gorman's notion of architecture as engineering of buildings. The building engineer was conceived as someone proficient in advanced construction techniques and architectural design, and whose skills – as opposed to those of university trained architects – would better respond to Mexico's needs for urban infrastructure.[14] Largely developed by O'Gorman, the curriculum provided him with the opportunity to apply his philosophy of functionalism at a larger institutional scale and was characterized by the suppression of almost all "humanistic" and "artistic" courses. Indeed, anticipating Gropius' more moderate initiatives at Harvard, the ESC offered no courses on history except for one dedicated to the "History and Geography of Mexico."[15] Conversely, the curriculum abounded in technical courses: nomography, statics, geology, hydraulics, topography, railways, roads, ports, sanitation, drafting, building techniques, and administration. Similar to the university, however, architectural design (*composición*) remained the core of the curriculum taught throughout its four years. Yet without the standard "visual" preparatory course other than one on sketching and *relevé* (surveying and drawing of historical buildings), architectural design was treated as a problem solving matter focused on the distribution of spaces in plan. Moreover, the buildings selected for *relevé* needed to be "rationally planned."[16]

While O'Gorman invited likeminded professors to teach the different topics of the school, he put himself in charge of its only other humanistic course: architectural theory. This course, however, consisted of the unpacking of his functionalist theory hinging on the thesis: that "architectural composition, its form, and elements, are determined by human needs and building procedures.[17] Emulating the pedagogy of his teacher Zárraga, O'Gorman defined architecture as "the shelter and locale for the work and rest of man." The first lectures were dedicated to an explanation of the school's goals (a "technical" education as opposed to an "academic" one) and included a session on standardization, industrialization, and Taylorism. Taken from Le Corbusier these topics were nevertheless seen through O'Gorman's anticapitalistic lens. Other introductory lectures were devoted to the "elements of composition," which for O'Gorman consisted of program, site, terrain and human needs. Abstractly conceived, the latter topic amounted to "areas of use," "circulation" and "unroofed areas," and their design explained as a process of "reduction to their minimal dimensions." Besides an overarching emphasis on economy, concrete aspects of human praxis were limited to the themes of visibility and acoustics in auditoriums. The introductory lectures also included sessions on style, proportion, art, regionalism, and the Greek Orders, but discussed in a way that highlighted their "dangers," yet, the bulk of the course was dedicated to the "elements of architecture:" walls, openings, doors, windows, supports, roofs, floors, vaults, domes, furnishings, and machinery. Both in name and in spirit, this aspect of his theory course derived from Julien Guadet's *Elements et Theorie de l'Archiecture*, a textbook used at the university since the turn of the century, assigned to O'Gorman as a student, and listed in his syllabus as a textbook. In addition to Guadet, O'Gorman also recommended four books by Le Corbusier: *Vers une Architecture*, *L'Art Decoratif d'aujourd'hui*, *Une Maison une Palais* and *Precisions*. These were precisely the books devoured by him as a student at the beginning of his career and were included to compensate for an otherwise encyclopedic reference. The character of the course, however, was closer to the latter; the only Corbusian topic being the "free plan" but solely conceptualized as the product of modern techniques.[18] The combination of the rather antithetical figures of Guadet and Le Corbusier didn't seem to have been problematized by O'Gorman nor put in historical context.[19] Indeed, as historian Rafael López Rangel has pointed out, there was neither in O'Gorman's course, nor in the school in general, "any systematic knowledge of history that could aid in the comprehension [of the complexity] of the architectural process."[20]

O'Gorman's bold pedagogical enterprise provoked a reaction in the architectural establishment of Mexico. Less than a year after the ESC was founded, the Society of Mexican Architects organized a series of "talks" to debate the state of architecture in the country. Its purpose was to address these questions:

> What is architecture and what is functionalism? Can functionalism be considered a definitive stage or as the embryonic beginning of all architectural becoming? Can the architect be considered a simple building technician or, also, a promoter of the general culture of the people? Is architectural beauty the necessary result of a functional solution, or does it also demand the creative will of the architect? What must be the architectural orientation in the country?[21]

Formulated by the organizers the questions were meant to put O'Gorman and his radical colleagues on trial, an opportunity that they nevertheless took gladly, making sarcastic comments directed to their hosts.[22] Arranged as a series of presentations, the talks did not allow for debate and were instead monologues of mutual indictment. Whether upholding beauty as architecture's eternal essence or denying it on the grounds of technique and social responsibility, the speakers paradoxically exhibited a deeper commonality in their shared belief on a dual nature for architecture. More negatively, they indulged in generic definitions of architecture without addressing any specific topic of design or theory.

But while O'Gorman was busy defending his theory of functionalism, his private practice was following less restrictive paths. The experience of the schools familiarized him with a scale of building and institutional representation that matured him as an architect. While he continued designing Le Corbusier inspired buildings, whimsical gestures were no longer included in the buildings and they acquired more articulated physiognomies. The 1935 Toor house, a variation of *Maison* Cook, was a series of stacked floors subtly revealing the vertical route organizing the building. Similar "phenomenal transparency" strategies were rehearsed on the contemporary Union of Mexican Cinema Workers (*Sindicato Mexicano de Cinematografistas*) (Figure 17.4). Accessed through an open ground floor, featuring in a balcony for political speeches and military defense on the third floor, and terminated by a library and a terrace on its uppermost level, this building exhibited greater hierarchy and an implicit narrative of solidarity, political autonomy, and spiritual emancipation. The 1936 project for the *Confederación Mexicana de Trabajadores* (CTM), the largest labor union in the country, was another Corbusian exercise, this time inspired in the Centrosoyuz building in Moscow, that despite its almost exact replication of elements, closely responded and transformed to the site and the monument of the Revolution recently built next to it. The CTM building was also the first project in which O'Gorman proposed a system of cladding after years of "stripping" down buildings.[23] This gave to the project a figurative and material character that anticipated many of his future preoccupations, as well as the work of other Mexican architects during the 1950s and 1960s. Despite O'Gorman's later disparagement of the project as a demagogic showpiece for the incumbent union leader, the CTM was probably his most accomplished project.[24] Working before the takeover of labor politics by the Mexican State, it was a provocative representation of the aspirations of an important actor in the Mexican Revolution and post-revolutionary politics.[25]

By 1936, however, O'Gorman began to realize that his functionalist theory, based as it was on an instrumental type of rationality, shared a similar logic as capitalism.[26] By this time other, less socially committed, architects were erecting functionalist *style* buildings for the middle and upper classes of Mexico. As the building industry (now benefitted by a nascent building boom) saw the advantages of building economically and efficiently as O'Gorman first proposed, functional architecture suddenly "turned into a

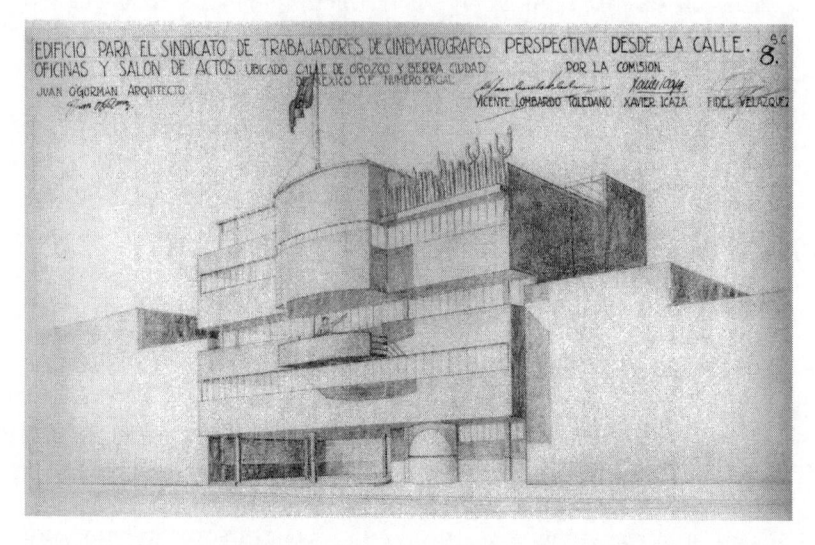

Figure 17.4 Juan O'Gorman, Union of Mexican Cinematographers, Mexico City, 1935

Frankenstein" for him.[27] Thus, shortly after the completion of the CTM project, O'Gorman decided to retire from architecture and turn his attention to painting.

During the next decade O'Gorman produced a series of frescoes in the Mexican-realist style, which strengthened his friendship with Rivera, but paradoxically led to his return to architecture. In 1939, through Rivera's workings and in a series of episodes that mirror his work under Nelson Rockefeller, O'Gorman was invited by the son of U.S. businessman Edgar J. Kauffman, Edgar Kauffman Jr., to paint a mural cycle in a building on their property in Pittsburgh.[28] For this project O'Gorman's envisioned a criticism of capitalism as decadent and a eulogy of the working class in their struggle for socialism. Finding his work too incendiary, Kauffman eventually dismissed O'Gorman, yet his stay in the United States was immensely important. Regularly visiting the Kauffman's recently built house in Bear Run, O'Gorman operated a further change of mentality that reshaped his view of functionalism. From here onwards his criticism ceased to be only about cooptation by economic forces and more about functionalism's deficiencies in topographical and cultural matters. In Fallingwater, O'Gorman "discovered" Frank Lloyd Wright and the value that his work, as opposed to Le Corbusier's, had for Mexican architecture. Visiting the United States at the height of the "good-neighbor" policies, O'Gorman saw in Wright the most faithful interpreter of the continental landscape and the true heir of Pre-Columbian architecture.[29]

After his retirement and even after his Wrightian epiphany, O'Gorman continued teaching at the ESC, now transformed into the ESIA. Surprisingly his theory course didn't change. If anything its structure was refined and its positivistic message strengthened. By 1950 it revolved around the idea that the discipline of architecture consisted of three "techniques": distribution, construction, and installation systems.[30] His decision to deliver similar content was based on the realization that the functional aspects of architecture were at the end "the most objective" and easily transmittable, whereas the "subjective" ones, in which he included the now more positive themes of proportion, aesthetics, and all things "delightful to the senses and the mind," could not be taught and depended on the architect's individual learning and personal imagination.[31] O'Gorman's criticism of functionalism therefore was rather a flight from a profession that was becoming intolerable to him. After his return from the United States his criticism became more focused yet this only inverted the terms of the problem without questioning its premises.

O'Gorman returned to architecture in 1949. In that year he was commissioned with the design of the most symbolic building of the new campus of the university: the central library (Figure 17.5). Simultaneously, he began designing his own house. Both buildings were covered with murals displaying mythical and nationalistic themes, using a mosaic technique borrowed from Rivera (Figure 17.6). Although similar in many ways, the two buildings were different, and not just in size, program, or shape. Carved out from a natural grotto, the house was a literal interpretation of Wright's ideal of organic continuity. The library, for its part, was a freestanding slab with a more assertive presence but with a subtler relation to the ground. Thought of as a domestic refuge, the house embodied O'Gorman's escape from the profession and the world. Located in the most prominent site of the university, the library was an open institution acting as a fulcrum for the campus and the entire country. While the former represented O'Gorman's exasperation, the latter reflected his internalization of architectural principles now largely autonomous from his theories. His eulogy of the house (a "truly Mexican" work) and his criticism of the library (a "*gringa* dressed in native clothing") are testament to O'Gorman's blindness to his own achievements and his constant subordination of architecture to ideology.[32]

By the mid-1960s Alberto Pérez-Gomez entered the school that O'Gorman founded thirty years earlier. Despite a number of reforms and the firing of O'Gorman himself in 1955, the school retained much of its original pedagogy. More than a decade later, when Pérez-Gómez finished his doctoral dissertation at the University of Essex, the thesis contained in it

Figure 17.5 Juan O'Gorman, University Library, Mexico City, 1949–52

revealed, beyond the acknowledged debt to his advisors, a deeper if indirect connection to Mexico in its explicit criticism of functionalism. Pérez-Gómez, however, produced a more compelling thesis than O'Gorman's reactionary one. Yet in its tone it retained echoes of O'Gorman's rebelliousness and uncompromising spirit.

In an interview with Edward Burian, Pérez-Gómez reflected on his education within the broader context of modern Mexican architecture.[33]

Figure 17.6 Juan O'Gorman, O'Gorman house, Mexico City, 1952

In the interview Pérez-Gómez discusses the pervasiveness of positivism in twentieth century Mexican architectural theory while at the same time acknowledging the creativity of Mexican architects for being able to produce "fascinating" buildings regardless of the theories that drove them. The conversation revolves around the idea (introduced by Burian and later applied to O'Gorman) that Mexican modern architecture operated along a theoretical vacuum, and that its richness relied more on an intuitive or tacit understanding of cultural and topographical conditions than on ideological imperatives. It is both paradoxical and understandable that one of the most important contemporary theorists emerged from that context.

Notes

1 Alberto Pérez Gómez, La Génesis y Superación del Funcionalismo en Arquitectura (Mexico City: Limusa, 1980).
2 On O'Gorman see Clive Bamford Smith, Builders in the Sun: Five Mexican Architects (New York: Architectural Book Publishing, 1967), 16–50; Edward R. Burian, "The Architecture of Juan O'Gorman: Dichotomy and Drift," in Modernity and the Architecture of Mexico, ed. Edward R. Burian (Austin: University of Texas Press, 1997), 127–149; Valerie Fraser, Building the New World, Studies in the Modern Architecture of Latin America, 1930-1960 (London: Verso, 2000), 38–82; and Luis Carranza, Architecture as Revolution: Episodes in the History of Modern Mexico (Austin: Texas University Press, 2010), 119–167. The

main sources in Spanish are Mauricio López Valdés ed., O'Gorman (Mexico City: BITAL-Américo Arte, 1999); and Antonio Luna Arroyo, Juan O'Gorman, Autobiografía, Antología, Juicios Críticos y Documentación Exhaustiva sobre su Obra (Mexico City: Cuadernos Populares de Pintura Mexicana Moderna, 1973), from where much of the biographical information derives.

3 The School of Architecture was the heir of the Architecture Section of the Real Academia de San Carlos. Founded in 1781 under the model of the Real Academia de San Fernando in Madrid (itself inspired by the French Academy) the Mexican Academy contained the first architecture school of the American Continent. During the nineteenth century it became an upholder of the pedagogy of the École de Beaux Arts.

4 In the tradition outlined in Reyner Banham, Theory and Design in First Machine Age (New York: Praeger, 1960), 14, 23–34.

5 Luna Arroyo, Juan O'Gorman, 100.

6 Juan O'Gorman, "Más Allá de Funcionalismo," in La Palabra de Juan O'Gorman: Selección de textos, ed. Ida Rodríguez Prampolini (Mexico City: UNAM, 1983), 125.

7 As embodied for example in Hannes Meyer's description of his collaborative entry for the 1926 League of Nations Competition: "Our building symbolizes nothing. Its size is automatically determined by the dimensions and conditions of the program." Quoted in Claude Schnaidt, Hannes Meyer, Buildings, Projects and Writings (Teufen, Switzerland: Arthur Niggli, 1965), 25.

8 Frank E. Brown's insights on Roman architecture may be appropriate: "[Roman] architecture was of a particular functional sort. Of its very nature, it not only contained the specific action it was framed for; it required it, it prompted it, it enforced it." Frank Brown, Roman Architecture (New York: George Brazillier, 1971), 10.

9 See Joseph Rykwert, "Lodoli on Function and Representation," in The Necessity of Artifice (New York: Rizzoli, 1982); and Alberto Pérez-Gómez, Architecture and the Crisis of Modern Science (Cambridge, MA: MIT Press, 1983), 253–258.

10 Stanford Anderson, "The Fiction of Function," Assemblage 2 (February 1987): 18–31.

11 For Stanford Anderson the cultural relevance of twentieth century functionalism was stronger in buildings whose display of functional elements possessed a "higher level of organization" that transformed them from the level of iconography to that of fictions or stories. Ibid., 22–29.

12 Narciso Bassols, Mexico's Minister of Education from 1931 to 1934, was instrumental in the, ultimately failed, project to educate Mexican children under an "exact and rational conception of the universe and of social life." See Gerardo Sánchez Ruiz, "Las Condiciones Sociales que Exigieron la Opción Técnica de las Escuelas Bassols-O'Gorman," in Juan O'Gorman: Arquitectura Escolar 1932, ed. Víctor Arias Montes (Mexico City: UAM-A, UNAM, UASLP, 2006), 36–51.

13 On the ESC see Rafael López Rangel, Orígenes de la Arquitectura Técnica en México, 1920-1933: La Escuela Superior de Construcción (Mexico City, UAM, 1984).

14 O'Gorman's initiative was not entirely original but resuscitated a short-lived nineteenth century initiative when, under the initial influence of positivism and the rising social status of engineers, the Mexican Academy transformed the title of architect into that of architect–engineer. The mastermind of this project was the German-trained Italian Saverio Cavallari. On Cavallari see Gabriella Cianciolo Constino, Francesco Saverio Cavallari (1810–1896): Architetto senza Frontiere tra Sicilia Germania e Messico (Palermo: Edizioni Caracol, 2007).

15 López Rangel, Orígenes, 92.
16 Ibid., 114.
17 See Juan O'Gorman, "Programa de Teoría de la Arquitectura. Escuela Técnica de Construcción, Ciclo Fundamental y Ciclo Especial (1932)," in Ideario de los Arquitectos Mexicanos, ed. Ramón Vargas Salguero and J. Víctor Arias Montes (Mexico City: UNAM – INBA – Conaculta, 2011), vol. III, 48–69. See also López Rangel, Orígenes, 113–114.
18 For Hanno-Walter Kruft, Guadet's book represented a "synthesis" of the École des Beaux Arts' architectural theory. Hanno-Walter Kruft, A History of Architectural Theory from Vitruvius to the Present (New York: Princeton Architectural Press, 1994), 288.
19 At any rate, O'Gorman warned his students that all the books listed were "written in French and thus no reading could properly serve as a textbook in the course." O'Gorman "Programa de Teoría de la Arquitectura," 68–69.
20 López Rangel, Orígenes, 114.
21 The talks were published in Pláticas sobre Arquitectura, 1933 (Mexico City: Sociedad de Arquitectos Méxicanos, 1934), and have been republished with commentaries in J. Víctor Arias Montes ed. Pláticas sobre Arquitectura, 1933 (México: UNAM-UAM, 2001), and Pláticas sobre Arquitectura, 1933 (Mexico City: Conaculta-INBA), 2001. On the talks see Valerie Fraser, Building the New World: Studies in the Modern Architecture of Latin America 1930-1960 (New York: Verso, 2001), 51–52; and Luis Carranza, Architecture as Revolution: Episodes in the History of Modern Mexico, (Austin: University of Texas Press, 2010), 151–158.
22 These architects were Juan Legarreta and Álvaro Aburto, both of whom were invited by O'Gorman to teach at the ESC.
23 O'Gorman's schools were characterized by Esther Born as having "no frills, no fuss, and no feathers," and "stripped for action." Esther Born, The New Architecture of Mexico (New York: William Morrow, 1937).
24 Luna Arroyo, Juan O'Gorman, 124.
25 See John Mason Hart, Revolutionary Mexico: The Coming and Process of the Mexican Revolution (Berkeley and Los Angeles, University of California Press, 1987), 52–73.
26 "It is easy to realize the productive value that a principle like maximum efficiency with minimal effort" has for the capitalistic system. Juan O'Gorman, "Arquitectura Capitalista y Arquitectura Socialista" Edificación 2, no. 6 (November/December 1935) and Edificación 3, no. 1 (January 1935/February 1936), 11–17, 14.
27 "'Abandoné la arquitectura porqué se me convirtió en un Frankenstein': O'Gorman," in Prampolini, La Palabra de Juan O'Gorman, 212–216.
28 On O'Gorman's Wrightian conversion see Keith Eggener, "Towards an Organic Architecture in Mexico," in Frank Lloyd Wright: Europe and Beyond, ed. Anthony Alofsin (Berkeley: University of California Press, 1999), 166–257.
29 Smith, Builders in the Sun, 18.
30 O'Gorman, "Más Allá de Funcionalismo," 125–131.
31 Ibid.
32 See "Comentarios acerca de la casa de la Avenida San Jerónimo no. 162," and "Dijo O'Gorman de sus murals en C.U. 'Por lo menos que fuera una cosa que no disgustara al público,'" in Prampolini, La Palabra de Juan O'Gorman, 157–159, 298–301.
33 "Mexico, Modernity, and Architecture: An Interview with Alberto Pérez-Gómez," in Modernity and the Architecture of Mexico, ed. Edward Burian (Austin: Texas University Press, 1997), 13–60.

18

ARCHITECTURE OR ACCELERATION

Position as opposition

Anne Bordeleau

When a physician talks about a crisis in the condition of a patient, he is describing a moment when it is unclear whether the patient will survive or succumb. In a true sense, this is now the condition of Western culture. In the last century and a half, man has done his utmost to define the human condition and ironically has lost the capacity to come to terms with it; he is unable to reconcile the eternal and immutable dimension of ideas with the finite and mutable dimension of everyday life.[1]

Alberto Pérez-Gómez

In order for the patient to survive from the crisis Alberto Pérez-Gómez diagnosed in 1980, a decision had to be made.[2] When I consider the phrase *Architecture's Appeal*, I can only think that the title must point to our responsibility as architects to constantly appeal a decision that appears to have been made. Pérez-Gómez was specifically building upon Husserl's reading of the crisis in European sciences, but the necessity for architecture to plead and plead again, i.e. to put forward a formal answer or objection, is relevant in light of another use of the term crisis. Since 1780, crisis has been applied to history to express "a new sense of time which both indicated and intensified the end of an epoch."[3] Acceleration, this sense of time that ascended over the last 200 years as a child of modern sciences, now dominates not only political and economic dimensions, but also everyday life, the perception of culture and even more fundamentally how we situate ourselves in the world as mortal beings.[4] The idea of reconciliation, whether or not it is still possible, implies a relation between the temporal and the eternal, two realms traditionally mediated through architecture. Positing the possibility of mediation at the heart of architecture's relation to time, in this paper I first question the impacts of acceleration to then glimpse at architecture's appeal: how it exerts its power to address itself to "chora" as a "space of ontological continuity," wherein the transience of becoming writes itself against the immutable figure of Being.[5]

Acceleration and depth

In a critical research on acceleration, the sociologist Hartmut Rosa ascertains the existence of our late-modern experience of time through a study of its social, theoretical and political underpinnings.[6] Some of Rosa's observations on the socioeconomic dimensions of acceleration will be familiar. Indeed, it is widely accepted that the growing rate of production and technological innovation fuels a greater level of consumption along with the insatiable sense of unfulfilled desire. The perception of acceleration has far-reaching consequences that include individual and collective senses of a scarcity of time, the conditions of the non-simultaneity of the simultaneous between (and often also within) specific social groups, the institutional adaptation in the form of exceptional powers as well as the experience of a growing distance from tradition. Implicitly, Rosa's study also points to the troubling nature of the relation between surface and depth. Over the past decades, architectural theorists such as Antoine Picon, Sanford Kwinter and Joan Ockman have considered how an unchallenged technological will rests at the core of the relation between the fluid surface and the petrified depth.[7] In *Polar Inertia*, Paul Virilio also addresses the stiffening effects of technology.[8] Paradoxically, the technology that propels the perpetual attraction for change and novelty also leads to the eternal return of the same. The technological promise of emancipation ultimately congeals in a new form of oppression that calls for alternatives to former conceptions of salvation. Identifying the daunting and ultimately oppressive nature of endless movement, voices both within and outside architecture – Marshal Berman, Hilde Heynen or David Harvey – have alluded to the persisting need for some redeeming figure of stability.[9] This figure, however, takes the form of an aestheticization of politics, a longing for the eternal, or a spatialization of time. The reference is no longer the possibility of ontological or even historical continuity, but rather the frozen moment of an endless present. We have moved from a time defined through duration, sequences and rhythms to what Manuel Castells describes as *timeless time*: a time without depth.[10]

The loss of depth, a real depth in the sense advocated by Pérez-Gómez, is directly related to the transformation of our relation to time. It must be understood in light of the shifting conception of, and changing relation between, time and eternity. From the sixteenth to the nineteenth century, the ability to measure time verified impressions of a temporal foreshortening that were gradually transformed from an experience based in eschatological Christian expectations of an end fixed from outside, to progress in the natural sciences that could be measured within history. In the words of historian Reinhart Koselleck, the Christian apocalyptic conception of a "foreshortening of time . . . became a metaphor for acceleration. . . ."[11] Rosa adds that in a secular conception wherein eternity refers to a world that will continue after our fast-approaching death, the ability to live faster, that is to live more options, eventually serves "as a functional equivalent to eternity." Functionally, the "almost infinite plurality of forms of life" that a late-modern individual embraces to match transformations in their changing world becomes synonymous to "traditional ideas of an 'eternal life.'"[12] In a strange reversal, the "open, experimental, and fragmentary images of the self" that one adopts to keep up with incessant changes pose as the figure of eternity, whereas stability in one's identity is avoided, doomed to be anachronistic.[13]

The redefinition and relocation of eternity is dramatic in at least two crucial ways. First, and fundamentally, the new secular conception negates the formerly implied transcendental dimension. From a temporal perspective, the quality of meta-narrative that any ideology tends towards is inevitably endowed by a certain sense of eternity. Plurality of fragmented approaches – like the "almost infinite plurality of forms" at the level of the individual – now replace former attempts to hint at some shared stable ground. Second and paradoxically, the secular location of eternity within accelerated time actually fuels an alienation from time. The experiences lived in accelerated time do not carry mnemonic depth; they disappear from memory as quickly as they vanish with the present.[14] This lack of reference leads to a form of self-alienation. To avoid becoming anachronistic one must constantly focus on the new, one must move with time's flow. In "Le Cygne," Charles Baudelaire was referring to the life of things that we behold in our memory once we have experienced them, a life that he then considered could outlive the objects themselves.[15] Along with the stable figure of eternity, even Baudelaire's memories – as heavy as stone – now evaporate.

Architecture's compensation: territory, the everyday and the fragmentary

The demystification of infinity in relation to human orientation in space has its temporal counterpoint in the ascending importance of acceleration. The former implies the superfluity of a larger cosmological order; the latter brings eternity within time at the expense of the lived-time of experience. As we witness the fragmentation of architectural practice and its expansion into larger fields, we can discern two apparently opposed tendencies. Current practice is polarized between tactical interventions and infrastructural urbanism, between ephemeral installations and metabolistic approaches to the territory, between explorations of digital materiality and ecological urbanism. At the punctual and ephemeral end of the spectrum, the emphasis is on the "everyday." At the other end, different definitions of "perpetuity" form the temporal framework inherent to broad and operational interventions. But whether in their investment in the everyday or in longer sustainable cycles, how far do these approaches reinforce or resist the intrinsic processes of our late-modern temporal regime?

Small-scale intervention, playful or parasitical projects that emerge and vanish quickly – lasting the time of a day, a festival or a season – projects rooted in the everyday typically rest on the participation of a willing crowd. Digital architecture is often the motor of production; mass customization, freedom in permutations and apparently limitless possibilities of appropriation frequently characterize the installations. When these projects are published, users are invariably represented. The architecture of the everyday must be shown in use, the crowd it gathers is the measure of its success. But they gather, how? Given the alienation engendered by the secularization of "eternity as acceleration" and its effect on the experience of time, how meaningful can the everyday remain? With the absence of an Other, of eternity as an immutable idea, isn't the everyday merely existing on the skin that time has already shed? In Virilio's words: "in our ordinary everyday life, we are passing from the extensive time of history to the intensive time of an instantaneity without history made possible by the technologies of the hour."[16]

If the temporal site of the architecture of the everyday is the flow of time experienced by individual users, projects operating at larger scales are situated against some greater flux of time. To overcome the thrilling but overwhelming sense of the ever changing, emerging architectural practices expand to embrace ecological urbanism, infrastructural urbanism or landscape architecture, leaving behind the single building to tackle greater scope and broader territories. Framed against geological time, ecological time or global time, the projects are conceived as processes that have the ability to respond or perhaps even to control anticipated changes. In the past few decades, large parks such as the Duisburg-Nord Industrial Landscape Park in Germany, the Olympic Sculpture Park in Seattle as well as Fresh Kills have rightly been heralded as successes. These projects take ownership, and with some delight, of the aestheticization of the forces at play – whether natural, economic or social. In other scenarios, alternate programs grow on the corpse of defunct infrastructure. For example, the High Line in New York offers promises of a renewed life for the old tracks but also for the buildings surrounding the elevated line. Notwithstanding its positive impacts on the city, High Line in all its bustling activity strangely museifies itself, the city and its past. Literally, the project promotes musing in a redefined urban museum. On top of this petrified image of a former life, the new path and everything that comes along with it – the rules, the new crowd, the rise in property value – have effectively replaced what was no longer relevant.[17] Like the territorial interventions, the project offers minimal resistance to economy and productivity, the driving forces of acceleration. As these projects sustain existing economic processes, the characteristics of acceleration persist despite, or perhaps even precisely through, the subservient changes of a deeper infrastructural core or larger territorial expanse.

In an attempt to recover depth, different practitioners hark back to the social theories of Michel de Certeau and Henri Lefebvre, or to the idea of the relational presented by Nicolas Bourriaud and Bruno Latour. For example, atelier d'architecture autogérée implements projects that "take time" – a meaningful slowness in the context of acceleration. The firm looks for the emancipatory potential of the relational over the search for quick profit that characterizes commercial endeavors, it seeks to foster depth through rituals, repetition and continuity.[18] Elizabeth Meyer likewise advocates an approach that includes if not the opposition to, at least the recognition of consumption and production, valuing confrontation of a collectivity or an individual as a means to effect changes.[19] Striving for another kind of agency in large landscape projects, she calls for projects that make bare the "invisible consequences of our needs and desires," allowing uncertainty and risk to frame our perception. Revealing discontinuities, making invisible forces uncomfortably tangible, allowing the moment to be fraught with tensions, accepting the irremediability of the gap: there is indeed great strengths in some of the projects that challenge the traditional domain of architectural practice to emphasize the ephemeral and the territorial. And yet, as interventions in the everyday or processes of territorialization, they are all rooted in the fluidity of time, projects and subjects of acceleration. The diversification of architectural practice may be rooted in a desire to address our modern relation to time, but as it moves along with everything else, or even as it anticipates and reacts, architecture remains subservient to the processes of acceleration, caught between a depthless time and a subsumed eternity.

When considering the possibility of an architectural resistance in temporal terms, it is precisely the concepts rejected or avoided by the architecture of acceleration that seem to be most promising. Today, to conceive of architecture as synonymous to a beautiful, useful and durable building is absolutely anachronistic. The same anachronism that plagues the stability of one's personality undeniably tints the relevance of beauty often equated with aesthetic trend, of usefulness defined in flexible function, or durability approached as the ability to endure change. But the anachronism that brushes history and time against the grain may be one of the ways in which we can resist being subsumed in time. For Giorgio Agamben, relating anachronistically to time is to keep a firm grip on it precisely by maintaining a distance, and "the ones who can call themselves contemporary are only those who do not allow themselves to be blinded by the lights of the century, and so manage to get a glimpse of the shadows in those lights, of their intimate obscurity."[20]

The projects in which this negative element is sought – the absent whole that lies in the shadow of the fragmentary presence – are certainly if intangibly hinting at some form of a shared pre-existing ground. Oscillating between a positive but fragmented presence and the implied potential whole that lies in its shadow, architects can not only reassert the position of the fragment in the present but also its indexical reference to what was or what could be. Examples range from the Gulag Stone in Moscow that literally and physically sets up a link with the history it represents,[21] Pierre Soulages' series of thick black paintings that reflect bright white light, or the simple joint at Peter Zumthor's Gugalun House, homage to the aged wood that housed an older generation, humility of the new wood that merely extends and will weather, holding both stability and time, continuity and transience. Echoing a passage from a section that for me was undeniably the most vivid expression of the inextricability of our temporal anchors in the experience of space, we can say that these works appeal to "our capacity to under-stand the co-incidence of presence and absence, space and substance, light and shadow."[22]

Position as opposition

When Alberto Pérez-Gómez used the term crisis, he clearly used the concept as the Greek did to imply the necessity of choice, judgment and decision. But today, the categorical dimension of the concept is subdued in an ambivalent wish to defer conclusion. "The concept of crisis, which once had the power to pose unavoidable, harsh and non-negotiable alternatives, has been transformed to fit the uncertainties of whatever might be favored at a given moment." This is Koselleck's conclusion in his essay "Crisis." And that, "a tendency towards vagueness and imprecision" is what he sees as a larger symptom of our current historical critical situation.[23] Deferring conclusion is again allowing the flow of time to preside over the impossibility to claim a meaningful position in time. It amounts to accepting the transformation of the fundamental dialectics between time and eternity into a self-propelled deferred image of eternity.

In *Phenomenology of Perception*, Merleau-Ponty addresses the necessity of a double direction between time and eternity. "[A] two-way relationship that phenomenology has called Fundierung," it is a relation between a founding term (time) and the founded (eternity).[24] In this conception, neither time nor eternity precedes one another but both take their full meaning from the existence of the other. Neglecting the necessity of this double movement between the founding and the founded, the embrace of acceleration as the promise of the eternal creates a situation wherein both time and eternity are consumed. Acceleration consumes lived-time; accelerated time consumes the figure of eternity. We need to return to time as the primary element. In relation to landscape, authors such as Mark Treib, Denis Cosgrove and James Corner have been urging architects to carefully tune the temporalities of architecture against those of nature.[25] Turning to digital representation and to the Internet as an archive without sedimentation, Antoine Picon has revealed the inability of digital architecture to become the register of collective memories, encouraging practitioners to question some of the larger physical and metaphysical contexts within which they chose to operate.[26] But time, whether conceived through epistemological interactions or as the motor of the phenomenological encounter, loses its significant depth if considered singularly. It must carry resonances that hark back to history as well as to the depths of our memory.

When Merleau-Ponty points to the tendency to equate depth with breadth, he also contrasts the emphasis of one single perspective over the necessary movement between two realms. Only a view from eternity, an ubiquitous divine vision, would ever support a vision in which breadth would indeed match depth.[27] In order to explicate the fundamental nature of depth, the phenomenologist suggests a temporal understanding of its quasi-synthesis: " . . . just as memory can be understood only as a direct possession of the past with no interposed contents, so the perception of distance can be understood only as a *being in the distance* which links up with being where it appears."[28] For Pérez-Gómez, an architecture of resistance "celebrates dreams and the imagination without forgetting that it is made for the Other, and aims at revealing depth not as homologous to breath and height, but as a significant first dimension that remains mysterious, and reminds us of our luminous opacity as mortals in a wondrous more-than-human world."[29] Indeed, the revelation of depth implies a double relation between architecture and what it seeks to bridge – human life and some figure of transcendental truth, a form of immanent order in the larger cosmos. Rather than accepting acceleration and adopting the instrumental, quantifiable, efficient and productive approach to practice, architects must take responsibility both for the past and the future by positing history as the only viable opposition to eternity *as* acceleration.[30] But what does it mean to recover history, and is it still possible? We are quick and keen on remembering the technical and measurable, but it is of course much harder to hold on the intangible and immeasurable. History is getting squeezed out of programs, we are experiencing the 1930s anew to make room not for new forms but new dogma: technology, skills, and measurable outcomes. In this context, position becomes opposition: not to go with the flow, and firmly siting oneself within and against historical continuity. This may imply the careful selection of projects, refusal to participate in certain ventures, an awareness of the means we employ, a commitment to take the time that it takes, a pledge to acknowledge what is already there.

Architecture or acceleration

In the choice between "architecture or acceleration" lies a plea to consider anew the strengths of the anachronistic, the quality of durability and the need for some form of historical continuity. Perhaps it is only so-considered that approaches that privilege either the everyday, the fragmentary, the participatory and even the territory can be emancipatory. Indexical figures of continuity and discontinuity, fragments can oscillate between their presence in an ongoing dynamic and their ability to reference potential pasts and futures. Anachronistic also can be architecture's durability, its unchanging form and resulting recognizability. A project like the Biblioteca España in Medellin, Columbia gains half its felicity by offering a counterpoint to the growing transit networks: from a space of production subservient to the larger economy of the city, the library is a place of contemplation, a break in scale and in temporality. Significantly, the project bears at its core the ambition to act as reference against the change it hopes to foster.[31] Here, architecture assumes its representational and historical role within and against a world otherwise dictated by productivity. Architecture can be this figure of continuity through which time is revealed, a hyphen that lets us glimpse at the eternal by allowing time to unfold.

Notes

1 Alberto Pérez-Gómez, *Architecture and the Crisis of Modern Science* (Cambridge, MA: MIT Press, 1983), 4.
2 Pérez-Gómez, *Crisis*, 3–14.
3 Reinhart Koselleck, "Crisis," *Journal of the History of Ideas* 67, no. 2 (2006): 358.
4 Reinhart Koselleck, "Is There an Acceleration of History?" in *High Speed Society, Social Acceleration, Power and Modernity*, ed. Hartmut Rosa (University Park, PA: Pennsylvania State University Press, 2009), 113–134.

5 Alberto Pérez-Gómez and Louise Pelletier, *Architectural Representation and the Perspective Hinge* (Cambridge, MA: MIT Press, 2000), 10–11.

6 Ulrich Beck, Anthony Giddens and Jurgen Habermas, posit the late-modern against notions of post-modernity to rather suggest a continuing modernity, hence a "late" modernity.

7 Antoine Picon, "Digital Architecture and the Temporal Structure of the Internet Experience," in *Chrono-topologies, Hybrid Spatialities and Multiple Temporalities*, ed. Leslie Kavanaugh (Amsterdam: Rodopi B. V, 2010), 222–236; Sanford Kwinter, *Architectures of Time, Toward a Theory of the Event in Modernist Culture* (Cambridge, MA: MIT press, 2002); Joan Ockman, "The Yes Man: Can Rem Koolhaas Make Consumerism Safe for Intellectuals? Harvard, Prada and Conde Nast all think so," *Architecture* 91, no. 2 (2003): 76–79; and Joan Ockman, "Between Ornament and Monument, Sigfried Kracauer and the Architectural Implication of the Mass Ornament," *Thesis* (Weimar: Wissenschaftliche Zeitschrift der Bauhaus-Universität), no. 3 (2003): 74–91.

8 Paul Virilio, *Polar Inertia* (London: Sage Publications, 2000), 17.

9 Marshall Berman, *All that Is Solid Melts into Air: The Experience of Modernity* (New York: Penguin, 1988); David Harvey, *The Condition of Postmodernity: An Enquiry into the Origins of Cultural Change* (London: Wiley Blackwell, 1992); Hilde Heynen, *Architecture and Modernity* (Cambridge, MA: MIT Press, 2000).

10 Manuel Castells, *Communication Power* (Oxford: Oxford University Press, 2009).

11 Koselleck, "Acceleration," 116.

12 Rosa, *High Speed Society*, 9–11.

13 Hartmut Rosa, *Aliénation et acceleration – Vers une théorie critique de la modernité tardive* (Paris: La Découverte, 2012), 101.

14 Rosa, *Aliénation,* 132.

15 "Paris changes!" Baudelaire admitted, "but nothing in my melancholia has changed! New palaces, scaffoldings, blocks, old towns, all is becoming allegory for me, and my dear memories are heavier than stones" (*Paris change! mais rien dans ma mélancolie – N'a bougé! palais neufs, échafaudages, blocs – Vieux faubourgs, tout pour moi devient allégorie – Et mes chers souvenirs sont plus lourds que des rocs*). Charles Baudelaire, "Le Cygne" (Tableaux Parisiens), in *Les Fleurs du mal* (Paris: Gallimard, 1972), 119.

16 Virilio, *Polar Inertia*, 25.

17 The High Line is called a "postmodern monument," charming as it masks history by Rachel Stevens, "The High Line: Monument to Modern Ruin," *Afterimage: The Journal of Media Arts and Cultural Criticism* 38, no. 2 (September/October 2010): 4–8. According to Adam Sternberg, "The project is the result of a perfect confluence of powerful forces: radical dreaming, stubborn optimism, neighborhood anxiety, design frenzy, real-estate opportunism, money, celebrity, and power." Adam Sternberg, *New York Magazine* (2007) as quoted in *Resilience in Ecology and Urban Design*, ed. Pickett, Cadenasso, and McGrath (New York: Springer, 2013), 277.

18 *Doina Petrescu*, "Relationscapes: Mapping agencies of relational practice in architecture," *City, Culture and Society* 3, no. 2 (2012): 139.

19 Elizabeth K. Meyer, "Uncertain Parks: Disturbed Sites, Citizens, and Risk Society," in *Large Parks*, ed. Julia Czerniak and Gearge Hargreaves (New York: Princeton Architectural Press, 2007), 59–82.

20 Giorgio Agamben, "What is the Contemporary?" in *What Is an Apparatus and Other Essays*, trans. David Kishik and Stefan Pedatella (Stanford: Stanford University Press, 2009), 44–45.

21 Laura Mulvey, "Reflections on Disgraced Monuments," in *Architecture and Revolutions*, ed. Neil Leach (New York: Routledge, 1999), 219–227.

22 Pérez-Gómez and Pelletier, *Architectural Representation*, 322–368.

23 Koselleck, "Crisis," 399.

24 Maurice Merleau-Ponty, *The Phenomenology of Perception* (London: Routledge and Kegan Paul, 1972), 394.

25 James Corner, "Eidectic Operations and New Landscapes," in *Recovering Landscape, Essays in Contemporary Landscape Architecture*, ed. James Corner (New York: Princeton Architectural Press, 1999), 152–169; Dennis Cosgrove, "Mapping Meaning," in *Mappings*, ed. Dennis Cosgrove (London: Reaktion Books, 1999), 1–23; and Mark Treib, ed., *Spatial Recall: Memory in Architecture and Landscape* (New York, London: Routledge, 2009).

26 Picon, "Digital Architecture," 235–236.

27 Merleau-Ponty, *Phenomenology of Perception*, 255.

28 Ibid., 265.

29 Alberto Pérez-Gómez, "The Historical Context of Contemporary Architectural Representation," in *Persistent Modelling: Extending the Role of Architectural Representation*, ed. Phil Ayres (New York: Routledge, 2012), 23.

30 Elsewhere, I have taken up the idea – advocated by Pérez-Gómez and going all the way back to Vico – that history, in the form of continuity, is indeed the only trace of eternity that we may still hold in common. Anne Bordeleau, "Monumentality and Contemporaneity in the Work of Tarkovsky, Goldsworthy, and Zumthor," in *Chora: Intervals in the Philosophy of Architecture*, vol. 7, forthcoming.

31 Giancarlo Mazzanti, "Biblioteca España," in *Landform Building, Architecture's New Terrain*, ed. Stan Allan and Marc McQuade (New York: Lars Müller Publisher, 2011), 106.

19

BUILDING UPON LOVE IN AN AGE OF INNOVATION

Peter Olshavsky

It is banal to devote oneself to an end when that end is clearly only a means.[1]

Georges Bataille

With recent efforts to recuperate modernity, innovation has been thrust into the foreground. While this effort might hold value for society, it can become pathological when innovation is mistaken as an end in itself. Evgeny Morozov has leveled insightful criticism against Silicon Valley's obsession with this thinking.[2] Yet, within architecture the recent shift towards post-critical practices has opened its own version of this pathology. This dilemma has consequences for designers that need to be discussed from a position other than complicit approval. My position is that we can't simply accept reductive forms of practice that blindly promote innovation. Using the work of Alberto Pérez-Gómez, I will argue for a richer approach. This will shift focus from foreground intelligence to a hermeneutic position that draws on a less articulate background to innovate appropriately.

Disciplinary shift

The dominant architectural conversation has shifted away from what Anthony Vidler describes as an "Age of Discourse." Architecture in "the knowledge society," Michael Speaks argues, is no longer propelled by "grand ideas or theories realized in visionary form."[3] As an early critic of Euro-American discourse, he and others point to the troubles of the critical project, which derives from the work of Manfredo Tafuri, Jacques Derrida, Theodor Adorno and various others. Specifically, he criticizes ineffectual concepts that sought "resistance" and "negation" of consumer society and metaphysical or political hegemony. "There is in the deepest motivations of architecture," Rem Koolhaas similarly observed, "something that cannot be critical."[4] However, Speaks quickly moves past K. Michael Hays' notion of "criticality," to question theory as a whole.[5] "Theory was interesting," he says, "but now we have work."[6]

Looking at academically inclined practices of the past forty years like Peter Eisenman and Diller+Scofidio, Speaks believes too much was being said and too little being done. The orientation of theory is supplanted by the demand that architecture "just works!" if I can misappropriate a quote by Steve Jobs, the patron saint of innovation. This is supported by the claim that "use-value," as Speaks notes, is more important than "truth content."[7] Setting aside the fact that Speaks' new found pragmatism reeks of rupture talk, it suggests that one must consciously build upon the teachings of our age. Architects should reshape their practices to innovate because global society demands nothing less. Speaks' view indeed might help some academics and practitioners frame their practices outside of "criticality." What has gone unmentioned is how he devotes himself to an end that is only a means, which neglects the background for the sake of the foreground, as he frames practices that are "after theory."

Design intelligence

Design intelligence was coined by Speaks to characterize a diverse group of practices from Asymptote to George Yu and Neil Denari. It appeared, he says, in the 1990s but was "inaugurated" by the events of September 11, 2001. He contends that the multitude of knowledge generated during the design process is valuable to the business of architecture. But this knowledge is frequently overlooked in favor of the design. Contrasted with the earlier vanguard, he promotes a less object-focused practice.[8] The "dislocative" possibilities of formal novelty, central to the earlier vanguard, are framed as a retreat from relevance. Instead design intelligence, he advocates, offers an important area for design research without rejecting the reality of current technologies and economy.

Design intelligence, he explains, is manifest through versioning or scenario planning that creates a set of "possible solutions."[9] These options are sought primarily through "prototyping." Architects work rapidly with prototypes to physically test design solutions. This discourages practices that first critically assess an existing situation and act secondly. Instead action and thinking purportedly happen in unison. Speaks describes this as "thinking-as-doing." This should not be confused with "making" in the sense of Giambattista Vico. Human truth, for the latter, is more knowable because it is made. Making, Vico suggests, was anti-Cartesian, not simply technical and pointed to the need to understand the historical background from which practices arise. Speaks' "thinking-as-doing" codifies studio-based production and brands its feedback and output as intelligence. Promoting instrumental production, Speaks has little concern for an individual craftsman, as his focus is the market viability of this knowledge. But Vico is after a reflective model for an individual's self-understanding because it provides a "practical wisdom" so a maker is able to act prudently.[10]

Speaks has little concern for prudence. Design intelligence, Speaks argues, is limited only by technical exigencies. Practitioners in this vein hold "no philosophic or professional truth, making use of no specialized theory, these practices are open to the influences of 'chatter' and are by disposition willing to learn."[11] The pursuit, control, and application of intelligence are what matters. The architect sacrifices adherences for the sake of realpolitik and solution-focused instrumentality. Adhering to philosophical values can create situations where one might have to compromise their stance for the sake of action. In place of a stance that might (and often does) create conflicting situations, openness and acceptance to information are foregrounded to face rapidly changing "real world" circumstances.

By claiming a monopoly on the "real," Speaks is able to frame practice as chiefly neutral. The ostensible monopoly and the attending neutrality soften, if not hide, the ideological nature of the architect's efforts. But to meet requirements, articulate needs or market demands, I argue, one has to recognize the complexity of the present situation, what came before, and how to act or "project" by employing design intelligence. But these actions suggest a point of view and a range of complex ideologically motivated evaluations. Even the basic belief that architects' intelligence is valuable and can contribute to society stems from a brand of ideology. Ideology, as I use it, is what constitutes one's intentions and actions even in the most normative sense. This constitution allows the architect to make sense of their practices and act. If we fail to recognize this ideology, can we be so sure we are not excluding outlying or exceptional intelligence?

Chatter and information

Even practices open to what Speaks calls "chatter" run the risk of excluding information. The term chatter describes contemporary reality as it is intertwined with digital information. Chatter might be "published on the web, found in popular culture, gleaned from other professions and design disciplines."[12] The term, according to Speaks, tries to account for the ability to process massive collections of information, analyze it instantly, and draw sometimes-surprising outcomes from such information. This diverse information and views opened by increasing access to chatter potentially escalates contact with alternatives. Information, as Cass Sunstein observes, might open a person to "a range of chance encounters, involving shared experiences with diverse others, and also exposure to materials and topics that they did not seek out in advance."[13] But exposure is countered by the capacity to filter information based on one's tacit background, preferences as well as control methods in a pre-determined or unknowing way. I might be able to diagram the demographics and spatial conditions of an under-privileged neighborhood but tell you nothing about the people, architecture and their stories. In other words, I might be cherry-picking information that appears in the foreground of chatter while overlooking harder to see values that constitute the background. In short, chatter can offer surprises but it can equally exclude, obscure or reinforce what one already knows.

From Speaks' various writings one can surmise that information dredged up out of the chatter can inform the boundaries of inventory, analysis, who participates, types of practices, ideas, visualizations, feedback loops, and the shaping of design innovation to name a few instances. But these are not simply neutral actions. Even simple information extracted from chatter is beholden to a specific orientation. The fact is that no matter how consciously reflective, one's ideological position manifests how apophenia in any of the above settings is structured. One's present position includes a range of issues, including our sediment past, future expectation, and the fact that we "are" our bodies.[14] Ideological biases are part of being human. They inevitably shape the patterns we discover. This is not always an a priori problem. In fact, phenomenology teaches that consciousness is itself intentional. Any practice, even if entirely open-ended or scientifically inclined, Hans-Georg Gadamer explains, is beset by prejudices.[15] These are not necessarily the heinous sort, but the tacit judgments cast pre-reflectively that open us to experiences. Even a seemingly banal act like collecting information assumes there is something to be found and perhaps taken away. Indeed these pre-judgments help make sense of one's design practice, but they also shape its orientation.

In the Euro-American West, information drawn from chatter can become a veil of legitimacy operating under the broader protections afforded to techno-science. Information, though fabricated, can be reified as fact. This further veils its orientation. Recall the multitude of American and British "intelligence" after 9/11 that buttressed the call to war. If information is reified, it can be placed outside of personal and political change. Referencing CIA intelligence gathering, Speaks claims that information impacts practice, which makes practice more adaptable. Yet, practices do not seem to impact information, which implies that information is placed beyond purposeful shaping. It becomes impervious to critique or worse seems "natural." Intervention can be dismissed as interference with its natural order. Attempting to manage or reconfigure it becomes a hopeless enterprise. We simply must listen and obey.

Innovation of design intelligence

While theoretical discourse, as Speaks suggests, can become perverted as intellectual posturing, in certain circles, including the Essex School, it was and still is understood as a way of orienting oneself and one's work.[16] Thus it was interpretative, open to argumentation and never a static construction. Yet, Speaks frames it as a straw man. "Theory is not just irrelevant," he says, "but was and continues to be an impediment to the development of a culture of innovation in architecture."[17]

To articulate his definition of innovation, Speaks cribs the ideas of Peter F. Drucker, a prolific writer and renowned organizational management consultant. Speaks uses Drucker's framework to distinguish between "innovation" and "problem-solving." Problem solving reactively addresses an issue whereas innovation is a pro-active approach. Innovative designers do not simply address an existing problem. They "add something unexpected, something not given in the brief or competition guidelines."[18] An innovation is a "change that creates a new dimension of performance," which might lead an innovator beyond a present predicament to new products, services, and perhaps new businesses.[19] It offers clients "alternative solutions" to their problems. This, Speaks claims, makes design intelligence "inherently innovative." In other words, innovation is framed as nearly an autonomous pursuit. It is valued outside of virtually any framework, except that it creates monetary value and "new potential for satisfaction."[20] In this way, it papers over its solution-focused core while distracting us with refrains of technological progress and speculative promises of capitalist morality.

The specifics of how innovation happens are not as important as the underlying ideology and its implications for architects. In fact, the ideological issues associated with innovation raise more questions than answers. Are innovative designers after the best chances for impact, meeting client's demands, publications, funding, or fame? Does the urgency to innovate actually attenuate the discussions on what constitutes our dilemmas? Does this urgency not promote practices that overlook the messy background, which as Jeremy Till suggests, always beset architecture with uncertainty and contingency?[21] Are we simply innovating for the sake of innovation?

Consider "the world's first eco-city" by William McDonough and Partners in Huangbaiyu, China. McDonough is best known for the 2002 book *Cradle to Cradle: Remaking the Way We Make Things*, co-written with Michael Braungart.[22] This book puts forward a biomimetic account of innovation where people should act like communal leaf-cutter ants and architecture is at its best when it patterns itself on a cherry tree. McDonough had the chance to plant numerous works in Huangbaiyu as China's broader effort to urbanize 250 million rural residences. The innovative design of the eco-city was, however, inappropriate. It did not account for the historically constructed social, cultural, and economic demands of the villagers. From plots of land that are too small to farm or tend livestock, to garages for people lacking the means to afford cars, its failures have been made plain by Shannon May.[23] In Huangbaiyu, the architect's innovative solutions created an untenable situation.

Equally, what is framed as a site rife for innovation, Morozov suggests, might be a characteristic or compromise that makes a situation work for the parties with a stake in that setting. This has been the case with graffiti. Typically, graffiti is seen as an irritant in the smooth operations of many cities due to its associations with urban blight and the cost of its removal. Over the years, it has been suppressed with surveillance, defensible well-lit spaces, buildings networked to the authorities, and smarter anti-graffiti materials. But these have not and will likely never eliminate graffiti. New paint, adhesives, and other forms of marking will be invented or co-opted. This raises the question why and for whom does one innovate? But perhaps this unmanageable element might enable positive personal, cultural or economic developments? The rise of Street Art is a case in point. Not every kid with a spray can merit the esteem of Banksy or Barry McGee, but that's not the point. Some neighborhoods, like Belleville, Paris, have embraced graffiti to cultivate a social and economic scene, instead of attempting to employ another graffiti fighting innovation.[24] This example suggests that the desire to problem solve through innovation can veil alternatives that better respond to how competing interests are played out through the contested domains of our selves, buildings, and cities. But to recognize when and where innovation should occur, should an architect not account for more than design intelligence allows?

Innovation built upon love

Many people assume our crises are so overwhelming that they tie our hands and force us to innovate. While the assessment of our situation might be true, it does not mean an innovative practice must be reductive. In fact, I will articulate an ethical praxis drawn from the nuanced and historical orientation found in Alberto Pérez-Gómez's book *Built upon Love: Architectural Longing after Ethics and Aesthetics*.[25] To distinguish its orientation from design intelligence, I will outline key distinctions – interpretive orientation, phronetic knowledge, meaningful innovation, and questioning – that show Pérez-Gómez's stance as a more appropriate way to foster innovation.

Chatter / interpretive orientation

"An agent free from all frameworks," Charles Taylor explains, "rather spells for us a person in the grip of an appalling identity crisis."[26] Without orientation, one would be set adrift in the space of appearances. An architect would be unable to judge or make informed qualitative evaluations necessary for action. Design intelligence assumes that being set adrift is positive because it empowers the architect to be informed by chatter. Yet, what emerges from this ungrounded view does not guarantee positive behavioral, socio-political or disciplinary change. It might in the end encumber all of these.

"Genuine innovation," as Pérez-Gómez suggests, "requires a wide-ranging hermeneutic of the discipline (a historical understanding of form, program, and intentionality) that provides the architect with an appropriate language to verbalize a position."[27] This orientation goes beyond a flippant engagement with chatter. "The architect," as Pérez-Gómez notes, "requires a broad cultural foundation to be able to generate an ethical response."[28] A personal imagination is placed in dialogue with the intentions of contemporaries, different cultures, and other historical epochs. Through dialogue involving interpretation, which is always courteous and critical, an architect can establish a ground from which meaningful agency springs.

Design intelligence / phronetic knowledge

Architects should offer more than the speculative promises and capitalist morality because "consumption and possession" are the "bastard aims of desire."[29] Contrary to this view, Pérez-Gómez argues for practical philosophy. "Only work grounded in . . . practical philosophy," he says, "is capable of contributing effectively to cultural communication, becoming authentic innovation rather than mere fashionable novelty."[30]

Practical philosophy is rooted in "phronetic knowledge," which comes from the Greek word *phronēsis* meaning practical wisdom. Phronetic knowledge is cultivated "through a profound comprehension of history and culture."[31] It is embodied and transmitted by specific stories, like Francesco Colonna's *Hypnerotomachia Poliphili*. This knowledge comes from the bottom-up and is based on understanding normative conditions, including values, habits and the background from which information and practices emerge. Phronetic knowledge is not dogmatic nor does it dictate to practice. Rather it evokes sound judgment and seeks out what is meaningful. So, in place of instrumental concerns of how an architect *might* innovate, it shifts to ethical considerations of why an architect *should* innovate.

Innovation / meaningful innovation

Innovation, contrary to Speaks' suggestion, is not an end in itself. To avoid this shortcoming, Antoine Picon argues, "architectural innovation" must "make sense," therefore it should be attentive to "meaning."[32] According to Pérez-Gómez, "meaning" should not be construed as a sign or intellectual construction. It is "more than merely information; it is knowledge of the world and its sensuous materiality understood by the body: a carnal, fully sexual, and therefore opaque experience of truth."[33] It appears during a work's reception. Meaning is "both the experience of something new, even destabilizing, while also recognizing the experience as familiar."[34] "True innovation" is described similarly to meaning as "a work that appears new and unexpected, yet familiar – a work that lasts."[35] Thus innovation is genuine, I would argue, when it is meaningful.

Creating meaningful innovation is similar to love. "Love and, by analogy, creation," he argues, "have their origins in the deeply felt experience of beauty itself, sometimes destabilizing and never in line with the principles of logic."[36] It is not tied to any given aesthetic, rationalized practice or code of conduct. No matter how hard one attempts to systematize genuine innovation for the sake of professional interests; it will not fit comfortably in normative design models, methods or production. This should not be lamented but celebrated.

When meaningful innovation in architecture – Antoni Gaudí's Casa Batlló, John Hejduk's masques, or Frederick Kiesler's endless architecture – appears in the space of lived experience, it speaks to one's most profound sense of existence. This is "an architecture that might be both beautiful and just, responsive to cultural contexts and genuinely creative, [therefore] the architect must recognize its medium is the space of desire. Thus architecture can inspire emotion and induce pathos, being both compassionate and erotic."[37] Thus a truly innovative work has the capacity to reconcile ethics and poetics in a way that reveals and transcends its conditions in a singular fashion. It, as Pérez-Gómez suggests, "lovingly provides a sense of order resonant with our dreams."[38] It might even change one's life.

Problem solving / asking questions

Focusing on problem solving, whether it adds something new or not, is like being equipped with a hammer; it's only a matter of time before one contrives all sorts of nails to drive. Instead of eagerly "projecting," as Reinhold Martin suggests, architects should ask themselves "just what sort of world they are projecting . . . ?"[39] In short, when facing a crisis, there is more to doing good work than enthusiastically "making a difference." It is not only important, as Teju Cole recommends, to "reason out the need for the need," but to demand a more enduring commitment.[40]

My criticism of design intelligence should not be misconstrued as advocacy against the newfound faith in architectural knowledge or as an avoidance of problems. Nor am I promoting a retreat into criticality. "Design," as Pérez-Gómez argues, "is neither problem solving nor mere formal innovation."[41] Instead of these false alternatives, it is important to seek questions worthy of consideration. These are often older than we think. In fact, reformulating questions, Pérez-Gómez maintains, "have contributed imaginative, poetic responses to our universal call for dwelling – answers from which we can learn and develop an ability to act here and now."[42]

Rather than a means without an end, asking questions from a grounded position is an attempt to respond to the true complexity of our situations where the paths to change are sometimes slow, full of ideological traps, and always tied to a fuller background against which our practice make sense. These differences are crucial, I believe, lest we solve precisely those things that make possible an architecture built upon love.

Notes

1 Georges Bataille, *The Tears of Eros*, trans. Peter Connor (San Francisco: City Lights Books, 1989), 19.
2 Evgeny Morozov, *To Save Everything, Click Here:The Folly of Technological Solutionism* (NewYork: Public Affairs, 2013).
3 Michael Speaks, "Intelligence afterTheory," *Perspecta* 38, 2006, 106.
4 Rem Koolhaas, quoted by Beth Kapusta, *Canadian Architect Magazine* 39 (August 1994): 10.
5 For an examination of the critical/post-critical debates see George Baird, "'Criticality' and Its Discontents," *Harvard Design Magazine* 21 (Fall 2004/Winter 2005): 16–21; and Jane Rendell et al., eds., *Critical Architecture* (London and New York: Routledge, 2007).
6 Michael Speaks, "Theory Was Interesting . . . but Now We Have Work," *Architectural Research Quarterly* 6 no. 3 (December 2002): 209.
7 Michael Speaks, "Intelligence afterTheory," 104.
8 Michael Speaks, "Design Intelligence. Part 2: GeorgeYu Architects," *A+U* 388, no. 1 (January 2003): 150.

9 Michael Speaks, "Design Intelligence. Part 1: Introduction," *A+U* 387, no.12 (December 2002): 16.

10 Giambattista Vico, *On Humanistic Education: Six Inaugural Orations, 1699–1707*, ed. Gian Galeazzo Visconti, trans. Giorgio A. Pinton and Arthur W. Shippee, intro. Donald Phillip Verene (Ithaca, NY: Cornell University Press, 1993), 8.

11 Speaks, "Intelligence after Theory," 106.

12 Speaks, "Design Intelligence – Part 1," 18.

13 Cass Sunstein, *Republic.com* (Princeton: Princeton University Press, 2001), 11–12.

14 Maurice Merleau-Ponty, *The Primacy of Perception: And Other Essays on Phenomenological Psychology, the Philosophy of Art, History and Politics*, ed. James M. Edie (Evanston, IL: Northwestern University Press, 1964), 3–5.

15 Hans-Georg Gadamer, *Truth and Method*, trans. Joel Weinsheimer and Donald G. Marshall (London & New York: Bloombury, 2013), 289–292.

16 The Essex School refers to the Master's courses formed by Joseph Rykwert with Dalibor Vesely in the Department of Art at the University of Essex. Their approaches, underwritten by hermeneutic and phenomenological frameworks, have influenced several generations of architects, historians and educators, including Daniel Libeskind, David Leatherbarrow, Alberto Pérez-Gómez and many others. See Helen Thomas, "Invention in the Shadow of History: Joseph Rykwert at the University of Essex," *Journal of Architectural Education* 58, no. 2 (Nov. 2004): 39–45.

17 Speaks, "Intelligence after Theory," 74.

18 Speaks, "Design Intelligence. Part 2," 150.

19 Peter F. Drucker, *Innovation and Entrepreneurship: Practice and Principles* (New York: HarpersBusiness, 1993), 30–36.

20 Peter F. Drucker, *Management: Tasks, Responsibilities, Practices* (Oxford: Butterworth-Heinemann, 1974), 60.

21 Jeremy Till, *Architecture Depends* (Cambridge: MIT Press, 2009).

22 William McDonough and Michael Braungart, *Cradle to Cradle: Remaking the Way We Make Things* (New York: North Point Press, 2002).

23 Shannon May, "Ecological Crisis and Eco-Villages in China," *CounterPunch* (Nov. 21–23, 2008), accessed June 10, 2013, www.counterpunch.org/2008/11/21/ecological-crisis-and-eco-villages-in-china.

24 "Mur de graff au square Karcher," *Mairie20.Paris*, accessed November 20, 2013, www.mairie20.paris.fr/mairie20/jsp/site/Portal.jsp?page_id=1104.

25 Alberto Pérez-Gómez, *Built upon Love: Architectural Longing after Ethics and Aesthetics* (Cambridge, MA: MIT Press, 2008), 187–201.

26 Charles Taylor, *Sources of the Self: The Making of Modern Identity* (Cambridge: Harvard University Press, 1989), 31.

27 Pérez-Gómez, *Built upon Love*, 201.

28 Ibid.

29 Ibid., 5.

30 Ibid., 110.

31 Ibid.

32 Antoine Picon, "Architecture, Innovation and Tradition," *AD* 83, no. 1 (January/February 2013): 133.

33 Pérez-Gómez, *Built upon Love*, 109.

34 Graham Cairn, "Conversation with Alberto Pérez-Gómez," unpublished manuscript, unpaginated.

35 Pérez-Gómez, *Built upon Love*, 185.

36 Ibid., 28.

37 Cairn, "Conversation with Alberto Pérez-Gómez."

38 Pérez-Gómez, *Built upon Love*, 4.

39 Reinhold Martin, "Critical of What?" *Harvard Design Magazine*, 22 (Spring/ Summer 2005): 4.

40 Teju Cole, "The White Savior Industrial Complex," *TheAtlantic*, March 21, 2012, accessed February 01, 2013, www.theatlantic.com/international/ archive/2012/03/the-white-savior-industrial-complex/254843.

41 Pérez-Gómez, *Built upon Love*, 210.

42 Ibid., 209.

20

CONTENT AND CRAFT

What do we do when we do the history of architecture?

David Theodore

In *Built upon Love*, Alberto Pérez-Gómez begins his chapter on the brothers Jean-Louis and Charles-François Viel with a reference to the work of another historian. He discusses Jean-Marie Pérouse de Montclos, who in 1966 marshaled evidence to argue that the brothers, active in post-revolutionary Paris, were indeed two distinct persons. For Pérez-Gómez, Pérouse de Montclos's attribution was helpful, but his analysis was not, for it seemed "to miss the profound implications of the multiple layers of his [Charles-François's] critique."[1] This is a curious but telling opening; it metes out praise for archival, documentary fact-finding research, while simultaneously denigrating it as secondary: what matters is whether the historian makes the right judgment, and the right interpretation. Pérez-Gómez's own chapter brings no new evidence to bear on this historical incident; he sets out instead to offer a textual re-reading, searching in the past for a meaningful understanding of the present. Here, then, rhetorically, is a brilliant opening flourish that invites – perhaps compels – us to read what follows as a model for doing history. In miniature, it is a brief manifesto of what we should do when we do the history of architecture; namely, it is not enough to get the facts and the story right, we must also receptively grasp the problems raised by the text and which the text addresses.

This essay describes, compares, and elucidates what Pérez-Gómez does when he does history at two moments: in his first book, *Architecture and the Crisis of Modern Science* (1983), and in the chapter on *les frères* Viel in *Built upon Love* (2006). I wish to comment briefly on how he uses documentary evidence, evaluates sources, enters into debates with other scholars and secondary scholarship, and constructs historical arguments. Rather than focus on his content and conclusions – his passionate exhortation to use history to orient ethical practices today – the essay seeks to understand his craft: how does his immersion in hermeneutics, history of science, and phenomenology constitute how he works as an historian?[2]

The question of Pérez-Gómez and historiography appears quite starkly today against the background of the recent transformation in the kinds of historical research undertaken in architecture schools. Contemporary architectural historians, liberated from the constraints of style-based art history, now aspire to the standards and procedures of research undertaken elsewhere in the academy.[3] As an architecture-school-based holder of a doctorate, Pérez-Gómez was an influential exemplar in the development of this trend. He was part of an earlier second wave of university-trained historians who sought a history of architecture distinct from art history in terms of method, heuristics, and philosophical sophistication. And yet his approach to doing history, rooted in his education at the University of Essex, goes against many of the conventions and standards of professional history as practiced in the university today. He makes a crucial contribution, on the level of craftsmanship, to showing how one might practice an alternative or oppositional model of historical writing, one free from the technocratic and formalist trajectories characteristic of the specialist historian.

One way to introduce the issue of method and technique in architectural history is to look at this "history of history." We can start by recounting the story about how "architectural" history emerged as an academic department after World War II, taking on institutional forms distinct from both professional programs and art history departments. The celebrated program at the University of Essex, led by Dalibor Vesely and Joseph Rykwert, was but one graduate architecture program focused on history and theory as the proper subjects of advanced degrees.[4] While Essex was famously nomadic and peripatetic (sometimes by choice), early programs in the United States had stronger institutional homes in architecture schools. Historians in programs at the University of Pennsylvania and Princeton, as well as slightly later ones at UC Berkeley and MIT, experimented with how history might be written.[5]

Architectural historians were not alone in the desire to create new histories and new academic departments. Historians of science and of medicine, too, also split off from their close associations with professional training and began to incorporate concepts and goals from social and intellectual history. Relying on arguments and strategies from anthropology, sociology, and philosophy, historians across the university aligned their work with the interpretive social sciences, and away from questions of connoisseurship and fact-finding. They worked assiduously to specialize and professionalize, changing the ways they assessed evidence and positioned themselves within the academy. Cultural and social historians especially sought to better understand the ways that people, whether ordinary citizens, philosophers, or architects, made sense of the world in distant historical periods.[6]

While there are problems specific to the writing of professional *architectural* history (e.g. the structure of the peer-review publication system or the opposition between avant-garde and social history), it is the character of Pérez-Gómez's craft within the broader view of the professionalization of history that concerns me here.[7] To that end, I want to discuss three key features of Pérez-Gómez's historiography he promotes that go against the conventions of specialist historical research. First, his interpretive practices are bounded by an understanding of meaning given by twentieth-century phenomenology. Second, he understands history as marked by metaphysical changes more strongly than economic, political, or social changes. Third, he reads the long tradition of writing architectural theory, especially since the rediscovery of Vitruvius in the Renaissance, as internally coherent. Each of these three parts provides, in circular fashion, the grounding for the other. For the sake of clarity I will discuss each part individually, pointing out only the obvious ways in which they connect to each other, but bear in mind that both conceptually and as a matter of prose style they are deeply intertwined.[8]

For Pérez-Gómez, phenomenology is not just a theoretical framework chosen from among rivals; consequently, he does not, as part of writing history, include any argument for adopting this way of thinking. He simply opens Crisis with a declarative, apodictic paragraph about perception, experience, and meaning.[9] Rigorously following phenomenological thinkers, he argues near the book's end, allows historians to disengage from technocratic, instrumental, formalist, and dualist thinking.[10] Indeed, Pérez-Gómez's historical propositions will make sense only if the reader develops a sophisticated understanding of a wide range of phenomenological thinkers. Two distinctive characteristics of Pérez-Gómez's work follow. First, there never arises an issue in the historical documents Pérez-Gómez examines that puts phenomenology to the test; history always reveals the truth of embodied meaning.[11] Second, there is never cause to engage with other theories of meaning either to repudiate or rehabilitate them.[12] But note also that Pérez-Gómez himself will not be the guide to understanding phenomenology. Pérez-Gómez's approach obliges the interested reader to actively read *Crisis* alongside the thinkers he recapitulates but does not elucidate.[13] This engagement with theory, strikingly distinct from other scholarly practices, is one of the most significant ways Pérez-Gómez's working methods, and not just content, should be understood in opposition to the conventions of professional history.

A second feature of Pérez-Gómez's craft is his insistence on ordering historical time into epochs. These epochs are mostly described by metaphysical distinctions, not social, cultural, political, or material changes. He derives them from historians of science, specifically, from Georges Gusdorf and Alexandre Koyré, adopting the forceful notion of a Galilean revolution.[14] In Pérez-Gómez's categories, a first fundamental change occurred in the seventeenth century with the scientific revolution and René Descartes's influential emphasis on the difference between *res extensa* and *res cogitans*; a second occurred at the beginning of the nineteenth century with J.-N.-L. Durand's combinatorialism and Gaspard de Monge's descriptive geometry.[15] Note that Pérez-Gómez's periodization does not arise out of his close scrutiny of texts, but rather guides and precedes his reading.[16] In *Love*, too, he explicitly and implicitly argues for the ongoing validity of a vocabulary of scientific crisis and epistemological revolution. By contrast, we can look at what happened in the history of science around the time *Crisis* was published. Historians of science had begun to question the schema of continuity and gaps, and, more profoundly, the coherence of "science." The idea of a Galilean scientific revolution, especially a metaphysical one, was shedding its cogency.[17] By 1998, the idea was thought of as a "zombie," a lifeless construct that nevertheless manages to live on outside of professional history, revived for administrative or publicity functions, but no longer an active theme engaged by working historians.[18]

A third structural feature of Pérez-Gómez's writing is his notion of hermeneutic continuity, or, the overlapping of cultural horizons throughout the history of architecture in the West. Despite using a framework of metaphysical epochs, Pérez-Gómez rejects the idea of *incommensurable* historical gaps or breaks. When reading a text, its meaning can be recovered (through hermeneutics).[19] In particular, Pérez-Gómez sees the development of French architectural theory from roughly 1500 to 1900 as "normative for European culture during this period."[20] The underlying philosophical homogeneity of contemporary Europe is the model for a similar notion of the underlying continuity of the western architectural tradition.

Next, I want to discuss Pérez-Gómez's attitude to four key characteristics of contemporary professional historiography: secondary scholarship, archival documentation, the scholarly apparatus, and image analysis. Each of these is sometimes strikingly absent from Pérez-Gómez's work. Yet the presence or absence of these characteristics of professional history is a crucial issue. Pérez-Gómez writes history in opposition to instrumental and formalist methods. It would be disastrous, therefore, if his own historical work was symptomatic of these ways of thinking. The external question concerns whether Pérez-Gómez's kind of history can achieve its goal of opening up a symbolic world that is richer than the world opened up by other kinds of history; the implicit critique is that the professionalization of historiography has as an ideal an empiricist notion of historical truth.

The treatment of Pérouse de Montclos referred to earlier illustrates an important characteristic of Pérez-Gómez's model that goes against current academic practices, namely, the lack of direct discussion of the work of other historians. In his history of footnotes, Anthony Grafton writes, "Only the use of footnotes enables historians to make their texts not monologues but conversations in which scholars, their predecessors, and their subjects all take part."[21] Of the sixty-nine footnotes in the chapter on les frères Viel in *Built upon Love*, there are only six that refer to publications later than 1966.[22] The Frenchman is essentially the only historian mentioned. Pérez-Gómez's practice of disengagement stands starkly against the directive in professional history to position one's argument in reference to the body of contemporary scholarship.

Secondly, although Pérez-Gómez argues for the importance of epistemological contexts he has an unconventional attitude to original research in archival materials. One powerful attribute of *Crisis* is his comprehensive and thorough reading of architectural treatises, published and unpublished. Yet he does not return to the archives in order to deepen his sense of his protagonists' worldview. Archival material, including wills, diaries, letters, newspapers, government reports and so on, the evidential paper trail so prominent in academic history, is absent from his practice. Instead, both chapters on the Viels follow the tenet, outlined in the introduction to *Crisis*, that the texts themselves be allowed to speak. So for instance in reference to Charles-François he writes: "Unlike most of his contemporaries, he understood that architecture could not be reduced to specialized knowledge."[23] But he provides no documentary evidence to allow the reader to gauge his insightfulness in characterizing Viel's "contemporaries" with this short epithet.

In her own discipline, the history of science, Lorraine Daston has nicknamed the current practice of positioning historical writing amongst archival materials and other scholarly writing as a move towards "better footnotes." Historians today seek a sustained engagement with the protocol and contents of the scholarly apparatus that surrounds a historian's central narrative. "The improved craftsmanship of the footnotes alone would signal a steep rise in disciplinary standards," she writes, "footnotes being to historians what joints are to carpenters, that is, the place where the trained eye looks first to test the quality of workmanship."[24] A third characteristic of Pérez-Gómez's craft is that he bucks this trend. But in this respect he is also following a tradition among architectural historians, conserving an older way of working as much as resisting a new one. The works of his predecessors such as Peter Collins, Reyner Banham, and Sigfried Giedeon are all decidedly not up to the standard of documentation required in the humanities today. And Pérez-Gómez's contemporaries, historians such as Manfredo Tafuri and Frederick Karl, publishing around the same time as *Crisis*, likewise make few references to other architectural historians.[25]

Finally, a fourth characteristic that distinguishes Pérez-Gómez's model from contemporary scholarly ideals is the lack of attention given to visual sources. His histories eschew detailed analyses of buildings or drawings, arguably the characteristic skill of the professional architectural historian. Pérez-Gómez's chapter on the Viels, for instance, has no illustrations. In fact, there are none anywhere in the book. His disdain for iconography also goes against the wave of visual culture studies that now examine images as a way of deepening and sometimes changing our understanding of scientific and artistic activity.[26] For Pérez-Gómez, the work of an architectural historian is tied to hermeneutical problems of architectural texts.[27] His analysis, then, is of words and texts, which aligns with his assertion that architecture's predicament demands language to "verbalize a position."[28] The theoretical reasoning behind this approach is subtle, and it appears more blunt than it is only because in his writing (though not in his lectures) Pérez-Gómez adheres so rigorously to the practice.[29] This reluctance to use iconography nicely aligns with his theoretical concerns with image-making and the hegemony of vision, and simultaneously forces readers to become aware of precisely what he does *instead of* doing what architectural historians characteristically do.[30]

Given these seven characteristics of Pérez-Gómez's historiography (three promoted and four contested), we can begin to evaluate the possibilities for historical work opened up by his example. One significant ambition almost lost to professional history but very much alive in Pérez-Gómez's writing concerns scope. For professional historians today, particular stories cannot exemplify whole epochs. As Daston puts it, "Gone are the case studies in support of one or another grand philosophical or sociological generalization about the nature of science."[31] But such generalizations are precisely what Pérez-Gómez has kept. He argues that architecture can be "locally significant and universally eloquent," and so can historical writing.[32] While professional historians have turned to micro-histories, avoiding any evidence of sweeping generalizations, in *Love* Pérez-Gómez writes about all of history from the early Greeks to the present. Micro-history has also led to an explosion of detailed knowledge, which poses a challenge to Pérez-Gómez's historical ambitions. For it would be quite impossible to put into one book – especially a short one – the breadth of history undertaken in *Love* and simultaneously to attend to the constant revisions in the historical scholarship on which he relies.[33] Concomitantly, it is not enough to read what he says; we must understand how he writes it. Examining Pérez-Gómez's history-writing craft allows us to better grasp what we ourselves might do when we do the history of architecture.

Notes

1 Alberto Pérez-Gómez, *Built upon Love: Architectural Longing after Ethics and Aesthetics* (Cambridge, MA: MIT Press, 2006), 167. Pérez-Gómez cites Pérouse de Montclos in the same fashion in *Architecture and the Crisis of Modern Science* (Cambridge, MA: MIT Press, 1983), 369 (note 20).

2 Just to be clear: the present essay is not concerned with evaluating Pérez-Gómez's conclusion that Charles-François is "the first critic of the rationalist doctrines upon which modern architecture was to be generally based" (*Crisis*, 323). For other interpretations, see e.g. Hanno-Walter Kruft, *A History of Architectural Theory: From Vitruvius to the Present*, trans. Ronald Taylor et al. (New York: Princeton Architectural Press, 1994), 157–58. Pérez-Gómez also writes about Charles-François Viel in the essay *Architecture and Ethics beyond Globalization* (Hamburg: Hochschule für bildende Künste, 2003). His evolving thinking could perhaps be traced in three articles he published before *Crisis*: "Charles-François Viel and the Instrumentalizing of Architectural Theory," *Dichotomy* (Detroit: University of Detroit 1980); "Charles-François Viel, primer representante de la reacción anti-racionalista," *Arquitecturas-Bis* 22 (Barcelona, Spain 1978); and "Charles-François Viel: primer arquitecto anti-racionalista del siglo XIX," *Cuadernos de Ciencia y Cultura* 1, COFAA (Mexico City: National Polytechnic Institute Press 1977).

3 See Anthony Grafton, "History's Postmodern Fates," *Daedalus* 135, no. 2 (2006): 54–69.

4 On the formation of the history and theory program at Essex, see Helen Thomas, "Invention in the Shadow of History: Joseph Rykwert at the University of Essex," *Journal of Architectural Education* 58, no. 2 (2004): 39–45. Note that Vesely had no formal position at Essex (ibid., 41). And for the background from which the program emerged, see also George Baird, "Introduction: 'A Promise as Well as a Memory': Toward an Intellectual Biography of Joseph Rykwert," in *Body and Building: Essays on the Changing Relation of Body and Architecture*, ed. George Dodds and Robert Tavernor (Cambridge, MA; London: MIT Press, 2001), 2–25.

5 About fifteen years ago, Mark Jarzombek wrote a series of articles analyzing the state of architectural history in the wake of its professionalization and institutionalization within schools of architecture: see "The Disciplinary Dislocations of (Architectural) History," *Journal of the Society of Architectural Historians* 58, no. 3 (1999): 488–93; "Prolegomena to a Critical Historiography," *Journal of Architectural Education* 52, no. 4 (1999): 197–206; and "The Saturations of Self: Stern's (and Scully's) Role in (Stern's) History," *Assemblage* 23 (1997): 6–21. Yet bear in mind Jarzombek's well-known objection to phenomenology in architectural history based on his claim that adherence to phenomenological tenets can cause scholars to fall into simplistic aesthetic inspiration; see his *The Psychologizing of Modernity: Art, Architecture, and History* (Cambridge: Cambridge University Press, 2001), 9.

6 Two key examples that appeared around the time of *Crisis* are Robert Darnton, *The Great Cat Massacre and Other Episodes in French Cultural History* (New York:

Basic Books, 1984); and Carlos Ginzburg, *The Cheese and the Worms: The Cosmos of a Sixteenth-Century Miller*, trans. Joan and Anne Tedeschi (Baltimore: Johns Hopkins University Press, 1980). While both of these works are concerned with recovering the worldview of illiterate folk, the same technique is common to the search for the oblique or obscure in other kinds of history; see Dominick LaCapra, "Rethinking Intellectual History and Reading Texts," *History and Theory* 19, no. 3 (1980): 245–76.

7   On the history of history in the twentieth century university, see Thomas Bender, Philip Katz, and Colin Palmer, *The Education of Historians for the Twenty First Century* (Urbana and Chicago: University of Illinois Press, 2004).

8   That is, I am aware of the violence involved in decorticating Pérez-Gómez's story, perpetuating an analytic method that the story itself is meant to oppose. But my authority here is his introduction to *Crisis*, and especially the closing sentence: "Being aware of the dangers involved in identifying order in history, I have nevertheless done so convinced that this is a fundamental dimension of historical research" (*Crisis* 13).

9   Pérez-Gómez, *Crisis*, 3.

10 Ibid., 324–25.

11 K. Michael Hays makes this objection in his brief introduction to an excerpt from *Crisis* in *Architecture Theory Since 1968*, ed. K. Michael Hays (Cambridge, MA: MIT Press, 1998), 462–64. Similar (but far less cogent) objections can be found in Christopher Hight, *Architectural Principles in the Age of Cybernetics* (London: Routledge, 2008); and Jorge Otero-Pailos, *Architecture's Historical Turn: Phenomenology and the Rise of the Postmodern* (Minneapolis: University of Minnesota Press, 2010).

12 Pérez-Gómez's strategy here is to focus on the architectural texts themselves, rather than debating theoretical concepts, and thus avoiding Peter Carl's lament that "architecture hardly has a discourse of its own"; Peter Carl, "On Palladio and Le Corbusier," *Architectural Research Quarterly* 13 (2009): 89. Cf. Fredric Jameson's use of other historians' work as a means of clarifying and presenting his own, e.g. in his 1982 lecture published as "Architecture and the Critique of Ideology," in *Architecture, Criticism, Ideology*, ed. Joan Ockman, Deborah Berke, and Mary McLeod (Princeton: Princeton Architectural Press, 1985), 51–93. Intellectual historians, in particular, are finding it fruitful to study phenomenological thinkers in their *interactions* with theorists of other stripes; see e.g. Peter E. Gordon, *Continental Divide: Heidegger, Cassirer, Davos* (Cambridge, MA: Harvard University Press, 2010).

13 For instance, *Crisis* contains no works of Heidegger in the bibliography. Footnote 5, p. 328, refers readers to Belgian phenomenologist Alphonse de Waelhens's widely read introductory text *La philosophie de Martin Heidegger* (Louvain: Editions de l'Institut supérieur de philosophie) (also not included in the bibliography), a book that first appeared in 1942 (i.e. before the publication of the "late" Heidegger's essays addressed more directly at architectural matters).

14 See Pérez-Gómez, *Crisis*, footnotes 19–20, 329–30. In *Built upon Love*, Pérez-Gómez cites Koyré's posthumous book *Metaphysics and Measurement: Essays in Scientific Revolution* (London: Chapman and Hall, 1968), a collection of his highly influential essays published in French between 1935 and 1938. As well, Pérez-Gómez approvingly cites books by historian Paolo Rossi (Rossi was a student but not a pupil of Koyré); see Pérez-Gómez, *Crisis* note 20, 332.

15 Pérez-Gómez, *Crisis*, 10–12.

16 It is helpful to compare this process with other strategies that relate close reading with historical meaning, for instance, those used by Lorraine Daston and Peter Galison in *Objectivity* (New York: Zone Books, 2007). Their history of objectivity in scientific image atlases leads to a periodization substantially independent of pre-established schemas.

17 See David C. Lindberg and Robert S. Westman, eds., *Reappraisals of the Scientific Revolution* (New York: Cambridge University Press, 1990), which was based on a 1981 symposium held in Los Angeles.

18 Mario Biagioli, "The Scientific Revolution is Undead," *Configurations* 6, no. 2 (1998): 141–48.

19 In *Crisis* he cites Hans-Georg Gadamer's 1960 book *Truth and Method*, which appeared in English translation in 1975 (trans. Joel Weinsheimer and Donald G. Marshall [London: Sheed and Ward, 1975]). Architecture is perhaps a good candidate for what Charles Taylor, writing of Gadamer, calls a "human science"; see "Gadamer on the Human Sciences," in *The Cambridge Companion to Gadamer*, ed. Robert J. Dostal (Cambridge: Cambridge University Press, 2002), 126–42.

20 Pérez-Gómez, *Crisis*, 13.

21 Anthony Grafton, *The Footnote: A Curious History* (London: Faber and Faber, 1997); on the history of footnotes, see also Anthony Grafton, "The Footnote from De Thou to Ranke," *History and Theory* 33, no. 4 (1994): 53–76; Robert J. Connors, "The Rhetoric of Citation Systems, Part I: The Development of Annotation Structures from the Renaissance to 1900," *Rhetoric Review* 17, no. 1 (1998): 6–48; and Robert J. Connors, "The Rhetoric of Citation Systems, Part II: Competing Epistemic Values in Citation," *Rhetoric Review* 17, no. 2 (1999): 219–45.

22 Three footnotes refer to *Crisis*, one to a work on music criticism, one to Gianni Vattimo's notion of "weak" theory, and one to an article by Ramla Ben Aissa [sic], "Erudite Laughter: The Persiflage of Viel de Saint-Maux," noted as forthcoming in *Chora*, the book series on philosophy and architecture of which Pérez-Gómez is an editor; it appeared in *Chora: Intervals in the History of Philosophy*, Alberto Pérez-Gómez and Stephen Parcell ed. (Montreal: McGill-Queen's University Press, 2005), vol. 5, 51–80.

23 Pérez-Gómez, *Built upon Love*, 183.

24 Lorraine Daston, "Science Studies and the History of Science," *Critical Inquiry* 35 (2009), 809.

25 Jarzombek, although making a very different argument from mine, notes the same phenomenon in histories of some of Pérez-Gómez's contemporaries: "For example, in their eminently analytical *Modern Architecture*, Manfredo Tafuri and Francesco dal Co do not mention a historian, nor does Frederick Karl in *Modern and Modernism*, or Matei Calinescu in *Five Faces of Modernity*"; see "Prolegomena," 201.

26 For a quick introduction to the vast literature on visual sources in the humanities, see Gillian Rose, *Visual Methodologies: An Introduction to Researching with Visual Materials* (New York: Routledge, 2012); and James Elkins, ed., *Visual Practices Across the University* (Munich: Wilhelm Fink Verlag, 2007).

27 Helen Powell contrasts Rykwert's "intellectual and textual" approach with Colin Rowe's "visual and formalist" techniques; see "Invention in the Shadow of History," 42. On the issue of the relationships between text and world, a vexed topic at the time *Crisis* appeared, see Dominick LaCapra, *Rethinking Intellectual History: Texts, Contexts, Language* (Ithaca: Cornell University Press, 1983).

28 Pérez-Gómez, *Crisis*, 201.

29 Pérez-Gómez's approach to images in his writing differs from his approach in teaching and in public lectures. He discusses his "dialogical" attitude, grounded in the priority of speech, in Marc J. Neveu and Saundra Weddle, "Interview with Alberto Pérez-Gómez," *Journal of Architectural Education* 64, no. 2 (2011): 76–81.

30 For a sustained historical examination of these issues, see Alberto Pérez-Gómez and Louise Pelletier, *Architectural Representation and the Perspective Hinge* (Cambridge, MA: MIT Press, 1997).

31 Daston, "Science Studies," 809.

32 Pérez-Gómez, *Built upon Love*, 205.

33 For instance, Descartes today is not always the Cartesian dualist seen in *Crisis*, nor do his metaphysics (or Galileo's) play an untempered causal role in accounts of the emergence of modern science. On the "new" Descartes, see e.g. Matthew Jones, *The Good Life in the Scientific Revolution: Descartes Pascal, Leibniz, and the Cultivation of Virtue* (Chicago: University of Chicago Press, 2006), and for other forces active in early modern science, see e.g. J. A. Bennett, "Practical Geometry and Operative Knowledge," *Configurations* 6, no. 2 (1998): 195–222.

Interlude E
Two Poems 2000–2011

Ricardo L. Castro

Ο φίλος μου, ο αδελφός μου, στην υγεία σας!

On the Way to Aegina (12-V-2000)
I think of Silence
before the horizon
when light softly,
touches the clouds.

The sea is calm and dark.

Slowly, first there,
in the distance, the mountains
begin their conversation with the nearby tree-tops.

The sea is quiet.

Like a vast mirror, it reflects the world above.

I think of light, now,
when the silence has vanished
in the vast horizon.
And the cicadas have begun their daily laments.

The sea begins to breathe and colors the wind.

It is midday, the hour of the "misameri" ghosts,
when silence is eloquent.

There, in the distance again,
the horizon plays with sky and water.

The sea talks, the light listens,
while the wind works.

I think of Silence,
after the horizon,
when light and wind
cease their daily quest

Friendship (11-V-2011)
The fireflies, which lit one's footpath
In the dark and dense forest.
The cicadas, which in a hot summer afternoon
set the melody of one's stride.
There are no cicadas nor fireflies here.
How I miss them.
How much solace they give me in a hot summer afternoon
and later in the dark vesper.

Figure E.1 Tomb for a seaman killed in the battle of Salamina, Aegina. In the distance, the Peloponesus (photo by author)

Figure E.2 Aegina, Greece. Tomb for a seaman killed in the battle of Salamina (photo by author)

Figure E.3 Epidaurus, Greece. Stadium . . . mountain (photo by author)

INDEX

eBooks
from Taylor & Francis

Helping you to choose the right eBooks for your Library

Add to your library's digital collection today with Taylor & Francis eBooks. We have over 50,000 eBooks in the Humanities, Social Sciences, Behavioural Sciences, Built Environment and Law, from leading imprints, including Routledge, Focal Press and Psychology Press.

Free Trials Available

We offer free trials to qualifying academic, corporate and government customers.

Choose from a range of subject packages or create your own!

Benefits for you

■ Free MARC records
■ COUNTER-compliant usage statistics
■ Flexible purchase and pricing options
■ 70% approx of our eBooks are now DRM-free.

Benefits for your user

■ Off-site, anytime access via Athens or referring URL
■ Print or copy pages or chapters
■ Full content search
■ Bookmark, highlight and annotate text
■ Access to thousands of pages of quality research at the click of a button.

eCollections

Choose from 20 different subject eCollections, including:

- Asian Studies
- Economics
- Health Studies
- Law
- Middle East Studies

eFocus

We have 16 cutting-edge interdisciplinary collections, including:

- Development Studies
- The Environment
- Islam
- Korea
- Urban Studies

For more information, pricing enquiries or to order a free trial, please contact your local sales team:

UK/Rest of World: **online.sales@tandf.co.uk**
USA/Canada/Latin America: **e-reference@taylorandfrancis.com**
East/Southeast Asia: **martin.jack@tandf.com.sg**
India: **journalsales@tandfindia.com**

www.tandfebooks.com